Watching the Flag Come Down

Susanna Hoe has also written:

Lady in the Chamber (Collins 1971)

God Save the Tsar (Michael Joseph/St Martin's Press 1978)

*The Man Who Gave His Company Away: A Biography of Ernest Bader,
Founder of the Scott Bader Commonwealth* (Heinemann 1978)

*The Private Life of Old Hong Kong:
Western Women in the British Colony 1841–1941* (Oxford University Press
1991)

*Chinese Footprints: Exploring Women's History in China,
Hong Kong and Macau* (Roundhouse Publications Asia 1996)

Stories for Eva: A Reader for Chinese Women Learning English
(Hong Kong Language Fund 1997)

The Taking of Hong Kong: Charles and Clara Elliot in China Waters
(with Derek Roebuck) (Curzon Press 1999)

Women at the Siege, Peking 1900 (HOLO Books 2000)

At Home in Paradise: A House and Garden in Papua New Guinea
(HOLO Books 2003)

Madeira: Women, History, Books and Places (HOLO Books 2004)

Crete: Women, History, Books and Places (HOLO Books 2005)

Watching the Flag Come Down

An Englishwoman in Hong Kong 1987–97

Susanna Hoe

)KS

`ORY PRESS

Published by The Women's History Press
A division of HOLO Books
Clarendon House
52 Cornmarket Oxford OX1 3HJ
www.holobooks.co.uk

www.centralbooks.com

British Library Cataloguing in Publication Data
A catalogue record for this book is available
from the British Library

ISBN-10   0–9544056–7–6
ISBN-13   978–0–9544056–7–0

Designed and produced for
HOLO Books: The Women's History Press by
Chase Publishing Services Ltd
Fortescue, Sidmouth EX10 9QG
Printed in the European Union

For the women of Hong Kong, past, present and future, especially those who appear in this book.

CONTENTS

HONG KONG

N

km
0 10

CHINA
Guangdong
province

CHINA

Beijing
Shanghai
HONG KONG
MACAU

Tin Shui Wai

Pat Heung

NEW TERRITORIES

Tai Po

Shatin

Whitehead

Tsuen Wan

KOWLOON

Kwun
Tong

North Point

HONG KONG
ISLAND

Jardine's
Lookout

Aberdeen

Tsim Sha Tsui

Rennies Mill

Peng Chau

Chek Lap Kok

Lantau

x

PREFACE

An English friend lived for some years in Pakistan where she was married and had two sons. From time to time we met somewhere in the world and caught up. Once I eagerly asked her, 'You do write everything down, don't you?'

Her face set and she stared at me reproachfully. 'Of course not,' she replied.

I suppose the main difference between us is that she was part of the community into which she had married. That has its own rewards and obligations. I lack those and I do need to record new experiences in new places. It is not so much that I'm part of a long tradition of expatriate women diary keepers and letter writers: I can't help it.

My husband, Derek Roebuck, and I lived in Hong Kong for ten years – those leading up to the return, in 1997, of the British colony to Chinese sovereignty. I didn't keep a diary there as I did when we spent five years in Papua New Guinea – a record that 20 years later resulted in the publication of *At Home in Paradise: A House and Garden in Papua New Guinea* (HOLO Books 2003). Instead I wrote the 'letters' that follow.

Soon after we arrived in Hong Kong in 1987, I wrote to a friend in England, Margaret, whom I had first met in Papua New Guinea when I asked if I could write a weekly literature column for the page she edited on the local paper. I told Margaret about the historical study I was just starting to research, later published as *The Private Life of Old Hong Kong: Western Women in the British Colony 1841– 1941* (Oxford University Press 1991). I added a bit about my new life and some local colour.

Margaret was then editing women's pages on an English provincial paper. She replied by asking me to write a monthly column – 'Letter from Hong Kong'. That is how these letters started.

I wrote regularly from 1988 until 1991 when the first Gulf War and the recession forced cuts on the newspaper; thereafter I contributed a piece when I had something particular to say – usually when I travelled outside Hong Kong in the region; (those pieces are not included here, apart from a visit to the 1995 UN Women's Forum in Beijing). But, although my column had formally come to an end, I continued to write regular 'Letters from Hong Kong', hoping they might one day be published under the title of this book.

When you first arrive to live in a place you are inevitably ignorant and detached; the writer has to go looking for her subjects – and that may show in the earlier pieces. Gradually, if you are determined, aware and absorbent, you begin to bed down – the subjects start to seek you out, become part of you and your development. That process itself may be of interest.

Unavoidably, I lived the typical comfortable life of a colonial expatriate but soon suspected that there must be more to explore than that; over the years, therefore, I snuffled out more enriching experiences. I found them mostly among other women in Hong Kong – Chinese of varied backgrounds, progressive expatriates, Filipina domestic helpers, Vietnamese refugees. I gravitated from sitting at home re-creating women's history to also being a founder member of a new women's campaign group and teaching Chinese women English.

Some may feel that what follows invades the privacy of those about whom I have written, that it is even an appropriation of their lives, but I see it neither as a betrayal of confidence, nor of sisterhood. As often as possible I have given individual women a copy of what I have written, and a chance to make comments and changes and give me their blessing. Not only that, as one committed to the re-creation of women's history, I believe that these lives deserve this fleeting record. As for my perception of people and events, that is for the reader to judge.

I changed over the years, and so did Hong Kong. Progress there was fast and that was a time that had never been before anywhere and never can be again. I was dragged along in the current. Occasionally I caught the crest of a wave and felt the exhilaration.

We have been back to Hong Kong a few times since we stopped living there. This account ends with some impressions of what has happened since to the women and place I knew.

Oxford 2007

AUTHOR'S NOTE

I started to gather together photographs for this book but in the end decided against using them. Most of them are snapshots which would not have reproduced well. They were also patchy: several might have illustrated one piece but many pieces lacked a photographic record. I have also convinced myself that visual images are somehow inappropriate when, because of the word limit imposed on each piece at first from outside and then by me, word images were so minutely constructed. Except towards 1997, when I was somewhat demob happy, and in the epilogue, every word had to count.

Very often I have used only first names in the pieces. That was appropriate when I wrote them. But as this book is something of an exercise in reportage, and I have cleared the pieces with those about whom I have written, I have, in the index, put surnames in brackets next to the first names which usually determine their alphabetical place.

For practical purposes, I have had to finish the epilogue at the end of July 2006, with still nearly a year to go until the tenth anniversary of the Handover. I plan, therefore, to put any essential update on the website <www.holobooks.co.uk>; click on 'updates'.

The usual list of acknowledgements is unnecessary – those who have helped are in this book, and it is dedicated to them (the women at least).

1988

Hong Kong is quintessentially modern. And yet, as I sit on our balcony overlooking the harbour, I have the strangest feeling. My eyes skim over the skyscrapers that reflect each other in their mirrored towers and rest, instead, on the water, sometimes gleaming, sometimes grey, in the distance.

Hong Kong is one of the busiest ports in the world and there are always dozens of cargo ships riding at anchor. But, from a distance, and especially at sunset, they look like sailing ships. And when I see them my mind goes back 150 years, to 1839. I think of the women on those ships then.

In those days of the China Coast Trade many men came East from Britain to make their fortune. Some of the ships' captains and merchants brought their wives. For six months the men joined their families in the pleasant Portuguese enclave of Macau. The other half of the year they left them there and went to Canton in China to trade, mostly for tea which the British, even then, could not do without.

But in 1839 things changed. Those traders were trading opium for tea and the Chinese emperor resented the drug's effect on his people. He sent Commissioner Lin to stop the opium trade. The British in Macau learnt that Lin was coming and that the Portuguese governor could not guarantee their safety.

With little warning, men, women and children were bundled onto ships in Macau and spirited away – towards a small, rocky, almost treeless island 40 miles distant. For several months, on and off, they lived on board ship (returning to Macau when circumstances allowed). Finally, in 1842, many of them came for good to that island – 'the spoils of war'. Today it is Hong Kong.

So I look from my balcony and see the women in those ships and imagine what it was like: the tension, the sea sickness, cramped cabins, crying babies, bored restless children, poor food. How did you keep your underwear clean? How did you cope when you

1

menstruated? Some days it would have been far too hot, sweltering and stifling. A day later, the wind and rain would lash the deck with a ferocity rarely seen in Europe.

When the 'refugees' finally came ashore to settle, life was not as easy as it had been in Macau. Almost the only goods available were imported at enormous cost. Over the next 20 years or so, in spite of the fine houses that were built and the beautiful tropical gardens that began to surround them, many died from what we now know to have been malaria. Even when life became more settled, children were sent home to Britain for their well-being. The Chinese, both on the Island and the Mainland, were often hostile. House-bound women rarely called Hong Kong home.

As I look at the fans whirling in our spacious sitting room, at the air conditioners there for a really hot day, and into our kitchen full of modern conveniences, I am full of questions about how the past, present and future relate, for those technical advances are in some ways superficial. Many expatriate women today are caught in a time warp. For Chinese women the situation is rather different. Their position and role have changed radically over the past 150 years.

When Hong Kong became British there were something over 4,000 Chinese living on the island. That figure swelled immediately and dramatically but for some time men came looking for opportunity without their families. Those women who did come took advantage of that. 'Respectable' women arrived only slowly and then they lived a secluded life, constrained in every way, including bound feet.

Today, a Chinese woman, Lydia Dunn, is the Senior Member of the Executive Council – the Governor's 'Cabinet'. Women Legislative Council Members such as Rita Fan are read about daily. Cheung Man-yee is Director of Broadcasts for Radio Television Hong Kong (RTHK), and Winnie Yu is General Manager of Commercial Radio. You can see even from their names how British and Chinese influences tussle in Hong Kong. With only nine years to go before the Colony (as no one calls it!) becomes, again, part of China, I will try and make all these disparate strands lively for you.

THE DOMESTIC FRONT   *October 1988*

In a world where important things were automatically interesting, I suppose I would write to you this month about the recent elections and appointments to the Legislative Council. But it can be argued that, as there is no universal suffrage (or, as they persist in calling it here, 'one man, one vote'), not even the Legislative Council is important. Let me at least tell you that, out of the eleven members whom the Governor has appointed, four are women.

In describing a more accessible matter, I would like to introduce you to two women who have no vote – not because of their gender, I should hasten to add – and tell you of the fate of others who are the beneficiaries of a benevolent, if undemocratic government.

You may remember me mentioning our view over the harbour full of ships. What I left out of my description were the traditional Chinese villages nestling into wooded hills between us and the skyscrapers crowding the harbour. These villages have given us much pleasure. They made us feel almost part of unspoilt Hong Kong, of the real China, as we watched the people coming and going, often bearing carrier bags from the same supermarket that we use at the bottom of our road. At night, the odd light would twinkle up from the obviously cobbled together electricity supply.

The first night we were back from 'home leave' this summer, we went onto the balcony to glory in our view. We looked, and looked, then looked at each other. In the darkness we could see just a pale scar on the hilltop. The nearest village had completely disappeared. We were devastated at two levels. First, what had happened to the villagers? Second, presumably some wicked property developer was going to put up a monster block of luxury flats. I asked Danny and Theresa what had happened. These two are the only Chinese women with whom I can discuss such matters.

Danny 'does' for us two mornings a week. You might expect her to be a working class woman for whom the hourly wages we pay her make a bit of difference to her family's life. No, Danny is middle class. She works for us for *extra* pocket money. She lives with her son and daughter-in-law who both have well-paid jobs in smart Italian furniture shops.

Danny rather despises us because we don't have a television set – they have two; and because our rugs are 'old', not brand new. I fancy it's partly to compensate because she cannot read and write, though her English is not bad. I asked Danny what had happened to the village and its inhabitants. She replied, 'I hadn't even noticed that there was a village there.'

We had assumed that Theresa was uneducated. She sells flowers and plants outside our supermarket seven days a week, including most public holidays. But when she delivered two plants to us last Sunday, we discovered that she used to be an assistant in a pathology laboratory. How she came to change jobs I have yet fully to discover – she is intentionally keeping me in suspense; I will keep you posted.

Theresa told me that the village was a squatter settlement, that it had been set fire to and then bulldozed, and all the people moved into government housing. Yes, there would be a big block of flats going up. Downcast, we went to walk on the naked hilltop which we had always before felt inhibited from intruding upon. We stopped two women, one old, one young, both in traditional Chinese dress, on their way to another village. But we could not communicate. We really must concentrate on our Cantonese.

How to find out the official facts in a colony lacking certain administrative machinery, I was at a loss to imagine. But I was sure you would want to know, so I persevered. I discovered a most helpful housing manager in Development Clearance. Within five years, the government plans to move all squatters into public housing. He understood both my concerns. Most of the people were happy to move to housing with modern conveniences. No, there are no plans at the moment for development of the hilltop. We shall see. Hong Kong changes fast, and there is nothing one can do about it.

IN MEMORY OF FLORA SHAW   *November 1988*

I nipped into the supermarket last Saturday evening and came out with broccoli, strawberries, and cream. An important person was coming to dinner so I stopped, too, at Theresa's to buy some roses. They looked exquisite, cream but with a tinge of peach. 'No,' said Theresa, 'you can't have those.' I looked at her in what to me was bewilderment, to her was simple-mindedness.

She took me by the arm and drew me away from her other customers. 'They're a bit old,' she explained. I was far too gracious to reply, 'That hasn't bothered you before!' And who was our guest? Mary Stott, my co-columnist on this page.

I've known Mary by repute, of course, for some years. Of all the good women journalists Britain has produced, she is perhaps the most revered. All *Guardian* women readers, as well as many others, owe her a lot. And now, here she was coming to dinner, following a trip by boat with her daughter round the coasts of China, Korea and Japan.

Hong Kong on a Saturday evening can be hostile to social life. Horse race crowds eat up the taxis and block the cross-harbour tunnel. Mary, in a hotel on Kowloon side, could not get a taxi over to us on Hong Kong side. (We have no car.) I could hear from her voice on the telephone that she felt a bit threatened by this noisy and crowded city. I painted a picture of the joys of crossing the harbour on the Star Ferry. She braved it and, thereafter, I believe, could hardly be got off it. It's a marvellous way to enjoy the beauty of Hong Kong.

We had the sort of evening and the sort of talk that do not come often. Half way through I asked, 'Do you know Clare Hollingworth?'

'Of course,' Mary replied, 'but I haven't seen her for a long time. She's surely not here?' I explained that Clare, another grande dame of British journalism, now the Far Eastern Correspondent of the *Sunday Telegraph*, is based here for part of the year. We rang Clare and she and Mary met for lunch the following day. As our editor wrote to me about Mary's prospective visit here, 'I wish I could be a fly on the wall when you two meet.'

On Tuesday, I met Mary again, and this time her daughter Catherine, at the Foreign Correspondents' Club. It's thanks to this column, and to Clare who acted as one of my proposers, that I am a member there. The fish and chips is excellent.

That brings me to the original legendary woman journalist – Flora Shaw. You may not have heard of her, history being what it is where women are concerned. But she was an expert on African affairs in the late nineteenth century. She also wrote, and so highly regarded was she that *The Times* asked her to head one of its departments, which she restructured into their Colonial Desk. Then, in 1902, aged 50, Flora Shaw married Sir Frederick Lugard and in 1907 came with him to Hong Kong when he was appointed its Governor.

I recounted this story of success in her own right, and then virtual oblivion, in a paper I gave at the University yesterday called 'The Way We Were: How Much Have Expatriate Women in Hong Kong Changed Over 150 Years?' The women at the workshop, organised by the Hong Kong Council of Women and the Centre of Asian

Studies, had not heard of Flora Shaw, nor her reincarnation as Lady Lugard. But it was her work behind the scenes that founded the University of Hong Kong in 1912. That has been over-looked.

Now, perhaps, her reputation is due for a revival here. For a start, I'm thinking of starting the Flora Shaw Luncheon Club. Our first guest, and then I hope a member, must surely be Clare Hollingworth. And then, perhaps, next year Mary Stott will return. If any of you are passing through, you would be a welcome guest; you do not have to be a journalist.

INSULT TO INJURY   *December 1988*

Have you heard about a certain well-known dictionary insulting the whole Philippine nation? It is said to have defined 'Filipina' as 'domestic helper', instead of 'Philippine woman'. The fuss had a strong impact here because Philippine women far outnumber other expatriates. And most of them are domestic workers – *amahs*.

They come over on contract, live in and, from what one can see, work all hours. At 7am we see them cleaning windows and washing cars. Then, in the evening, when the children are in bed, there are the dogs to be exercised. That is another matter for social comment. One writer declared that people should not have dogs in flats unless they are prepared to walk them themselves. It is not good enough to leave it to the *amah*.

There is a funny side to that. Quite often we go for a walk before bed. At the top of our street is a public sitting out area and there can often be seen a bevy of Filipina *amahs* chatting, while at their feet lie assorted dogs which their owners think are out walking.

The network of friendship between Philippine women so far from home is important. On Sunday, thousands of them congregate in smart central Hong Kong. The noise is like a sky full of starlings and critics complain of the lowered tone and the litter.

I talk to domestic workers whenever I can because one gets a feeling of great homesickness, even though they are earning what, for them and their families at home, is good money. I'm still haunted by the woman next to me on the bus who poured out her heart about how her 'mistress' didn't understand her. Now she was five minutes late getting back from doing the shopping and would be in trouble.

When we came here, we decided against employing a Filipina to live in the hutch behind the kitchen which all middle class blocks provide for the domestic help. Chinese *amahs* working by the hour are rather rare. They are usually older women; the younger ones work in factories or shops and there is no unemployment. Enter Danny about whom I have written before. Whereas Philippine *amahs* give the appearance of 'knowing their place', Danny knows hers and it's not as a 'servant'. Thank goodness!

Fortunately, she wasn't here yesterday, and is not here today. The water went off at about 7am, just as I was about to wash my hair. Over 24 hours later it is still off in the whole suburb. In the afternoon a water cart appeared and streams of buckets made their way towards it. I was the only non-Filipina in the queue. As for the drudgery of it, I consoled myself by thinking that for centuries women in many parts of the world have collected all the water for the family, often from great distances. I was now part of that history.

This morning's gossip column in the local paper mocks people in the Champagne belt for having to wash their hair in Perrier water and queue for water. A picture shows a queue not of fur-clad or business-suited people, but Filipina *amahs*.

But, if you think that nicely ironic, how about the gossip piece last week. Most people go to work by public transport. Where we live, the little buses are not too bad but in some areas the pressure on them is ferocious and people queue for ages. Those with live-in *amahs* do not queue themselves, so we are told, they send their *amahs* to queue and then roll up in time to board the bus.

I can't see Danny doing that. I remember her telling me once that her previous employer used to pay for her taxi. 'Really,' I replied in a tone that she had to interpret across cultures.

1989

Theresa was not really concentrating on how she wrapped the striped, peach orchids. Later, when we went out to dinner, I felt embarrassed at handing them to our hostess. I had even hesitated to disturb Theresa because she was sound asleep on her stool between the dry cleaners and the supermarket. 'I'm not sleeping well at night,' she explained. 'I'm so worried about George. Can you help me find a new secondary school for him?'

Of course, families in every culture are concerned about the future of their children. But the Chinese still put family above all else in a way that is striking to an independent Westerner.

In Macau this week, parents who have fled to the Portuguese enclave from China over the years have responded overwhelmingly to a Government amnesty. They have put themselves at risk by coming into the open and registering their children. The parents will still be illegal, but not the children.

But family here is more than your children; it includes your ancestors. At the mid-autumn festival, families visit the graves of their forebears, bringing flowers, joss sticks and suckling pigs. Theresa is quirky about that. 'I didn't go and see my dead mother,' she explained. 'After all, she knows that I'm thinking about her. She doesn't need me to go all the way to her grave.' There are not many things Theresa would take a day off for.

Another time, it emerged that she does not cook. 'Your husband does it, does he?' I asked, interested.

'No, either my mother-in-law or my sister-in-law.' So, in what appears to be a small wooden house on the beach, there is Theresa's nuclear family (two sons), together with at least two female in-laws. How many more, I wonder. But that is not at all uncommon. How do they get on? I have not yet presumed to ask!

Danny's daughter-in-law with whom she lives is, by all the evidence, very kind to her. And rather long-suffering, too, I should think. But when my mother, staying for a few weeks, made some remark about daughters being disrespectful to their mothers, Danny, who only has a son, snapped back, 'It's very much worse when it's your daughter-in-law.' However badly or well the extended family gets on, older people are maintained, without question, within the family unit.

Elderly expatriates are traditionally rare in Hong Kong. Entrepreneurs and officials would come out for a certain period but retire early home to England, often in comfort. Since the Second World War and all the upheavals that have followed, there are older foreigners here, often impoverished. They fell through every social welfare net until the China Coast Community was set up in 1979. Now there is accommodation and care for those who have been in the region some since before the war. And care in their own homes, too, if they have one.

I've mentioned before that many younger expatriate women are caught in a time warp. Unless they have professional training that fits in, or unusual flair, determination and energy, women, with an *amah* to look after the home and children, can find themselves a bit at a loss. Many take to voluntary work. The China Coast Community is one of the objects of their attention. That is how, when I went to talk to Peggy the other day about pre-war Hong Kong, there were the following attendants, apart from me and the social worker who took me: a full time Chinese *amah* who had been with her for over thirty years, a part time English nurse (from an agency), a China Coast Community volunteer visitor, and another woman from the Samaritans. Peggy complained to me that she just wanted to be left alone!

There are pensioners in Britain who might find the position of Peggy, with her entourage, or Danny, permanently in her family's bosom, piquant as they sit lonely in front of their gas fire turned down low.

PENG CHAU   *February 1989*

Yesterday was a special day. The day before had been dull and overcast, chilly and a bit depressing, as it often is at this time of year. Today is much the same. But yesterday!

By the time we were seated on the open ferry deck, the sky was postcard blue and the sun glinted off the mirrored buildings on both sides of the harbour and off the dancing sea. It was warm and gentle on our shirt-sleeve-covered arms.

We had once caught a glimpse of Peng Chau – one of Hong Kong's 230 islands – when the ferry to the much larger, more populous and more popular Lantau put in there. It seemed at the same time both solitary and alluring and we vowed one day to return.

So here we were. The first women we met were selling fish along the pathway from the pier to the high street. Live eels, prawns, crabs and a dozen kinds of fish wriggled in containers of water. As we watched, the fishmonger would pluck a gleaming fish for a customer from the water, slap it on her board and stay its wild gyrations with a few well-aimed thwacks of the chopper.

Outside the temple, a woman sold gaudy woollen jackets. The colours were tempting and the garments well-enough-made but the quality of the cloth deterred us.

The main thoroughfare was not the width of a street and small, low-slung shops tumbled onto it, many of them selling vegetables. There are no cars and no tourists on this village-sized island.

A side alley intrigued us. It led to a porcelain work-shop where half a dozen young women sat on high stools, each with a piece of china under one hand, a paint brush in the other. They painted with impressive speed and lightness of touch, pausing to return our greeting in a friendly way but then hurrying on with their work.

Now we were off the high street. From all around came the clack of mahjong tiles as the older people whiled away the hours at one of China's best-loved games. Some older women simply sat on stools in the sun in their dull-black trousers and mandarin collars, their faces like paintings from time immemorial. They, too, returned our greetings.

An hour or so later, the thought of seafood could no longer be resisted. By this time, however, the wayside cafes had emptied and we could not even gesture to another diner's plate to show what we would like. We sat down tentatively, eyeing the owners. Before we were aware of anyone moving, a young woman appeared at our table. 'I've been asked to interpret for you,' she explained, her broad face alight with mischief. She was Dorothy from the island's only bank next door. She was in her element and by the time we had finished ordering had invited us to stay with her when we next visit Peng Chau.

Even before we had finalised the vegetables, which we later saw arriving from a nearby garden, Mr Wong was handed a bag of leaping prawns. And when we looked round again Mrs Wong had deposited a huge, steaming dish of now quiet, pink prawns on our table. Of all the meals that live in the memory over the years, that one will remain bright. But the day's experience was more than that.

It confirmed for me the importance of travel – however short the journey away from home. Travel provides insights that allow you to see a person as an individual, instead of a parcel with a label round that someone else has written.

Our ferry back that evening had come from Lantau and the open deck was full of rude, noisy teenagers. The behaviour of the 15-year-old girls bothered me most. As the heavily urbanised parts of Hong Kong are rather rough and tumble, too, it would have been easy during that rowdy boat trip to generalise about Chinese people, and about how Chinese womanhood was not in safe hands.

But the small sunny joys of our day on Peng Chau made sure that I saw things differently.

FRIENDSHIP CALLS   *March 1989*

There is a small corner of Hunan Province in China where the women have their own system of writing. Today, there are only two elderly women left who know and use the script but traditionally, in 20 or more villages, all the women did so. They used it to write letters to each other as 'ritual sisters'. They wrote to commiserate when a sister got married, to offer their condolences upon a death in the family, or to ask a new acquaintance they liked if she would be a 'ritual sister'. I heard all about this yesterday evening and it was rather timely because I had been considering writing to you this month about women friends.

During the past week or so, meetings with friends have brought home to me not just how important such friendship is but also that women have a particular facility for it which should be practised creatively, like an art or craft.

Meeting congenial women here is not easy. Most expatriates come for a short time. Often work contracts last only two years. Transience is not conducive to close friendship because of the hurt of constant partings. And why should a Chinese resident expend energy and let down defences between cultures for an expatriate who is here today, gone tomorrow? So let me tell you about some of the women with whom I have shared warmth this week.

I dropped into the History Workshop at the University to ask Elizabeth who runs it if I could do some research there that afternoon. 'What are you doing for lunch?' she asked, adding, 'I'm meeting Maria and Irene; why don't you join us?' I didn't know Elizabeth, a Chinese historian of Hong Kong, that well. I've met her through my work, which she has helped enormously, and through the Royal Asiatic Society which is joined by many expatriates, and some Chinese, who have an interest in the region. Her invitation was spontaneous and generous.

Maria is a German scholar who did postgraduate anthropological work in Britain, field work in China, and now teaches women graduates in China. She is always flying north, where it is often very much colder than here. And she often seems to be preparing for the 'flu she will catch or getting over it.

I first met her when she gave a talk on modern Chinese women and have since drawn on her expertise on *mui tsai*. These were young girls, both here and in China, sold by poor families to rich ones, until the practice was stopped, partly by the campaigning of some of the characters in the history I am working on. Maria had just published a book, based on interviews with survivors of the system, called *Concubines and Bondservants* (Maria Jaschok, Zed Books) which might interest you.

Irene is a young Chinese graduate who will soon go abroad for postgraduate studies. The day before, she and Maria had delved into some newly-sorted archives of a Chinese organisation that used to look after *mui tsai* when they got into trouble.

A day or two later, Joan rang to invite Derek and me to dinner. She is an American Oriental art historian and photographer. She let slip that she was giving a talk later that day about modern women Chinese artists. 'Would you like to come?' she asked tentatively. Out of friendship, I changed my plans and went. I was rewarded in terms of both friendship and learning.

Yesterday evening, we dropped by Theresa's before going to hear about the women's script, to buy roses to take to dinner afterwards at Joan's. Theresa was edgy. 'What's wrong?' I asked.

'I've been given notice to leave here by 15 March,' she replied. 'They won't renew my contract because of the re-building they've just started. Can you find me a job?' she pleaded. 'I'll do anything, even be an *amah*.' She has sold flowers and plants there for 15 years, seven days a week.

At dinner, a new woman acquaintance gave me the name of the managing director of the supermarket chain that has terminated Theresa's contract. I'm off to the telephone. Friendship calls.

NEIGHBOURS   *April 1989*

Gillian and Jennifer have gone, and with them an example of Hong Kong's fascinatingly cosmopolitan society. Although our two little neighbours are Chinese, they were not born here, nor their parents. The families left Indonesia after 1965 when there was an attempted coup for which the Chinese were blamed and punished. At least one set of grandparents came to Hong Kong but Gillian and Jennifer's parents studied in Britain before their marriage and lived there until recently. Between them, they have medical degrees from London, Liverpool and Edinburgh.

The family looks Chinese and their flat is decorated in Chinese rather than Western style, with huge tanks of tropical fish dominating the sitting room. And yet, I recently had a unique experience of their Europeanness.

Gillian and Jennifer are very shy and I don't see them often. When I do, I have to work hard at relations. On the day that I locked myself out of the flat only in a dressing-gown and slippers while trying to heave the Christmas tree into the hall, I was taken in next door and had a chance to discuss Jennifer's drawings with her. She showed me one of the sun and when I admired it she confessed that it was Gillian's. I asked if I could see her own work.

The next time we met, she ran off and came back holding something behind her. Shyly, she thrust it at me. I looked at the tower and blurted out, 'But that's Rapunzel's tower!' As soon as it was out I said to myself, what a clot you are! How could she have any idea what you are talking about? Now you have confused her and she will go even further into her shell. Jennifer didn't answer but scampered away and came back waving a children's book. I took it gingerly. RAPUNZEL it proclaimed in bold letters. Across cultures and years and goodness knows what else, we had communicated.

But not all has been sweetness and light between neighbours. Even though my abiding memory will be of Gillian standing by the lift like a faun, her dark hair clubbed about her face and her skimpy ballet practising dress clinging to her slender form, I won't forget, either, the sound of the piano.

I've suggested to you before that where we live is rather luxurious. But wide vistas, marble halls, the troops of security guards and Philippine *amahs* are only one aspect. The other is lavatories that don't work and every noise from one's neighbours overlaying that of the traffic and the nearest pile driver.

For three months in our first year, Mrs Ma was having the flat below gutted. That meant drills for more than eight hours a day, seven days a week, as they took up all the parquet and stone floors. Then came the electric saw to cut the black marble which was laid instead. Mrs Ma refused to talk to me about when it might be completed.

I never met her but she moved in with a couple of young daughters who took piano lessons. Every morning at 10.40 the scales would start, or it might be 'Baa Baa Black Sheep'. Then Gillian and Jennifer's mother acquired a grand piano. At the end of the first day, I gently explained to her that I could hear every single note that was played. 'I know,' she replied, 'but what can I do? The sound proofing is terrible but I must play the piano.'

She plays quite prettily but she starts at 9am when I start work, and again in the evening when we ache for peace. Gillian and Jennifer have lessons, too. And when the family is out their two Philippine domestic helpers strum.

I've described before the constrained lives of Philippine maids here. How can you complain about them occasionally relaxing on the big, beautiful piano? So I'm not altogether sorry that Gillian and Jennifer have gone.

Mrs Ma went some months ago. In her place has come an elderly Chinese couple. They don't drill or play the piano. They burn incense. It wafts upwards and down our throats, thick and cloying. What does one do?

4 MAY 1989   *May 1989*

When in future years I'm asked where I was on 4 May 1989, I can reply with pride, 'In Chater Gardens, of course.'

For the students in Beijing, this 4 May was relatively straight-forward. It was the 70th anniversary of the day that fired the intellectual movement that led eventually to the revolution of 1949. And it was the climax of their demonstrations to purify that revolution through the introduction of democracy.

Here in Hong Kong, the situation is more complicated. The most obvious question to ask about the recent demonstrations is, 'how do they affect us?' – both in the lead up to 1997 when Hong Kong becomes again part of China, and afterwards when 'one country, two systems' will prevail.

One of the straws that Hong Kong people have clutched at since the signing in 1984 of the Joint Declaration between Britain and China is the relative stability of China following the turmoil of the Cultural Revolution and the death of Mao Zedong. So, were the student demonstrations a return to an instability that would adversely affect Hong Kong's future? The Hong Kong stock market seemed to think so.

Foreign correspondents sometimes ask taxi drivers for their opinion. Not many here speak enough English for political discussion with foreigners, but one who drove me had the Beijing demonstration on his radio and he was raising a clenched fist in time to the chanting as he negotiated a hairpin bend.

Danny seemed a more obvious fount of wisdom. I interrupted her dishwashing to ask what she thought. 'I don't,' she replied, without taking out the earplugs of her walkman.

You may remember me mentioning Irene, a postgraduate student at the University. At lunchtime on 4 May, I went to listen to her talk about women and politics in China and asked how she felt about the Beijing demonstrations. 'Let them do what's needed as soon as possible,' she replied.

Later, I went to the City Polytechnic where students in the new Law School there had invited the Hong Kong 'opposition leader', Martin Lee, to address them on the implications of 1997. He leads the campaign to introduce universal suffrage in Hong Kong well before 1997, so that 'one country, two systems' could mean democracy and the protection of human rights in Hong Kong, whatever the situation in China itself. From the Polytechnic he and many of the students were to go to Chater Gardens for a rally to celebrate 4 May, express solidarity with the Beijing students, and advance the campaign here. Derek, who was chairing the Polytechnic meeting, and I were invited to join them. Thus, I came to be among 5,000 students from many institutions in Chater Gardens that evening – the biggest demonstration of its kind that Hong Kong has seen.

Chater Gardens used to be the Hong Kong Cricket Club. There, for more than a century, Englishmen dressed in white ran under the noonday sun, presumably to the amusement of the Chinese who have never taken to cricket. Now the space, a prime site in the centre of business Hong Kong, is a charming green and paved oasis.

As darkness fell, the lights came on in all the smart hotels and soaring banks that encircle it. For two hours, marching students thronged into the square, each group to be met with warm acclaim as they sat down on the hard paving and listened to speeches. Occasionally, we would rise to sing a snatch of anthem – quite a feat, I can assure you, in a straight white skirt and high heels!

I've suggested before that courtesy and gentleness are not features of Hong Kong life, as anyone who has travelled on the MTR (tube) can testify. But that evening there was not only the electricity that keen demonstrations can generate, but also a sweetness and a welcome towards us two foreigners that was quite striking. Bonnie, a woman law student, interpreted the speeches and songs for us and, when it was time for us to leave, took the trouble to escort us through the ranks of squatting students and thanked us for coming. One couldn't help but feel optimistic about the future.

LETTER FROM EXILE   *June 1989*

As we flew out of Hong Kong, the troops in Beijing were starting to massacre its citizens. Now, 7,000 miles away, on leave in London, I feel all the despair of an exile. It's a strange feeling when almost all I thought I had in common with the people of Hong Kong is that I am living there for a few brief years.

How intensely we lived that month of May, starting with the gathering on the 4th that I wrote to you about in my last letter. As I watch the scenes of devastation on television, I remember as if they were images from my youth, the progress of Hong Kong's political awakening.

In Hong Kong in April you couldn't get more than 500 people at a meeting calling for democracy. Then it was 5,000 for democracy, freedom, and solidarity with the Beijing students; then 50,000; then 500,000. 'I love China' was on many lips. On that last demonstration before the shooting started on 4 June, when we thought the Beijing students had nothing left to do but drift sadly away from Tiananmen Square, we walked the length of Hong Kong city with one million others.

Now, I sit in my safe London flat, with my British passport, and my British citizenship, and my British right of abode, and I think of the people of Hong Kong, most of them with none of that, for all the 150 years of British rule. And the prospect of 1997 is very stark.

Even before 4 June, the Joint Declaration of 1984 had prompted many of those who could afford it to move abroad – mainly to Canada, Australia and the United States. A former student of Derek's invited us to dinner soon after we first arrived. When we came to return the hospitality, we were told that he and his family had left for Canada three days before. The other day, Derek tried to go to the dentist who had treated me a few weeks ago – he, too, had emigrated.

But for most people that option does not exist. Hong Kong Chinese can have a British passport of sorts – but it is an apparently worthless document and certainly does not entitle its holder to take refuge in Britain after 1997. It should also be said that most people could not think of leaving their country for Britain, whatever happens after 1997; Britain is not a few days' sail away, like Hong Kong is for the Vietnamese Boat People.

How long ago it seems since Dame Lydia Dunn, Hong Kong's senior politician, lost control of her emotions in front of the House of Commons Foreign Affairs Committee, when she spoke of Hong Kong's brain drain and the failure of Britain to provide passports as a safety net which could stop it. And yet, it was only April.

How long ago it seems that we read of how the wife of the Chinese dissident Xu Wenli saw him for the first time in three years. 'I have never seen a man so thin,' said his 16-year-old daughter. On our front pages, a large picture of the crippled and fragile girl with her mother accompanied the heart-rending description of the meeting.

Three years from now, how many Beijing students will be lost and thin in China's prisons? And, after 1997, how many people who once lived secure under the British legal system in Hong Kong?

The press in Hong Kong became increasingly adventurous during May, but in April I heard the outspoken journalist Emily

Lau describe how freedom of the press was threatened even then in Hong Kong. She reported how a fellow journalist, questioned about self-censorship, replied, 'I don't have a foreign passport for after 1997.'

Hong Kong people showed in May that they are ready for democracy now. The old men who rule China have shown that the agreement between Britain and China that Hong Kong's way of life will not be touched for 50 years is meaningless. At least universal suffrage in Hong Kong and the right of abode somewhere in the world would give Hong Kong people the confidence over the next eight years to strengthen the ramparts round their future.

FOR MOTHER'S SAKE   *July 1989*

'Oh, oh!' Elizabeth put her hands to her head. 'I forgot to leave her some tea this morning.' We were sitting across from each other in Elizabeth's office and my Chinese historian friend was telling me about her dead mother.

Elizabeth's mother has been dead for three weeks now but the period of customary mourning, and the rituals that go with it, are by no means over, although Elizabeth, going against custom and, indeed, her own inclinations, is back at work. She looks pale and drawn and her dress was consciously dull in colour. Earlier in the week, I noted that she was wearing black linen trousers, the Western colour for mourning, and a white linen blazer, the Chinese – but it was inadvertent.

Of all my Chinese friends and acquaintances, Elizabeth, with her doctorate, her impeccable English and her sense of humour, combines the Western and the Chinese most conspicuously and with most conspicuous success. But it is the Chinese in her that is to the fore at this time.

The Chinese in Hong Kong, as I have suggested before, still practise religious rituals in the traditional manner. But I would not have expected it of Elizabeth. Her Chinese husband, a doctor, believes none of it but, as Elizabeth explained to me: 'I'm agnostic, but what if…? I cannot afford to take a risk, for my mother's sake.'

To describe it crudely, the Chinese worship their ancestors. The spirit of Elizabeth's mother is expected to return to the family hearth, or that family hearth chosen to house her portrait arranged on its funeral stand. In this case, it is Elizabeth's nuclear family flat.

Eventually – perhaps immediately, perhaps in 200 years' time – her mother's spirit will be reincarnated; that is a Buddhist element. Other rituals and beliefs that make up the whole are more eclectic, some of them older. In the meantime, her spirit must be looked after.

Following her death, she was cremated. Then her portrait was brought home from the funeral parlour and an expert consulted about when her spirit would return to visit the family. He used her date of birth and other factors to calculate it. On that night, Elizabeth, her two teenage sons, her husband and her brother, who had returned from abroad, all slept in Elizabeth's room. Across the door were knives to protect them, for her mother's spirit might return with guardians from the underworld who could be harmful. In another room, with the portrait, were dishes of food such as steamed fish and an avocado – food that her mother had enjoyed in life.

At the lunchtime seminar where we all take our lunch in a brown paper bag, I noticed that Elizabeth was eating an avocado. 'Rather an old one,' I observed, leaning over longingly, nonetheless, from my cheddar cheese and carrot. That is how Elizabeth started to tell me about her mother's food because the aging avocado was 'left over' from that ritual night.

'So your mother didn't touch the food?' I didn't mean to sound sceptical. Elizabeth was not offended. She is surprised to find herself so involved in these rituals.

'No, and nothing happened that night, although people do talk of rushing winds and guttering candles. I discussed it with a friend,' Elizabeth continued, 'and she says that sometimes one is given the wrong date for the return just to cause confusion. The night before, however, my brother did feel ill at ease.' 'But that's not all,' she went on. 'My sister, who lives in Japan, felt a great strangeness in bed on the right night, although she didn't know which was the one.'

What really worried Elizabeth about forgetting her mother's tea that day was what her 'baby *amah*' would say. This woman, though a servant, is completely part of the extended family. She has been with them since before Elizabeth's birth and such a woman is the institutional memory who directs a family, particularly a Westernised one, in the rituals that have been observed from time immemorial. It takes a long time for some things to change in China.

AFTERMATH   *August 1989*

If you were coming to Hong Kong now as a tourist you wouldn't notice any difference. Well, you might notice that there are fewer visitors; hotel occupancy is down 15 per cent. Apparently people have been frightened away by the 4 June massacre in Beijing. But Hong Kong is as safe as ever for tourists and their absence is serious for a place that depends heavily for its economic well-being on tourism.

Economic stability continues to be the watchword for Hong Kong though the balance is more difficult to hold. Rumours of Deng Xiaoping's imminent death sweep the stock exchange. Ordinary people want him dead but it would mean business instability, so down plummets the Market. But how have things changed underneath? Our taxi driver when we arrived back from leave was still full of 4 June. The implications of it mean much to him as 1997 draws nearer. My historian friend Elizabeth, however, could not talk about 'the events' when she rang me before going on holiday. 'I have grieved so much,' she said, 'that I must stop now. I have to get on with my life. I cannot talk about it any more.'

A waiter in a restaurant we frequent has faced a more practical problem. Previously, he and his wife went on holiday to China, where most people's families came from quite recently. But his photograph holding a mourning banner appeared in the press and he is frightened to go there now. 'They say nothing happened,' he told me. 'But I saw it on television. I know.'

Safety, now and in the future, that is the key. So there is still agitation for the right of abode in Britain. But, with the British Government's intransigence, a bitterness is growing which is reflected in insulting letters to the press about the British way of life. Sometimes I feel my sympathy slipping but I struggle to retain it, knowing how easy the future is for me.

In the moments when I feel critical, I think of the Vietnamese Boat People – over 50,000 of them in their barbaric camps and more of them still arriving. There is a local agitation against them that seems inhuman coming from people who are themselves seeking refuge.

I thought I had the answer to this ambiguity: that it was working class people, earning little money, living in over-crowded conditions and stuck here, who were complaining about the camps on their doorsteps putting further pressures on their communities. And that it was the middle class, those with money to buy a house and transfer their business or professionalism abroad, who were struggling to be given right of refuge. Recent events have made this issue less clear. When the Singapore government announced an invitation to skilled immigrants, blue collar workers besieged the consulate in their tens of thousands.

My Sinologist friend Maria confirms this broader trend. She shares a steam bath with a group of women in her block each of whom lives in two rooms – husband and wife in one, their children and Philippine *amah* in the other. They too are clamouring and clambering to get to Singapore.

And how about the Boat People? Well, they are Vietnamese. 'Lazy,' pronounced Danny as she attacked our ironing. I asked her how she knew. 'The men, anyway,' she replied. Tension is growing in the August heat.

The most logical step to improve prospects must be to continue to fight to establish democracy here before 1997, so that people can make decisions of their own. But most seem too frightened to show their heads above the parapet. Nor can they agree what to do. After demonstrations of a million people before 4 June, the most recent one roused 300. Those few glorious weeks of unity and purpose are now just a beautiful memory. Even the hero journalists are unwilling to unravel the recent past to help build for the future. They are too busy racing each other to get their Beijing massacre books written and published.

WAR REQUIEM*   *September 1989*

The nostalgia this month for the beginning of the Second World War is not as great in Hong Kong as it is in Europe. The war did not really impinge on daily life here until 1941. Then, just after Pearl Harbor, on 8 December, the Japanese crossed over from China into Kowloon. Peggy did not bother to wait for the fiftieth anniversary; she died a couple of months ago and, in my opinion, she had been more than willing to die for some time. That was the impression I got when I visited her last November. You may

*   This originally appeared in *Chinese Footprints: Exploring Women's History in China, Hong Kong and Macau* (1996).

remember I mentioned her when I wrote to you about the contrast in attitudes towards the elderly of Chinese and Western cultures.

The day after I met Peggy, I met Sister Lina, an Italian nun who was also in Hong Kong before, during and after the war. It is the contrast between those two women, and how they lived through the war and afterwards that comes to mind this month.

When I met Peggy she was 69, said she was 79, for reasons of her own, and looked 90. I know she would not mind my telling you that; she was a down-to-earth person. She was also an alcoholic and a chain smoker. As we talked, she constantly sipped neat gin. She sat on her bed in a shortie nightie, her legs akimbo – legs like sticks. She had been ill and not eaten for some time. But her mind was sharp and a bitter sense of humour strong.

I had gone to talk to her about pre-war life in Hong Kong. But whatever my purpose had been, she would have harked back to the war. Someone I talked to about her recently had known her too well, put up with her for too long, to be entirely sympathetic; but to me as a stranger, what happened then had determined the rest of her life, however she may have behaved in the intervening years.

Six months before the Japanese invasion, she married a Dutchman, after waiting the two years that companies then required their young male employees to do before marriage. When the Japanese overran Kowloon, before Hong Kong Island fell, and the Governor surrendered on Christmas day, Peggy became an auxiliary nurse. Her new husband was a private in the Volunteers. One night, sheltering in the basement of the hospital from bombs, Peggy distinctly heard her husband cry out for her. She never saw him again.

When she was already interned in Stanley Camp, his body was discovered, dug up and reburied in Stanley Cemetery. It was without a head. I don't think Peggy ever got over that. The years in Stanley were hell for her because of that image, as much as for the lack of freedom and food and the illness and anxiety. I think she died with that image stuck fast in her mind.

When I met Sister Lina, she was dressed in long white robes, her face smooth and pleasant, as only a nun's can be. She was Peggy's age. She talked to me about the world, about the book she had written on one of my historical characters, her life during the war. Then she took me to see the office where she works as her Mission's archivist.

During the war she was frightened, of course, and the nuns lacked sufficient food but, because Italy, Germany and Japan were allies, they were not interned. She remembers how they would go in twos to the Convent farm in the New Territories to pick up fresh produce. She hated to go out because of the bombs. The Convent hospital was bombed and some nuns died from disease and malnutrition. But the Mission's Chinese school continued, and the nuns who had run the English school managed to do a little private teaching. Today, Sister Lina stands proud and upright; I saw her a few weeks ago, her face smiley and serene.

It depends a lot on mental reserves how one comes through a war, and on luck. But as long as women like Peggy have experiences like hers, and die welcoming death with such open arms, we must not forget. And we must fight to prevent war

OUR FIRST WEDDING   *October 1989*

'Something old, something new, something borrowed, something blue' – all of us old married women remember that from our wedding day. Recently I had the chance of seeing what the equivalent symbols are for Hong Kong women getting married today.

The invitation came to us in gold letters on red card. Red was a good colour in China long before the Red Flag was raised, and that card harks back to when a wedding procession arrived at the bride's home, with a red missive tinged with gold from the bridegroom urging her to come. So we went.

There is a range of weddings in Hong Kong: from a traditional ceremony in an almost unspoilt village in the New Territories to a posh Christian 'do' in St John's Cathedral. The one we went to combined elements from both and took place at the registry office in Cotton Tree Drive.

A recent cartoon strip had half-prepared us for the scene that greeted us when we arrived at 11.25. I've suggested to you before that Hong Kong is not only crowded but that the crowd is not always solicitous of the individual. When we got married at a London registry office, I don't remember seeing another bride, nor her relatives and friends. At Cotton Tree Drive there were a dozen brides and grooms and attendants, all of them milling about in one narrow corridor. Like so much in Hong Kong, the building was in a state of flux and the accommodation cramped and temporary. No doubt something grand is on the drawing board.

We couldn't see our bride, and Derek, who knew her slightly from the solicitor's office where he's a consultant, wasn't sure he would recognise her dolled up. At the enquiry office, packed like a rush-hour bus, we learnt that neither of the names on the invitation was on the list for 11.30. Hong Kong people often have several names. Our bride eventually did arrive, in the very high heels which Chinese women never wear and a dress suitable for the climax of a Paris fashion show – yards and yards of oyster silk and lace. The pearls round her neck symbolised those which used to hide the bride's face as they hung down from her coronet.

When our young woman was extricated from 12 other identical beauty-salonned brides, we crowded into the marriage room and the ceremony took place to the strains of 'Softly Awakes My Heart' from the rather inappropriate opera *Samson and Delilah*. Then photographs were taken and it was the only time any of the brides seemed troubled by the competition for space, as two crinolines jostled for the same vantage point.

The wedding banquet was held in the evening. Many of the 300 or so guests had arrived at about 4pm. Then they would have seen our bride in her traditional red marriage robe. By the time we arrived at 8 o'clock, she was in a calf-length, full-skirted, purple satin dress with matching satin roses holding back her glossy chignon. Cards and mahjong were in full swing in the large banquet hall. We taught our table 'switch' which is accessible when not everyone speaks a common language. Some of us drank tea, others tumblers of neat Cognac – a twentieth century Chinese tradition.

The pork which opened the 14 course Chinese banquet was symbolic of the suckling pig which the bridegroom used to send to the bride's family the morning after he had satisfied himself that his new wife was a virgin. The oranges which closed the evening symbolised the orange tree traditionally placed in the bridal chamber and hung with emblems of fruitfulness and wealth. By this time, our bride had changed into a mini dress in ruched orange silk, with a big orange bow at her nape and she circulated each table exchanging toasts. At 11.30 she and the families were ready to say goodbye and within minutes 300 guests had dispersed.

It is not easy to gain access to the heart of Chinese family celebrations here, so it was a special day for us, one that delightfully bridged Oriental and Western custom and lost little in the process.

PRINCESS DI VISITS HONG KONG   *November 1989*

Princess Diana doesn't like having her hair washed by anyone but herself. And that's official; Danny gave me the news as she stood at the ironing board. She cannot read, so she must have heard it on television; thus you can see both the level of our television and the pap that was put out about this month's royal visit.

I'm sorry for Princess Diana because one of the pleasures in this frenetic town, where it is hard to get a good hair cut and where prices are astronomical, is having one's hair washed. Perhaps so the salon can justify its prices, the Chinese shampoo boys give the most gloriously sensual and healing scalp massage. I stopped going to one hairdresser because the boss stole my cutter's brilliant shampoo boy.

Before the Princess's arrival, I asked Danny what she thought of her. Chinese school girls, apparently, find 'Diana', as everyone here calls her, most appealing. 'But how about you?' I insisted. 'Are you going to see her?'

'What can she do for me?' asked Danny in her inimitable way.

'If she could do something for you,' I replied, 'what would you like it to be?' At the time, Danny was sitting on a kitchen stool turned on its side cleaning shoes. She turned round and looked at me reflectively.

'What I'd really like,' she said slowly, 'is a little house, which I don't have to pay for, which I can live in for ever, and where I can keep chickens. Somewhere I can have fresh air.'

In a city where six million people scramble for space, where the noise, air and sea pollution is chronic and unbearable, and where 1997 is as far as 'for ever' gets, her reply not only crossed all time and cultures but tightened my throat. 'You'd like to grow vegetables, too, wouldn't you?' I prompted, blinking. She nodded.

I asked her that because the dream of Theresa, our flower seller outside the supermarket, is to grow her own vegetables and walk in peace along the beach. Indeed, she nags me about that day when she and I are going to walk quietly along the beach where she lives, or go up to Victoria peak where the air is rarified, and where you can escape the crowds. Unfortunately, I'm too busy at the moment. That's life in Hong Kong.

Life this month has not only been the royal visit; it has also been the opening of the new Hong Kong Cultural Centre. It sits on the edge of the harbour, blocking the view of those who were on the shoreline before more land was reclaimed, but it has no windows at all looking out over that magnificent panorama. It is the traditional colour of women's underwear – you know, sort of dirty beige-pink – and it is shaped like a generous wedge of cheese. A pink elephant perhaps.

The entertainment has been splendid: Jessye Norman, the Alban Berg Quartet from Vienna, John Williams and his guitar, the Cologne Opera doing Rossini's *Barber of Seville* and Beethoven's *Fidelio* – beautifully. Then there was the National Theatre's *Hamlet*. A real feast of and for the human spirit.

The Royal Couple opened the Centre but did not meet any Vietnamese Boat People who have been providing an increasingly poignant and bitter drama of their own. I must write to you properly on this subject but it's difficult to know how to do so in a way that might be helpful to them as well as informative to you.

I learned from my hairdresser the other day that in the early days of the camps, when the numbers were manageable and seemed finite, and the countries of the Rich World were taking in refugees at a helpful pace, he used to teach some of them hairdressing, thus providing them with a trade which would be useful when they found a country of abode. That's been stopped, as have many other educational and fulfilling experiences. The 55,000 over-crowded, hungry people with nothing to do are no longer individuals, just a big problem.

JUST BEFORE CHRISTMAS   *December 1989*

'How could they do it just before Christmas?' someone asked when they heard of the 'mandatory repatriation' of 51 Vietnamese Boat People. But, of course, it isn't Christmas for the Vietnamese, whether they are Communists, Buddhists or 'pagans'. It's Christmas for the person upset on their behalf.

I make that point not to be cynical about genuine humanitarian instincts but I do feel that in writing to you on this subject I must look beyond my own emotional response to someone else's misery.

And I do think that some of the tirades against Britain and Hong Kong should be questioned.

The Hong Kong people are constantly frustrated at being at the whim of the British Government. Being handed back to China in 1997 is the most obvious example of that. But their frustration is equally intense when what they feel are their needs and rights are thrown in their faces by other agencies. In this instance, the response of the United States is causing great indignation.

People here are aware of several facts: that the US regularly sends back illegal immigrants from Mexico and Haiti. Many Mexicans are as poor as villagers from Vietnam. In Haiti, certainly in the recent past, people forcibly repatriated could face persecution, even death. They are aware, too, that US forces bombed Vietnamese villages to smithereens and destroyed large tracts of land. It is from the North that people are now fleeing.

They know that since the US Government was humiliated by the outcome of that war, it has blocked the endeavours of the Vietnamese Government to rebuild their shattered country – that there have been trade embargoes and the witholding of aid; and that the US has persuaded the rest of the Rich Western World to behave similarly.

The British Prime Minister, in defending her Government's action, talked of the Hong Kong people's 'terrible suffering'. She shouldn't have said that; it's not true and is on a par with the remarks made in the heat of the moment by those castigating her. The Hong Kong people are not suffering terribly from the influx of Vietnamese Boat People but this is how they see things: for some years now, there has been an agreement between China and Britain that any person illegally crossing the border between the mainland and the colony will immediately be sent back. Most of those who come do so from nearby provinces and many have relatives here, sometimes spouses. They are deported without appeal.

Although Hong Kong is superficially prosperous, there is much poverty. The non-elected government is benevolent as colonial governments go, and works hard to improve welfare, but many people are still without housing, facilities, and benefits. Those who do have a home often share a small space with a large extended family.

In 1939, there were 800,000 people here, now there are six million. It is very over-crowded and people's reactions to many things stem from that. Traditionally, Chinese and Vietnamese have not been good neighbours. Hong Kong people, therefore, resent money spent on the Boat People.

There are 13,000 Vietnamese refugees, those who arrived before June 1988, still awaiting resettlement. Their conditions are tolerable, and they have hope. Since then, 40,000 have arrived. They now have to prove that they are genuine refugees – that they would face political persecution if sent back; otherwise they will be classified as 'economic migrants'. Then there is no chance of resettlement. That procedure is causing anxiety and must be improved.

I ache for those in the detention centres. They are in large dormitories, sleeping in bunks. They are not allowed out to work or play. Violence is increasing. Few of them will be able to prove themselves eligible for resettlement. What then is their future? And, from March, thousands more people will arrive (with the change of season that enables boats to put to sea) unless they are deterred.

Who has come up with a solution? Now that Britain and Hong Kong have put a gun to the head of the world community, perhaps it will find one. Assistance in making Vietnam a homeland in which citizens would be content to remain would be a start.

1990

January 1990

Danny has gone. You may remember that she cleaned and ironed for us two mornings a week. Some of you may see me as a '*memsahib*' who deserves little pity. Others, recalling some of the reported opinions of that female Chinese Alf Garnett, may have wondered at our relationship.

I am writing to you not for sympathy because Derek and I, with a flat full of visiting family arriving and departing, are trying to work full time and keep the place habitable, but because of issues that have to be faced on such occasions by people of good will – issues such as the traditional role of women in the home, being an employer, and relations between women.

I believe that if a wife wishes to fulfil her traditional role of mother and housekeeper, she should be beyond question, as long as she has consciously chosen that option. I also believe that women have the right to adopt other roles more suited to their temperaments, needs and talents.

I have chosen to be a full time writer and, where there is time left over, a political activist. So, given that my spouse works full time outside, and at some distance from, the home, who should do the housework? I also believe that to employ someone to do it is the same as employing a lawyer or a plumber. It is not opting out of your responsibilities and exploiting another person but members of a household jointly hiring a professional.

That professional is, therefore, treated as an equal. And that is where the trouble started with Danny. It was compounded by the fact that I usually work at home; thus another of my beliefs, that relations between all women should be sisterly, came into play. But I was so busy putting my beliefs into practice that I didn't notice how uncomfortable they made Danny.

In traditional Chinese society, hierarchy is everything – at work, in the family, in society. Everyone thereby knows their place and their role, as they look up and down. To practise egalitarianism was to disconcert Danny and thus mean loss of face for her – the ultimate destroyer of balance and harmony. In addition, my craft was alien, even hostile, to Danny. To sit all day reading, writing and typing when she cannot read and write at all was constantly to confront her with her inability.

I remember the first time we were going away for six weeks and I asked her to dust the row upon row of books. She crumbled at first into sulks and then into tears. It took me a while to work out what was wrong. But putting my arm round her and trying to sympathise made it worse.

I won't bore you with the drama that took place last month but after weeks of deteriorating relations which I could not fathom, Danny did something completely contrary to an earlier request of mine, damaged precious objects, lied about it and, when I chided her, started abusing me. I can't say that I behaved as well as I would have wished but, as I went towards her to answer her ravings, my voice raised, she drew herself up and back as if in a melodrama and declaimed, 'Go on – slap me, slap me!'

To slap the face of a Chinese is, I understand, the ultimate humiliation to the person slapped and a dignified ultimate weapon for the person who slaps. In taunting me to do it, was Danny trying to establish the hierarchy between employer and employee that was the only relationship she could manage? I don't know.

All I do know is that it was me who was humiliated, at that moment and at how I had mishandled the whole of our two years' relationship. 'Please go … now,' I said, recovering my composure and giving her what I believed in the circumstances to be a reasonable sum of money. I had the brief satisfaction of seeing her surprise. She understood me as little as I understood her.

As I wash the kitchen floor, I worry that I really cannot behave differently next time, but perhaps I can be more sensitive.

LUCKY DAYS!   *February 1990*

If you ever dream of coming to Hong Kong to enjoy the full drama of Chinese New Year, change your plans. You would do better to visit Gerard Street in London.

In the past, we have taken advantage of the break to nip home to England for a week. This year we stayed behind for a visit from

Paul, one of my stepsons; we looked forward to showing off Hong Kong's most exotic attractions.

At every other time of the year, this is among the most busy, noisy, crowded, exciting places in the world. Shops stay open all hours seven days a week, shoppers throng the pavements like Oxford Street on the first day of the sales. You would be mad not to book at a popular restaurant and any service imaginable is yours in 24 hours. Not at Lunar New Year. For four days or more, Hong Kong is like the City of London on a Sunday. It is the most eerie experience.

It was not always quite like that. Traditionally, this festival is a private not a public affair. The family – in its most extended form – is everything. But in the past you could at least hear the families communing with each other as they let off the firecrackers that were so much a part of all festivals. For days, explosions would sound like an endless coup d'état. That was the trouble or, rather, the troubles of 1967 were the trouble. After that, by law there were no more explosions that sounded like gunfire.

In practical social terms, this ban on private firecrackers is sensible, avoiding injuries and fire. But, of course, not everyone obeys it. If you walk through villages in the New Territories, the streets are strewn with tell-tale red confetti left by firecrackers, which hang up in strings like Spanish onions. I even heard complaints on the radio from Chinese listeners that anti-social people were disobeying the law and letting off those dangerous and noisy explosions. How times change!

To compensate for this dampener on traditional joyfulness, there is now a public firework display, set off from barges in the harbour. For half an hour, an impressive show illuminated a clear dark night, competing with skyscrapers dressed overall in coloured lights, and a flotilla of little boats festooned in lights. We should have gone among the crowds on the waterfront but we have such a marvellous view from our balcony that we stayed put enjoying, too, the oohs and aahs from children in all the other flats.

Crowds did also come out on New Year's Eve, when the flower market is the prime attraction. The Chinese love flowering plants at all times of the year, but New Year is when the miniature orange and cumquat trees turn Hong Kong into a riot of orange and green, and the delicate down of peach blossom makes every lobby of a public building magical.

I wanted to buy one of those lopped-off peach trees but, when I turned up at Theresa's, she flapped her hands at me. 'Do you know how much they cost?' she asked. I looked uninformed. '$1,000 (£100), that's what.' So we had a little cumquat tree to go with our still-thriving poinsettia from Christmas. Soon I shall bottle the cumquats in brandy for next Christmas.

Even Theresa took four days off, an unprecedented phenomenon. There were 35 family members for dinner at her place on New Year's Eve.

We tried to follow the rules for luck: you have to pay all your debts; your house must be extraordinarily clean; you must wear new clothes; you must not use scissors or knives. Then there are the little red envelopes. You fill them with *lai see* (lucky money) and give them to children. It is also a time for thanking, rewarding, tipping. Then, traditionally, the children go out into the streets and there are ingenious men who appeal to the Chinese love of gambling and they take the lucky money off the children. Lucky them!

A MURDER IN ESSEX   *March 1990*

You may have read recently of the Hong Kong born woman living in Essex who is charged, after admitting the offences, with murdering her four children. I do not presume to comment on the facts of the case, nor even to suggest how the terrible incident could have occurred. But I cannot help imagining what life in Basildon must have been like for 32-year-old Oi Tai Ngai compared with that in Hong Kong.

When the issue of British passports for Hong Kong is discussed, I wonder if those hostile to the idea realise how much it would take to drive Chinese people away from here, especially to Britain which is not the mother country but a far away coloniser with responsibilities.

To take the most apparently trivial deterrent – the weather. Here, technically, we have the same seasons at the same time as you, but they are rather different. Apart from a couple of days during the year, not even an expatriate wears a winter coat. Central heating does not exist; indeed, air conditioning blows, often uncomfortably, through the year to stabilise temperature and humidity. On very rare days do I crouch in front of a blow heater. Exotic flowers continue to bloom.

Then, think of the cold, dank and dreary days that usually start in Britain in October and continue until April. Here they do not start until the end of January, and the rain does not come until March and continues until August, during most of which time one jumps over puddles with only an umbrella for protection. It is far too hot for a mackintosh.

Weather, as you know, influences mood, and incessant Essex wet and grey must be undermining to someone more used to worrying about rampaging typhoons which quickly pass. Having set the scene for mood depressants, who would a Chinese woman go to in Basildon to pour out her heart?

Here, she would probably be living in a small flat with not only her husband and four children but others as well. Our ex-cleaner Danny lives with her son and daughter-in-law; Theresa, as well as her nuclear family of husband and two sons, has her husband's mother and sister living with her.

Living-in women relatives share the problems, the chores and the expenses and can look after the children to give their mother a break. Not only that, the extended family lives close by in Hong Kong. Theresa had 35 family members for dinner at Chinese New Year. The two brothers who sell us vegetables from a van had 20.

Even if other unrelated Chinese families live nearby, Oi Tai Ngai might not be able to confide in them, for it would mean losing face. As for her British neighbours, how friendly would they be? She might not even speak much English.

Oi Tai Ngai's husband works in a Chinese take-away restaurant. That is not traditionally characteristic in Hong Kong either. Eating is the centre of communal life. At home, you eat produce bought daily and freshly cooked, or you eat out. Danny often told me about going out for breakfast and there are special restaurants that serve *dim sum*, rather different from 'English' or 'Continental' breakfast, all through the morning. It is a highly social meal.

Then there are cooked food stalls, or *dai bai dong*, with a couple of tables and chairs. They snuggle in the corners of street markets which fill narrow streets with crowds, constant movement and noise. Large bubbling vats of Cantonese delicacies breathe their perfume into the already hot damp air. For other occasions, there are huge, noisy, crowded rooms where you eat ten courses or so at large round family tables, or places where delectable seafood comes live from tanks.

So, when Oi Tai Ngai's husband left at 4pm one February day to serve in an alien take-away, she stayed behind with no relatives, even squabbling ones, to sustain her. Just four children, the four-month-old baby probably crying, an over-active toddler and, if it had not been retrieved by the bailiffs, a television set talking at her in English.

NOT MUCH TO ASK FOR   *April 1990*

You may remember me telling you last year about an amnesty in Macau for the children of illegal immigrants from China. As a result, mothers briefly came out of hiding in order to register their children, until then without status in that little Portuguese enclave next door to Hong Kong. Since then, those Chinese who are legally in Macau have been told that after 1999, when Macau is returned to China, they will have passports enabling them to reside in Portugal, and thus anywhere in the European Community.

This month, the Macau authorities announced, in addition, that the parents of those children who were registered last year could themselves be registered and thus receive the identity card that would allow them permanently to leave the twilight world of the illegal. Four thousand two hundred identity cards were available. Unfortunately, the authorities tragically miscalculated. The first day, few of the women and children who gathered outside the security headquarters qualified: the children had not been registered last year. What is more, word got around, and soon thousands were besieging the office.

Registration was moved to the dog racing track away from the centre of town. Soon, 45,000 people were trampling over each other to register. Fathers carrying babies were knocked over; pregnant women were crushed; some miscarried. In panic, the authorities locked the gates leaving thousands still outside fighting to get inside.

While the Macau authorities and their masters in Portugal are dreaming up a way out of the mess, a world hitherto unsuspected lies revealed. Exploitation has been rampant. Unregistered Chinese *amahs*, for example, have been paid a pittance and there was not much they could do about it; after all, they had a roof over their head, a job and relative security. Increased registration is certainly going to change the social fabric of Macau: no more two skivvy households!

Here in Hong Kong, controls are much stricter. Troops patrol the border and police raid construction sites. Those caught are sent straight back to China, unless they have committed some offence, such as working as a builder or returning a second time. In that case they are charged and face up to 15 months in prison.

In 1980, there was a general amnesty for illegal immigrants. Two days later, just too late, Chan Miu-ling sneaked in to join her husband who had been here since 1972 and had an identity card. In April 1987, there was an amnesty for illegal child immigrants and Chan Miu-ling surfaced to register her three children. She was arrested, together with more than fifty other women. That group of mothers was repatriated to China without their children in 1988.

But in March this year, 36-year-old Chan Miu-ling crept back into Hong Kong to rejoin her family. A day later, she was arrested and a week ago she appeared in court. She was sentenced to only a day in prison, so as not to affect her chances, said the magistrate, of eventually being granted a legal permit from her home in China. At the present rate, that could take her 22 years.

There has been a happier outcome for a 17-year-old Vietnamese woman, Nguyen Thi Thu Lan. Ten years ago, her family fled from Vietnam to China where they spent the next six years in refugee camps. In despair they fled again, to Hong Kong. But here they were not Vietnamese refugees, nor Chinese illegal immigrants. Without recognised status, the bright child growing to young womanhood in a detention centre has watched her future recede. Now, Norway has taken that family and some in a similar plight.

Lastly this month, there has been the arrival in Paris of Chai Ling, one of the leaders of the Beijing students. She has been on the run since the Tiananmen Square massacre of 4 June. The first pictures showed her looking ill and wretched but she has at last reached safety.

With all these images pressing on our senses here, you can perhaps understand why the words '1997' and 'refuge' and even 'passports' mean so much.

DOG WALK   *May 1990*

My lunchtime walks are over. Either it's too hot and humid, or it's pouring with rain – that's Hong Kong from now until October.

The walks are important for someone who works at home. To stay bent over books and papers and office machines alone all day is bad for you. Happily, in the view of experts, a brisk walk is as good as jogging or aerobics. I find, too, that you have to get out and about to keep the mind healthy.

I don't meet many people on my walks. Jardine's Lookout consists of tower blocks and large mansions behind high walls and electrically operated gates. But the world outside is refreshingly vibrant. There are usually Philippine *amahs* and their charges in our gardens. Often the children are being met off the school bus with their drawings to be admired. In the poorer parts of Hong Kong a major problem, as the extended family breaks down, is of children being left alone while both parents, or single mothers, go out to work. Frightful accidents are reported. But not in this area; here they are warmly supervised.

Our gardens, too, are well-tended. Last month the azaleas were out in their clear bright ballet dresses. This month, the more subtle, cinnabar ones are blooming alone, and the wattle trees, spindly shrubs three years ago, now laden with dark green leaves and furry mustard balls, exude a heady perfume. A wave to the security guard at the back gate and I'm onto the road outside. The verge is wild and the smell of liquorice grass overwhelming. Mind the dog mess, though.

Recently, I saw there a coucal or crow-pheasant – the most beautiful bird in Hong Kong. Its head, body and tail are blue black but a glistening chestnut design joins one wing tip to the other.

Jardine's Lookout is on a hill overlooking a valley, the city, the harbour, Kowloon and China. But rising above and behind us – part of a rugged country park – is a thickly wooded peak with protruding boulders. One of those is the legendary lookout where 150 years ago the *taipan* Jardine surveyed what was to become Hong Kong – that's my story, anyway!

Most of the big houses have guard dogs behind their locked gates. One shouldn't talk to them but over the months some who used to bark when I passed now look bored or wag their tails. When they are out walking with their minders, I ask their names, so I know Lika, who looks like a hyena when she barks, and Lucky, a Chinese *sha pei* more wrinkly than a boxer dog and with ears that waggle sideways and independently. *Sha peis* are too nervous and their ears too ridiculous to frighten anyone. Leroy is a proud Alsatian with mange. The postman and I exchange greetings outside his gate.

Every month the flowering trees change. In April, Hong Kong's national flower, the bauhinia, smothered the area in its delicate mauveness. In June, the flame trees will set the place on fire. The Chinese have always loved flowering pot plants. The mansions have dozens marching in rows against walls and along drives. They are regularly swapped and I pass the nursery which supplies them. I suppose the gardeners work in the cool of the day; at lunchtime there is always the frantic clack of mahjong tiles from inside the garden shed.

Opposite our front gate is a just-completed, colonnaded granite palazzo. We dub the style of this rich man's self-indulgence Peking Palladian. Down the road I wave to our cobbler who squats in a lean-to shack giving a timeless quality to a place that overnight changes violently amid noise and dust. Outside the supermarket I gossip with Theresa and buy a dozen roses or orchids.

Without my walks will I get flabby and slightly more doolally? Instead, at about 3pm, when my head is like concrete from concentrating, and before other people's children come home, I plunge into the big round swimming pool that sparkles beneath our balcony and dodge the swallows that swoop down to drink, staining their breasts turquoise with the reflection of the water. It's a hard life!

ANNIVERSARY   *June 1990*

On Saturday evening I wore white cotton trousers, an orange silk shirt with a multi-coloured cotton over-blouse, and gold high-heeled sandals. On Sunday afternoon I wore the same trousers, a white tee-shirt with a red slogan, a black belt and black cotton Chinese shoes. On Monday I wore a hand-embroidered white banana leaf shirt from the Philippines, black belt and white skirt. Those clothes were all carefully chosen.

On Saturday we went to a sixtieth birthday party held on a tram. The invitation said, 'dress, cool, casual, festive'. What our hostess, Joan, didn't know was that in the tram shed there's always oil on the ground and anything it touches stays touched. I had worn those white trousers to a previous tram party and it still showed. You should always learn from history.

Tram parties on the line that runs from one end of the island city almost to the other are popular at this time of year, as are junk parties which sail to an otherwise inaccessible island for a fresh seafood meal. But it nearly always rains on such occasions, which is why I wore a cotton over-blouse, and carried an umbrella. It's usually fun as well, particularly if the Margaritas flow.

We carried an umbrella the following afternoon, too, but we were lucky, it didn't rain. We walked almost the length of the tram line which we had followed with such gaiety the previous evening. This time our spirits were less high. Indeed, at the beginning, tears coursed uncheckable down my cheeks. It was Sunday 3 June and we were marching to commemorate those who were killed in Beijing and elsewhere a year ago. We had been asked to wear white, the Chinese colour for mourning, or black, the more international colour, and my tee-shirt, dating from last year, read, in Chinese characters, 'Liberty and Democracy for China'.

The organisers of the rally had told the press they expected 30,000 to attend. We were more pessimistic. Previous attempts to rouse the people of Hong Kong in the past few months have yielded a few hundred supporters. In the event, there were about 200,000 of us. You could tell those who had planned to come. We wore black or white or both. Later, passers-by and spectators joined in and other colours muted the effect. But there was still a strong image.

Before we set off from Chater Gardens, in the sombre quiet of the speeches, when faces were tense and wet, white cotton bands were reverently passed from hand to hand, so that each person could take one and tie it round their forehead or arm. And there was a forest of small black and white posters, some stuck on the end of umbrellas. We started off sadly but after some hours of what can only be called the 'democratic shuffle' spirits revived; stiff backs, singing and solidarity soon dry tears.

On, on we wended towards the New China News Agency, which represents the People's Republic of China here: young couples with linked fingers, mothers and fathers carrying babies, hand-held toddlers continuing to toddle long after it was natural, school girls swinging water bottles, elderly women limping and smiling bravely back when I smiled in sympathy, and sturdy youths grappling with huge, wind-tugged banners.

For a while in front of me was a knapsacked back decorated with a large badge. It depicted a black tank, before which stood, like a fearless bullfighter, the black figure of that young man who halted a column of tanks. They say he's dead now. So on Monday 4th I wore white, too, as I went about my working day. In the evening, from our balcony overlooking Victoria Park, we watched the silver sea of flickering candles as over 100,000 held a vigil in memory of the dead.

Those who don't care to antagonise China have castigated us for looking back, instead of forward. The answer is simple; as one poster put it, 'We do not want to remember, but how can we forget?'

A ROSE BY ANY OTHER NAME   *July 1990*

What's in a name? Quite a lot, sometimes. 'Her name is Petty Chan,' the employment agency told me. 'Are you sure?' I replied. 'Isn't it Patty or Betty?' He checked with her. 'It's Petty.' By chance that evening I read in a book review of how in the early days of the Russian Revolution Lenin called for an all out struggle by the New Soviet Woman against 'petty housework'.

'Marvellous,' I said. 'We'll call our new domestic helper Ms Petty Housework.'

When she arrived, with her smiling young face and lack of English, she thrust her identity card into my hand. 'Please,' she said. 'You see. Not Petty – Peggy.'

My disappointment was intense. 'Of course, Peggy,' I replied. But we call her Petty behind her back.

Her name could easily be Petty. Although mocking cultural quirks is usually taboo in a mixed society, laughing at the funny 'Western' names the Chinese often tack onto their Chinese names is permitted. Even my Chinese friend Elizabeth is faintly amused. My husband has a student called Helium and a newspaper recently delighted in reporting the existence of Utopia Law, Marmalade Tin and Motorbike Chan.

Westerners are as prone to name reinterpretation. My name, Susanna, still not very common in Britain, is surprisingly common here. What is more, the Chinese version, *Siu Sam* means 'Ice Heart'. By changing the tone used to pronounce *Siu* and changing the Chinese character to represent a new object, I am called in Chinese on my visiting card, more to my satisfaction, 'Book Heart'. But I once had a telephone call from a shop assistant who called herself not Susanna, not Susie, nor even *Siu Sam* or Ice Heart but Icey.

My ordinary, if uncommon, English surname 'Hoe' causes much confusion. It is assumed on the telephone that I have a Chinese husband called Ho and sometimes that means good service, and sometimes bad! My worst moment came when a Chinese woman wrote an awful letter denigrating Philippine *amahs* to the *South China Morning Post* and signed her name 'Susanna Ho'. The editor refused to print my letter disassociating myself from her sentiments. A week later I had to chair a meeting and introduce a Filipina talking about the problems of her compatriots. I felt mortified.

Our former Chinese *amah* was called Danny simply because, when she came here from China as a teenager in 1952, it pleased her image of herself. Those who read of the unpleasant ending to our relationship will be surprised to hear that recently Danny rang to ask if I wanted her back! I'm determined to be more circumspect with Petty. She works from 8 to 12, so no opportunity for me to practise offensive egalitarianism or sisterhood over lunch.

I was discussing with Elizabeth the Chinese aversion to touching. I never greet her with a kiss on the cheek. Then there was the occasion when Danny started crying after I asked her to dust all the books while we were away. I put my arm round her to comfort her – a terrible insult an expert told me: 'Mothers may touch their babies, but never a younger woman an older. She probably thought it was a lesbian pass.'

At that moment in the story, a colleague of Elizabeth's came into her office and was introduced to me. He found several excuses to touch me and I laughed about it as he left. 'A Chinese lecher,' explained Elizabeth.

Just after the demonstration to remember the Beijing Martyrs I asked Petty, partly by sign language, if she had been there. Stumblingly she expressed regret. 'I was,' I said. 'It was very hot and tiring.'

She took my arm in her two hands. 'Thank you,' she said, tears springing to her eyes. 'Thank you.' I put my arm round her and we sobbed together. 'Petty' has a new meaning.

SHIRLEY AND CO.   *August 1990*

I took my stepdaughter, Lucy, to my jeweller last week. If that sounds rather proprietorial, it's typical of Hong Kong. Nowhere in the world can there be a more irresistible array of personal services.

We discovered Alice the jewellers when we passed through as tourists some years ago and we have remained faithful to them. Using their own designer and workshop, they have made up unusual raw materials from unusual places and they have accommodated several friends and all three stepchildren – an engagement ring, pearls to express affection, and now Lucy's ring which needed new stones.

But, more than that, they have made us feel valued customers, however small our requirements. First there was Elyse who smiled and waved even when we were only passing; now there is Shirley, the boss, who told us so risqué a story with a table napkin that one day I'll get thrown out of an exalted dinner party.

Our original printer was called Ken. His pokey little shop on top of another which blares out pop music has been taken over by Nami, a lass you would think too young to be in business on her own. Letter headings and visiting cards are essential for even the most personal use in this part of the world, so that what seems cheap in comparison with Europe ends up making large holes in one's pocket. But one does feel smart!

Then there is the cobbler at the bottom of our road. He cobbles from nothing more than a shack by a running stream, in strong contrast to the dwellings around him. But he only does our heels and soles; Derek and I each have our own personal shoemaker. His is underneath a stairway in Causeway Bay and produces custom made shoes that fit like soft gloves at two thirds the price of those off the rack.

My shoemaker is in an alcove in Old Bailey Street. I take in one of a pair of beautiful high heeled sandals I bought in a sale in Bond Street in London ten years ago and which broke my heart when they wore out seven years later. For under £20 I have them copied exactly in any colour I choose. It's a wife and husband team: she does the negotiating, he the making. Her English is one step better than my Cantonese, so it's all done in sign language.

Not long ago, I found a new hairdresser just round the corner from my shoemaker. Doody's English is of the same kind, so I say, 'Crew cut, please,' which he understands from the acquaintance who recommended him.

You may remember me telling you of the extraordinary expense of the smart European hairdressers. Doody charges me £4.50 compared with £30. 'But what about the hygiene?' my American friend Joan wailed. Doody's fittings are a bit worn but I'm not sure he takes less care than hairdressers all over the world.

So, where's the rub in this apparent paradise of personal service? Well, Elyse disappeared one day from Alice the jewellers. First she had gone to Australia for a year. Now she has permanently emigrated. Shirley has recently sold half the shop in Tsim Sha Tsui, the tourist area full of rich pickings, for a large sum. The half-sized shop that remains wouldn't matter if it did not portend the imminent departure of Shirley as well.[*]

Although Nami says that Ken has only gone on a very long holiday, we know better. And when Nami follows, who will do our printing? Doody, the only hairdresser who really suits me, has just disappeared too.

As time runs out, is it only the taxi drivers – and all those other working class people whom we colonials rarely meet – who don't earn enough to emigrate, who will be left with us to hold the fort?

HOMECOMING   *September 1990*

If you've ever envied the regular traveller to foreign places, or even the expatriate living in an exotic clime, don't. Of course, there are advantages and adventures but, after a long journey, you vow you'll never move again. So, pity me, just back from a trip home to Britain, with a side swipe at the Soviet Union.

Last year, after Derek slipped a disc, we bought new suitcases – smaller and lighter than ever before. But one of the rewards of travelling is collecting mementoes, and stocking up on items that are more available or cheaper elsewhere. What made us buy antique library steps in Buxton? Or the sweetest china teapot in Moscow? And all those books from Hay-on-Wye, those stylish clothes, ranging from socks to suits, from you know where?

So picture our last week on our return from the USSR to London: my mother-in-law to be visited for the last time, days of research in Cambridge and the British Library to be done, endless telephone calls, last dinners with friends … packing.

Dead on our feet from too little sleep and too much travelling, we traversed the week. On Wednesday came a final, final demand

---

[*]   In January 2006 I went looking for any sign of the shop – and found no evidence that it had ever existed.

from British Telecom. Though the agent said the bill was paid, money had not been received. Negotiations for a stay of execution were successful. But when on Friday evening we limped home, the telephone was dead. In a far away telephone box that disgorged green cards more generously than it accepted them, we were told we were not disconnected: some bright spark had burnt down the rubbish area in our block cutting us all off.

The next morning, while I packed suitcases that bulged like the mouths of boys with gobstoppers, Derek made book parcels. When he reached the post office, every one of them was over the 5 kilo limit. Someone had snaffled the luggage balance that might have prevented that. Each box had to be repacked.

At Heathrow, the library steps, resembling a body, fragile as the finest glass, stared balefully at the check-in person. Did you know that you can have a fragile item specially treated? Staff could not have been kinder to us or it, as the queue lengthened behind us. But then there was the VAT reclaiming to be dealt with – a perk for those who live abroad made so difficult that only the very determined persevere. Unless you can wear or carry what you wish to reclaim on, you have to take your luggage for the hold through immigration and security checks, in case the VAT form-stamping-person wants to see your purchases. You know what an airport is like in mid-summer! Was it worth it?

The non-stop flight from Heathrow to Hong Kong is about 14 hours – that is if you don't wait for an hour or so on the tarmac. They say the human body is comfortable in an atmosphere of 50 per cent or so humidity; aircraft cabins these days are about 15 per cent. We slept fitfully, woken regularly as our necks snapped or the knees behind found our kidneys. We watched the start of three frightful films. Some metabolisms cope, and it must help if you fly business or first class with the added leg room and reclining seats. But after all those hours in cattle class, I stagger off with ankles and legs like barrage balloons.

Our suitcases came off early at Kaitak, but not 'the Body' which we assumed was lost. That came off last, specially treated – better than us if its condition when we unwrapped it was anything to go by.

So, did we tumble straight into bed when we arrived home? Hardly. A ring at the door revealed Petty, our treasure, who had made the flat look like a palace for our return. With her came her giggling twin daughters and her bouncy young son. She had forgotten to clean the vegetable compartment of the fridge, she smilingly informed us.

How could I explain our condition? Zombie-like I rummaged for the pens from England that we had taken all the way to the USSR for youths who wanted only dollars and chewing gum. The smiles were almost worth it.

TO EARN A CRUST   *October 1990*

Greta was thrown out of the house at 10pm on a Monday evening during the tail end of a typhoon. She had no money. She had been in Hong Kong for ten days.

Greta is a Filipina *amah* or domestic helper. There are nearly 60,000 of such women migrant workers here – most of them from the Philippines – and their position is, as I have suggested before, in many ways unenviable. How unsatisfactory was brought home to me more fully the other day when I attended a workshop set up by various Philippine workers' organisations and the Hong Kong Council of Women.

Fortunately Greta had a relative here to turn to and she has a friend who works for an expatriate so incensed over the general treatment of Philippine maids that he was only too willing to take up Greta's case. He brought her to the workshop. Before us stood a slender, clean-cut, young woman of 19 who looked some years younger, both vulnerable and spirited.

Greta's protector told how she had been expected to eat the leavings off the plates of her employers and she had been sacked because she had thrown away a piece of mouldy bread also given to her to eat. The fact that Greta is not alone in the world should enable her easily to survive here and find another job. But it is not as simple as that for domestic helpers.

They pay out a considerable sum to come to a job. Over-blown agency and other fees and sweeteners put them in debt for the first few months of employment. For that reason, if Greta had not been sacked, she would probably have done nothing about her ill-treatment.

Once unemployed, a woman is in debt, the family she is supporting in the Philippines is without the funds they counted on, and she has only two weeks in which to find another job. Without a reference, finding a job is virtually impossible. At the end of two weeks she is sent back to the Philippines. If she were to institute proceedings against her former employer, she might be granted a short visa extension, for a fee, but could not work while the case was pending. And the case could drag on, at the whim of the employer. Such a situation becomes so intolerable that recently a Filipina attempted to commit suicide from a Philippine consulate window.

The Two Week Rule is an iniquitous government directive that overshadows all other problems and it was what the workshop came back to time and again. Indeed, it ended by passing a Resolution calling upon the Governor to abolish the Rule, brought in to prevent 'job-hopping'. Of course, it is inconvenient when an employee hops off to another job, particularly when the employer has also expended money to an agency to hire the helper. But why had job-hopping become prevalent enough for employers to demand government action?

There is a minimum government wage for migrant domestic workers which is increased from time to time. The increase only affects new contracts, though. Workers would, rather naturally, break the old contract and enter into one at the higher rate with a new family. Now the penalty makes job-hopping impossible. But would it not have made more sense, been fairer, to introduce a mechanism for renegotiating contracts, so that helpers' wages increased as those of other workers do in line with inflation? Apparently not, for here the bosses rule.

The workshop was attended by officials from the Departments of Labour and Immigration. They listened but remained seemingly unyielding. Sitting beside them, I learnt later, were representatives from the Employers' Organisation. The two women remained incognito and silent. Since then, though, there have been several employers' letters to the press detailing the shortcomings of Filipina *amahs*.

The workshop was only a step – though a big and encouraging one – in a continuing campaign. It may be that at some stage you can help. After all, until 1997 Parliament in Britain is ultimately responsible for human rights in Hong Kong. I'll keep in touch.

LIFE BEGINS AT 70   *November 1990*

Will my mother forgive me for announcing to the world that she
has just turned 70? Probably not. In our culture the age of a woman,
even in these days of relative freedom, is a sensitive issue. Privately
we may rejoice at a landmark birthday, but not publicly – unless
it is the Queen Mother. Certainly Mummy has been dreading the
day. In Chinese culture it is somewhat different. We began to learn
about that when Ping came to discuss the menu for the birthday
party.

I sometimes wonder if the domestic help we have grates on
you. Not content with Petty who comes two mornings a week, we
have now discovered Ping, a cordon bleu cook who is available,
at a most modest rate, for dinner and lunch parties. To the
overworked husband and wife team in this household it is a magical
solution.

Ping's animation increased when she learnt the reason for the
lunch. The Westernness of her cordon bleu training and experience
mingled with her Chineseness, and the Chinese in her won.

For a Chinese man, 70 is the great age, for a woman it is 71. But
that is all right because Chinese babies are deemed 1 at birth. So
a British woman at 70 is Chinese 71. For the Chinese, advancing
age is advancing wisdom and status within the family, so much so
that if you die after 70 the mourning colour is not the white and
blue that equates with our black, but red, the lucky, happy colour.
Indeed, the funeral then is known as a smiling or laughing one. Of
course, we have the Queen's birthday telegram at 100 – but before
that there is a long grey period.

With Ping now into her Chinese stride, the menu became subject
to various rules and taboos. But it took a marked change in her
body language on the sofa beside me for me to realise what was
going on. We had discussed a fish dish done Thai style in coconut
milk, coriander, ginger and chillies, garnished with prawns, to be
served with fried rice and stir-fried vegetables, and a cold chicken
salad. That was to be followed by a chocolate birthday cake and
a Pavlova. Still Ping was agitating for more food. 'Why don't you
have a meat dish?' she asked more than once. I explained patiently
that too many of the ten guests did not eat red meat.

She wriggled and wriggled and finally, through my obtuse
Westernness, I asked, 'Is something wrong, Ping?'

She flushed a bit and apologised for being Chinese (a very unChinese approach). 'You see,' she explained, 'you've got four dishes, excluding the puddings, and "four" sounds the same as "death" in Chinese. You can't have it.'

Mummy and I were riveted. 'Of course we understand,' we chorused. 'What shall we have?' 'How about salmon mousse?'

It took a while then for us to understand why Ping kept on about cheese and biscuits as well as the two puddings. We fobbed her off but she said, 'Well, I'll just put a little in a dish – you won't notice it.' Without the cheese and biscuits there were seven dishes in all – not a good number. Now eight – that is the very best of all. Rich men fight to get an 8 car number plate. Flats on the eighth floor are at a premium. And the soaring Bank of China was 'topped out' on 8 August 1988. Our marriage on 18.8.81 has an added lustre.

The day before the menu discussion, my mother had arrived in Hong Kong with her leg in plaster after slipping and breaking a bone in her foot. Then there was jet lag. Her birthday was on Thursday and we had planned an evening out; Sunday was the day for the lunch celebration. By Thursday Mummy and Derek had 'flu. They staggered out of bed for a rustled-up birthday dinner.

By Sunday, however, they were much better and we had a marvellous party. Ping was a Good Fairy in the kitchen and the Chinese spirits seemed satisfied.

LEARNING TO TEACH   *December 1990*

Thank goodness that's over! Who would have thought that learning to teach English would have been so painful an experience for a native speaker whose profession is much to do with written expression in English?

But it is good for the soul to eat occasional slices of humble pie and, if I found my ability to analyse English grammar rather lower than I anticipated, at least the course has had unexpected benefits. I had the chance to learn from and relate to Chinese students for the first time.

The whole business of English in Hong Kong is fraught with difficulties and challenges. Here we have an international trading depot and financial centre which benefits from transactions in the international language of English. What is more, there are those who suggest that English is essential for Hong Kong's internationalism and, thus, well-being after 1997; and yet, only a small proportion of the majority Chinese population speaks it with any degree of fluency.

It is a perennial complaint in the letters columns of the English language newspapers, as new expatriates arrive and discover that taxi drivers and shop assistants have no idea what they're talking about. But if you have any sensitivity, you keep rather quiet, at least in public, because Cantonese is a fiendishly difficult language to learn and I am still unable, after three and a half years here, to tell taxi drivers how to turn left or right in their language.

Many Chinese are motivated to learn English, as the proliferation of English language classes testifies. In my limited recent experience two incentives stand out: one is so that mothers can help their children studying at English medium schools with their homework; the other is to help with emigration. Either the learners are going to emigrate themselves, or they have family members who have already done so. Not only will English make visiting them more enjoyable, but second generation Chinese emigrants – nieces and nephews – will probably not speak any Cantonese at all.

One of my assignments for my English teaching course was to pick out a student and analyse her English learning. To do this, you had to talk to the student at some depth and get to know her. Thus I came to talk to Susanna, whom I chose for our common name, and because she seemed bright in class. And so I came to know a little about a middle class Chinese housewife whom I would probably not otherwise have met. What was so interesting about this attractive 40-year-old was that she spoke English less well than I expected, given her bright demeanour in class. I had to try and understand why.

Is it because she was brought up in a family where the boys went to English medium schools, and then on to university, while the girls went to Chinese medium schools, with a strong leaning towards traditional values regarding women and anti-Western Chinese nationalism (linked to the Kuomintang who fled from the mainland to Taiwan in 1949)? Is it because her mother, her role model, still speaks only Cantonese, after 20 years in Canada with one of her sons and his family?

Or is it because Susanna is married to a Hong Kong University graduate who did postgraduate studies in Britain? Does he speak English so well that she feels inhibited? Does her son, who goes to an English medium school here, join with his father in nagging Susanna about her poor English? Is that why she is taking English language classes – and not progressing? Is she squeezed between her background and her foreground? Is there anything I can do to help?

It is fascinating being a teacher and using every ounce of your ability at all levels to create a breakthrough for individual students. And Hong Kong itself, with its people from so many different backgrounds and experiences, and their myriad motivations and inhibitions, is more fascinating than ever.

1991

Most big cities are full of obvious contrasts but the mix of East and West in Hong Kong is too striking to dismiss as a mere cliché.

Before the Second World War, East and West rarely met. Two exceptions were the racecourse and business, where the excitement of money ignored all barriers. While Chinese and expatriates today meet and mingle easily enough at a certain level of society, and money is more of a social divider than race, some of the contrasts between East and West are still strong. Two recent meals have prompted me to write to you on the subject. On Friday evening we dined at the Hong Kong Club and on Saturday in a 'village' in the New Territories.

The Hong Kong Club was founded within a few years of the creation of the colonial city of Hong Kong by a handful of British businessmen and, for well over a century, it remained a haven for their kind, and a bastion; it had no Chinese and no women members. Gradually, women were allowed through the portals on 'ladies nights', and eventually Chinese were accepted as members. Now a single woman can become a member, but a married one is still the appendage of her husband, and by no means everyone who applies is accepted. There are still places in the club, too, where a woman cannot enter. To dine there, if you are sensitive to issues of colonialism, race and gender is still to experience a slight shiver, though the external atmosphere is pleasant and the food superb.

On the night in question we had one of those French meals of 1001 courses, each dish delicate and delicious. The walls glowed warm and red, the flowers and glassware were impeccable, the tables far enough apart to protect you from other diners' talk and smoke.

The following afternoon we made our way to the New Territories for a Royal Asiatic Society outing. The Society, in spite of its name and long tradition of British imperial interest in Asian art and culture, is unpretentious and the only way people like us have a chance to glimpse through a gap in the fence the last vestiges of Chinese culture which has evolved over 3,000 years. Many of the indigenous people of this area were originally seafarers and there are several temples dedicated to their goddess, Tin Hau. The one we visited is common to 20 villages in the valley which joined together, with the name *Lam Tsuen* ('village in the wood'), a couple of centuries ago for mutual support. Every ten years they still hold a special joint festival.

For this festival – *Dajiao* – a 'village' springs up around the temple, the most outstanding feature of which is a giant red and gold opera house. The festival therefore becomes, for several days, a cross between a church service, a music festival and a fairground. Its ritual aim is to cleanse the district of 'hungry ghosts' and other hostile forces, and to renew through thanks the community's relationship with the gods and spirits, and with the cosmos at large.

Apart from the chance to hear Chinese opera and buy some unusual trinkets, we were able to watch age-old rituals led by Taoist priests in gorgeous red and gold robes, one of the climaxes of which was the release of a small bird from a cage. The bemused creature's first landfall was my trousered leg, which I took to be propitious.

It was a bright day but cold, becoming colder as night fell, and we were glad to accept the community's invitation to a vegetarian meal. Although out of doors, it was half protected by canvas and close to the fires on which the food was cooked.

As we left, the red and gold 'village' was on fire with fairy lights, and though we knew we were visitors, for ever outsiders, it has become part of our warm, rich memory soup.

GIVE PEACE A CHANCE   *February 1991*

Every Monday evening from 6 to 7 o'clock, a hundred or so people gather between the exclusive Mandarin Hotel and the Hong Kong Club. But those who meet are not yuppies or chuppies (the Chinese version).

The first time they met they tried to do so around the nearby war memorial. But the police, knowing they were coming, asked the Urban Council to rope off the memorial and put up notices warning against incursion. I'm not sure that those dead would have minded the intruders. After all, they were calling for an end to the latest war, so that men, women and children should not die, once again uselessly, in the coming weeks and months.

After an hour we moved towards the roped off memorial and, stretching forward on our haunches, placed our lighted candles just inside the rope – a small gesture of defiance. A larger one, we were told, would lead to charges and possibly two weeks in prison.

It was a pitifully inadequate gesture: to listen to rough and ready speeches, quietly to sing a couple of songs that suggest the futility of war – John Lennon's *Imagine* and *Give Peace a Chance* – and then to stand silently as end-of-the-day Central Hong Kong bustled past. But what else can one do?

The third week of the vigil, the organisers failed to consult the police, having made it clear that this would be a weekly event while the war in the Gulf lasted. Police were eagerly round the early arrivals at 6pm but smiling enough. That night, however, they called on the woman who had given her name and address to them, waking her at 11.30 to ask questions. She lives alone apart from an adopted Chinese baby and was made most anxious by the visit. That was no doubt the intention.

At the first meeting she had stood up, with her baby in a sling on her front, to talk to the small crowd about all the children who would suffer in and because of the war. You can imagine how subversive she sounded.

A couple of young expatriates in the audience wore black and white PLO scarves; there were even one or two listeners who might have been from the Middle East. Otherwise, there were a handful of Philippine domestic workers, a clutch of preachers, elderly and young, a sprinkling of people involved in voluntary organisations, some teachers, a string of students, assorted children, not totally controlled, but sweet in the candle light.

At one meeting a young man held a much-used CND banner with scenes of Viet Nam in the background. When asked how young he had been at the end of that war he replied that he had not yet been born.

As elsewhere, the war has saturated the news media here, desensitising people against its horrors. The Chinese on the mainland, one hears, in spite of their government's studied neutrality, are greatly excited by the war. Life has been a bit uneventful since June 1989.

Our greatest homegrown excitement has been the sum of HK$230 million (£15.3 million). This strange figure – perhaps two sides compromising between 200 and 250 – is what the Government proposed Hong Kong should give to the allied war effort. There are rather more sides now that the proposal is out in the open. Anti-war students have demonstrated outside the Legislative Council that none should go; some call it a colonial kowtowing. There are those against the war who say it should go for humanitarian purposes.

Then there are those who say, how can you expect the allies to give us passports for 1997 if we don't give them money now? There are those who say the donation will prove we are an international centre in our own right. There are those who point to how much vulnerable trade we have with the United States.

Such a lot of fuss over such a little money. But the donation is an important token in the eyes of the powers that be. Just as our weekly vigil is a token – a symbol of something bigger. And tokens of peace springing up in small patches all over the world could add up to something. It's better than nothing.

THE MAKING OF HISTORY   *June 1991*

When a vote is to be taken in the House of Commons, the Speaker intones, 'Ayes to the right, Noes to the left', and MPs file off into their own world, out of sight of the public gallery. Only when Hansard appears the following day can you see who voted how. Here, in our Legislative Council (Legco), things are done more intimately, and to be in the public gallery for an important vote can be even more exhilarating, as I recently discovered.

In September, for the first time in this 150-year-old British colony, two handfuls of seats in Legco will be up for direct election, as opposed to indirect (elite) election or appointment by the Governor. When a forthcoming election and a deterioration in law and order coincide, all sorts of creepy crawlies slither out of the woodwork; appealing to the popular vote becomes an irresistible option to those of them seeking election. The popular vote is angry and frightened about gangsters from China wielding guns in jewellery shops in Hong Kong. Thus it came about that a Legco member introduced a Motion to get the death penalty reinstated.

Since 1966 – following Britain's abolition of capital punishment – the Governor has automatically commuted all death sentences here to life imprisonment. But the ultimate cruel, inhuman and degrading treatment has remained on the statute book.

From time to time, people have been stopped in the street and asked something to the effect, 'The death penalty would deter all these violent robbers, you do believe it should be reinstated, don't you?' To which, not surprisingly, the answer has been 'Yes'.

You have to know that capital punishment has nowhere in the world been proved to have a deterrent effect and to be aware of various other scientific, practical and moral arguments to make an informed 'no' answer to that question.

Abolitionists rallied round to oppose the Motion of Hong Kong's best-known appealer to the lower instincts. We were somewhat anxious, for Legco has never seemed very fertile abolitionist ground. Even the reminder that China – of which Hong Kong becomes again a part in 1997 – uses the death penalty even for economic and political crimes usually fails to arouse much interest.

But somewhere those forces that determine the course of history were beavering away. An Amendment to the Motion was tabled by a brave man who constantly questions the status quo and the carefully constructed future. The Amendment called for increased support for the police but ended with a call for legislation that would 'abolish the death penalty and replace it with life imprisonment'.

Only a handful of Legco members were expected to take part in the Debate; the vote could go either way. I settled back in my seat in the public gallery having done my little bit, but not at all confident of the outcome.

As it turned out, 30 members of a legislative chamber of 56 (which includes ten officials) had put their names down to speak. And so they did, hour after hour – the majority of them unexpectedly against the death penalty but not all of them in favour of the abolitionist Amendment.

At 10pm, the Secretary for Security told Legco that if the abolitionist Amendment was passed, the Government would consider legislation to abolish the death penalty. The chamber became unbearably quiet and tense. There was suddenly everything to win. The Amendment was put. The Ayes shouted slightly louder than the Noes. The Acting Governor called for a vote. And then came this heart-stopping moment. The clerk sonorously read out each name, so the members, including the officials, who might have been expected to support the status quo, could call out their reply.

As they replied, I filled up the three columns I had feverishly drawn on my order paper with numbers: abstentions 5, Noes 12, Ayes 24.

The disbelief turned to triumph and my glasses steamed up with tears. All being well, in that instant the death penalty in Hong Kong became history. And the colony can hold up its head among civilised countries of the world.

THE PANGS OF PROGRESS   *July 1991*

So we are to have our new airport after all. Suddenly and unexpectedly, for ordinary people anyway, the answer is yes when we had become resigned to it being no.

I always had ambivalent feelings towards PADS – Port and Airport Development Scheme. It seemed so enormous, inhuman, money-devouring and environmentally unfriendly. And yet the business community saw it as essential if financial confidence underpinning prosperity and stability was to be maintained.

Then China got into the act. They were unhappy about not being consulted, unhappy that PADS would put at risk the monetary reserves they had counted on when they took over in 1997. The issue became deeply political.

During that hiatus – will it, won't it go ahead – the huge impersonal became personal when the delay meant a friend in the construction industry lost his job, and his wife hers too because they had to leave Hong Kong. I felt a bit ashamed that I more than half hoped the deadlock would not be resolved.

Now they claim everyone is happy except a few maverick democrats who say the people of Hong Kong have not been consulted about the new Sino-British deal, and those whose homes were on Chek Lap Kok island, the site of the new airport. It is that last group that I think about most, I suppose because they have most to lose at the most personal level and the least to gain from the long term advantages of Hong Kong's development.

Hong Kong, this great steaming cauldron of glass, concrete, money and flair, has communities on its fringes whose ways are still those traditional when Britain took the island 150 years ago: weather-beaten people who earn their living and live their life on the shore of numerous islands and the sea that laps into the Pearl River Delta.

When the airport was still going ahead last time, a deadline was issued for the removal of people and property from Chek Lap Kok. We went, with a group from the Anthropological Society, to visit the island the day before the deadline expired.

We left from the mainland on a junk – not the usual smart variety that companies own, or expatriate groups hire to go for a lazy day ending with a seafood dinner on an island, but a working boat. Strung over dozens of bamboo poles on the upper deck were thousands of small fish with green raffia loops round their tails, hanging up to dry, twinkling and tinkling in the sun and the breeze. The smell was real! The husband and wife team went about their daily business as they carried us to Chek Lap Kok. The woman wore the traditional silky pyjamas and broad-brimmed straw hat and handled the ropes with effortless skill.

The bulldozers were already on the island; already they had sliced the top off it, leaving a vivid orange burn mark. Several of those monsters were parked by the little Tin Hau (Goddess of the Sea) temple that had nestled in the seashore since the early nineteenth century. We were probably the last to see the statue in place. And we were the last to buy a straw hat from a woman selling soft drinks and knicknacks on the pathway that crossed the island, allowing visitors to enjoy quiet walks in an environment that still harboured rare species of insects and reptiles and archaeological digs. Nearly all the houses and gardens were already deserted and desolate.

The following day a Taoist priest conducted the statue of Tin Hau, protected from the sun by an umbrella, to her new home. Perhaps she will be happier than Wong Gwai, 79, and his wife Wong Chow Mui, 76, who have been forced from the simple community life of Chek Lap Kok to the confusion and isolation of Kowloon. 'Sometimes,' said Mrs Wong of her bereft husband, 'he sobs to himself and I cannot comfort him.'

As for the fisherwoman from our junk, I have seen her picture in the newspaper too. She was one of a mainland coastal village, adapting its traditions, caught selling hundreds of television sets to smugglers from China.

EMILY, ELSIE AND LEGCO   *September 1991*

As you rev up for a general election, see how it will compare with ours. We have just had our first democratic elections in 150 years –

but only democratic to a certain extent. The ordinary voter was only able to vote to fill 18 seats in the 60 seat Legislative Council.

And how, you may wonder, did women fare? Six out of 54 candidates to be directly elected were women. One was successful. She is Emily Lau, a former journalist who gave up her job for what was quite a gamble. She won because she is a fighter: she opposes all the governments who have power over the Colony: the British, the Chinese and the Hong Kong governments. The tide was in favour of those who spoke out against the powers that be. Democracy is, more than ever, demanded both from the old coloniser and those who massacred their citizens in Tiananmen Square. Most successful candidates belonged to a 'liberal' (business) party or group; and many of them won because of that. Emily won as an independent and an outsider. Her win is, therefore, a little startling and the only encouragement to women in what is otherwise a desolate scene.

Emily will have at least one 'sister' in Legco: Elsie Elliot Tu, another independent outsider. But while Emily is 39 years old, Elsie is exactly double that. In those extra years Elsie has fought many battles, and won an impressive number of them. She was born in Newcastle-upon-Tyne and arrived in China as a missionary just before the 1949 Revolution. Forced to leave there, she came to Hong Kong and set up a school for disadvantaged Chinese children which had endless setbacks, but which was ultimately a breakthrough in education here. Then she started fighting corruption in the Police force. She was branded a subversive, labelled a silly woman, and endured every insult in between. Her life was in danger.

Now, married to a Chinese man, and in a more harmonious phase of her life, she is an admired, even loved, institution. She has been returned unopposed in one of the 21 functional constituencies, the members of which are voted in by interest groups, rather than by the population at large. The groups are mostly professional and, therefore, male dominated.

Elsie is a known and valued campaigner for women's concerns. Emily is more of an unknown quantity but she will probably be receptive to good arguments on behalf of women. They have in common, apart from a neatness of size which should not be mistaken for vulnerability, courage, outspokenness, integrity, and a strong feeling for human rights.

The Governor will appoint 18 more Legco members (as well as three officials) to complete the numbers. On past record, several of them will be women. But these appointments tend to be more the sort of women who believe that because they have done well, all women in Hong Kong are doing well. They are not.

That is why some of us have set up a new group – AWARE (Association of Women for Action and Research). Our prime function is to encourage women to become more involved in politics and women's issues at every level.

We need a stronger women's lobby, leading to a Women's Commission. We also need more women to go against the pressures of family and society and stand for election. Women need the self-confidence to vote for women. This is hardly a new idea but it is one that has made little impact here, yet.

Petty voted for the 'liberal' winners. There was a woman candidate in her constituency but she is pro-Beijing and, therefore, unacceptable. 'Yes,' Pet said in reply to my probing, 'it's good if a woman gets in. But she must be a good woman.'

Hong Kong's next elections are in 1995. They will be little more democratic than this one but one important change is possible: plenty of women good candidates and a respectable number of women Legco members. There is a lot of work to be done.

WISHING WHITEHEAD AWAY   *October 1991*

Will the only woman I know in Whitehead Detention Centre be going home soon? And does she want to?

For people of sensitivity, the next few weeks and months may be difficult in Hong Kong. The large-scale forced repatriation of Vietnamese Boat People is now, more than ever, a real possibility.

You may remember that I once wrote to you about this from the point of view of Hong Kong people. Mostly they seem to be in favour of what is euphemistically called mandatory repatriation – after proper screening to distinguish between refugees and economic migrants, of course. Since I put forward their arguments, Italy has forcibly repatriated thousands of Albanians and the world community uttered nothing like the protests that greeted the Hong Kong Government's one flight nearly two years ago.

What I did not write to you about, because it would have been improper at the time, was a visit I made to Whitehead, and the interview I attended of a woman who may well find herself on one of those planes home.

The interview of Miss Thanh (not her real name) was conducted by Derek, one of several lawyers asked by concerned people to double check the screening process and, if appropriate, make an application to the United Nations High Commission for Refugees to exercise its Mandate. That is, the reassessment of the case of someone already screened out whose appeal has also been turned down. The internationally empowered body is a last resort.

What hits you first at Whitehead is sanitised stainless steel and barbed wire. As far as the eye can see is a camp, holding 25,000 people, of cold, hard silver which under the summer sun of Hong Kong must shimmer and glare like the gates of hell. But that grey day there was a tropical downpour that thrummed on the corrugated iron roof like a thousand hammers on a thousand anvils, drowning all our voices. Only the variegated, broken umbrellas leaping puddles from one bunk-filled barracks to another had a human dimension.

My first impression of Miss Thanh was unexpected, considering she had been cooped up here since 1988. She was wearing brand new blue jeans and a feminine pink and white blouse. Her nails were scrupulously clean and in good condition. Her skin was clear and her hair newly-washed and well cared-for, though with split ends. She was slender but not mal-nourished. She had not lost her self-respect, but she never once smiled. It was only after nearly two hours of careful, sympathetic questioning that the strength of her case emerged. How then would she have fared with an immigration officer with a heavy caseload?

We came away with scope for an appeal: Miss Thanh fears persecution if she returns. She is from a Southern family with the wrong political and military connections which led first to police surveillance and discrimination in all aspects of daily life and later, in 1987, to two short periods of arrest.

A letter was sent to the UNHCR and a long year later a negative reply came back. No reasons. There was no opportunity of telling Miss Thanh personally. I often wonder if anyone told her, and how she felt.

There is evidence that those 10,000 Boat People who have returned voluntarily have been reasonably received – not ill-treated nor discriminated against, according to UNHCR monitors. They have even been re-trained, but there are no jobs for them in Vietnam and, of course, everything they sold to flee is lost.

That, and the new agreement about forcible repatriation, may deter future seekers after a new life. But what of Miss Thanh? If she is forced onto that plane, there is unemployment, at the least, at home; if she stays here there is no chance of resettlement abroad.

The lifting of the trade and aid blockade against Vietnam, that would assist it to recover economically, is once again the only obvious solution.[*]

NOTHING BUT THE TRUTH   *December 1991*

Not many people know this, but the ditty 'I'm a little teapot short and stout' has a Cantonese version, sung to the tune of 'Frère Jacques'. I learnt this at the Christmas party we held at the Women's Centre at the end of my first term of teaching English there.

When we set up our new Women's group, AWARE, we realised that simply to say, here we are, we're going to put the world right, was a little naive and presumptuous. We needed standing within the community. So we asked the Women's Centre, set up eleven years ago by the Hong Kong Council of Women, if we might affiliate with them; and they were prepared to take us on. But, what can *we* do for *you*, we asked. Well, replied the social worker director of the Centre, Linda, what we really need at the moment is English teaching.

At last, I saw some use for the TEFL course which put such a burden on me last autumn; I volunteered to organise and teach. Another member of AWARE is an American student, Darcy, who has taught English in China and who plans to do the course I did, to formalise her qualifications, next year; Darcy took on the teaching of a second class, as part of her undergraduate studies.

Since October, once a week, I have made the three-quarter hour journey to the other side, to an area where I would never normally go, to the working class public housing estate (Lai Kok) where the Women's Centre is located. There, for twelve weeks my horizons have been steadily expanded, and for the first time I have felt in

[*]   Whitehead Detention Centre was closed in 1997. The last camp, at Pillar Point, was closed in June 2000 and the remaining thousand or so asylum seekers were granted residency in Hong Kong. Whitehead became a golfcourse, and was considered a site for Hong Kong's Disneyland.

touch with Chinese women in Hong Kong. It has not simply been that I have learnt about the women and their lives, though that has been of great sociological interest and emotional appeal, but we have experimented in what we have called women-centred teaching.

This is more than making sure that there are plenty of female pronouns and characters in the teaching material. It is also a question of discussing women's issues in the lessons, and learning to relate to each other as sisters. It is unashamedly part of AWARE and the Women's Centre's hopes of raising political consciousness among women so that at the next election, in 1995 – the last before Hong Kong reverts to China – there will be more women standing for election, women prepared to vote for them, and women anxious to question all candidates about their concerns.

My first priority when we started classes was to create a relationship of trust. When I was doing my TEFL course, I was impressed by one teacher I observed. She was teaching her class the words for members of the family and had brought in a pile of photographs of her family as teacher's aid. Her lesson was marvellously slick, interesting and involving and afterwards I congratulated her adding, 'I do envy you; I have such a funny family that it would be impossible to use my family members to illustrate a lesson.' 'Don't be silly,' she replied. 'So have I; none of those were my family.'

What a clever technique, I thought then. But, when I came to teach my Classmates I had to reject it. Everything had to be true between us, or else how could we move forward. So I taught them about divorce and stepchildren in a society where they are still not commonplace, certainly in their milieu.

After one lesson when I had played a tape of a discussion between an interviewer and Derek about a Christmas trip to England, a Classmate asked me what we were doing for Christmas. 'But you heard it on the tape,' I replied. 'You mean that was the truth?' she asked, her eyes lighting up. 'Of course,' I replied. 'Everything is.' I saw it sink in.

It is hardly surprising, then, that my first real experience of teaching English has been rather rewarding. The best bit is I think the Classmates feel the same.

1992

January 1992

'I felt as if every illness I'd ever had had come back,' explained a stalwart journalist on returning from a five-day trip to Tibet. Another hardy soul added, 'I knew then what it was like to feel old.'

You don't have to suffer from altitude sickness during a visit to Lhasa, 12,000 feet up in the Himalayas, but many people do. Of our group of 90, the majority went under to a greater or lesser extent.

Travelling from the West to exotic places has become commonplace. Articles proliferate about the sights to be seen, the experiences to be felt, the heat and food to be enjoyed, the lush vegetation to delight in. I wonder, though, how far the new traveller takes account of what awaits the body. After Tibet, I feel I should pass on some hard-gathered wisdom.

I laughed at my father when he advised me to clean my teeth in mineral water in Naples in the sixties. In Iran, I learnt the hard way about drinking water provided in a bucket for a desperately thirsty traveller. In retrospect, it took me many years to recover completely. My first trip to China, in 1976, was not helped by the after effects of a cholera injection. I should have had it earlier, or not at all. Some people don't take well to prophylactics. One of the reasons we left Papua New Guinea was that five years of anti-malaria drugs were enough.

We try to keep our tetanus injections – which last five years – up to date. There is little more worrying or likely to disrupt a journey than a cut or graze received where tetanus may be prevalent. Now, in Hong Kong, where hepatitis B is endemic, we have been persuaded to have vaccinations because our blood held no anti-bodies at all. I reacted badly to the injections.

A chance to visit Lhasa, where it has so often been impossible to go over 150 years, and even over the past four years, seemed heaven sent. We knew about altitude sickness and we had some idea how to combat it: Take it easy the first few days, until your system becomes used to the lack of oxygen at 12,000 feet; drink water constantly; take 2 diamox – a mild diuretic used by doctors of the Himalayan Rescue Association in Katmandu – just before you arrive, and just after.

But when you are in Lhasa from Wednesday lunchtime to Sunday at dawn, how do you take it easy? When you are taking a diuretic and drinking pints of water, what do you do when there are no lavatories in the 1,000 room Potala Palace? And when you have that limited time, how do you face the disappointment of staying in bed with a splitting headache and an upset tum?

I, who have a headache at the drop of a hat, felt better in Lhasa than I'd felt in years. Derek, who is usually gratifyingly healthy, had difficulty breathing throughout our trip, and could barely shuffle along the corridors of the comfortable hotel for breakfast.

There is no way of knowing who mountain sickness will hit. You are likely to suffer it anywhere over 8,000 feet, from Bogotá to Ladakh, from Mount Kenya to Lake Titicaca in Peru.

But there is more! On our last evening, people round us started succumbing to colds; then Derek and I fell too. We were delayed at Lhasa airport in buses in the freezing cold for six hours; delayed in damp Chengdu for nearly 24.

I waited to write this to see how long it would take for the cold, caught in a place where hygiene is lax, to clear up. I have it still – a sore throat, catarrh and a cough. It lingered for many others too.

So my advice: Listen to the experience of your body. Make sure you take enough vitamin C, painkillers and tummy medicine, and find out what prophylactic is recommended. Try Mexico City at 7,400 feet before Lhasa. Be sissy rather than sorry. The effects of a holiday abroad should nourish you for ever – make sure they don't dog you!

BAD VIBRATIONS   *February 1992*

The women have won! Who would have thought the elderly women of a New Territories village could beat the property developers? After all, these same women are usually defeated by the law in all things before they start.

When the New Territories were leased by the British government from the Chinese in 1898, following the taking of Hong Kong island by force of arms in 1841, and Kowloon in 1861, they were not to be administered according to the Hong Kong variety of English Common Law, but according to the Chinese customary law that had prevailed for some centuries.

That law, for the most part, still plays a strong role in the New Territories, and is not exactly favourable to women. Indeed, one of the reasons that CEDAW (Convention for the Elimination of All Forms of Discrimination Against Women) has not been extended to Hong Kong, though both Britain and China have ratified it, is that, under Chinese customary law, women cannot inherit ancestral property. The reason for this succession law has its logic in traditional society, for women marry out of the clan. Their husband's family becomes their family, and that of their male children. If women inherited, the property would be seen as lost to its original clan.

Although such discrimination is not exactly acceptable in the modern world, the Heung Yee Kuk, the male organisation that is so strong in the New Territories, insists that things remain as they are. Thus, CEDAW, with its international obligations of implementation, monitoring, and reporting the progress of appropriate anti-discrimination reform, is a bit of a hot potato here.

So, what has been happening among the old women of the New Territories? Nothing to do with inheritance, unfortunately. The government suggests that it has not had complaints from New Territories women about inheritance law, although at least one case has been reported in the press. Instead, the women have been fighting a property developer which planned to build a £3.5 million columbarium (repository for human ashes) to house 40,000 urns in the village of Pat Heung. Not only did they plan it, but they lashed out millions of dollars – they actually began to build it – before all the planning hurdles had been jumped.

This need not have mattered; the authorities had already given the go ahead for 'unspecified use'. But the villagers decided that the repository would bring very bad *feng shui* – natural vibrations – to the village. Having the spirits of thousands of ancestors – not even connected with the village – brooding over their homes would not only do them great harm, but six villagers had already died suddenly because of it. And they were not having it.

All the village was up in arms, but it was the old women – some of them in their late seventies – who fought, would not give up, and won. They started by blocking the entrance to the site, and when that did not have the desired effect, they attacked the construction workers with sticks and excrement. They were taken to court and charged, but they refused even to promise to behave themselves.

They got so much publicity that, even though the building was almost complete, the town planning board was forced, based on recently introduced building controls, to reconsider the issue. The re-appraisal went against the property developers on the grounds of traffic congestion, particularly at the time of *Ching Ming* (festival of the ancestors).

So it came about that people of any sensibility gave a chuckle over their breakfast papers, for Hong Kong is ruled and ravaged by property developers, those harassers of our heritage. And we raised our cups to the old women of Pat Heung.

Now all we need is for the youngsters to start flexing their muscles, and demanding their inheritance rights. That way we will knock down one more obstacle to the extension of CEDAW. And when we have that, and the Women's Commission and anti-discrimination legislation that will go with it ...

THE WOMEN'S MARCH   *March 1992*

International Women's Day has just extended over a long weekend, the diversity of activities reflecting not divisiveness but solidarity. We all went to each other's events and thus created a memorable womanfest.

It wasn't just a celebration of women, for it isn't only those of the New Territories who have less legal protection than in many other countries. There is no anti-discrimination legislation here at all and no one body looking after women's interests. And there's more to it than the fact that CEDAW, the Women's Convention, has not been extended to the Colony; our new Bill of Rights only protects the individual against the government – and unequal pay and sex discrimination are features of the private sector.

The festival started up-market: On Friday, the Association of Business and Professional Women held a lunch for 150 at a smart Central hotel. Executive women, mostly expatriate, elegantly dressed and coiffed, listened to orderly speeches over a carefully chosen light lunch in a chandeliered ballroom. You had to ask, 'Is this all there is? Is this all we are?'

All afternoon it rained and we organisers of AWARE and the Women's Centre wondered if anyone would turn up to our rally; rain is a highly negative force in the emotional life of many Chinese women. We needn't have worried; but there was another hurdle. We had set much store by organising an event where Cantonese would be the dominant language. A delicate balancing act of translation would be required not to alienate Western participants. Happily it worked and, at that crucial question, in both languages: 'We're here to discuss the setting up of a Women's Commission, do you want one, or shall we go home now?', every hand shot up amid grins of delighted sisterhood.

We ended with the message to the Government: 'Give us a Women's Commission now.' And we sealed it with Ethel Smyth's suffragette anthem, 'The March of the Women', renamed 'A Women's Commission' and with new words, and stickers which carried the same demand.

On Saturday the theme of the Hong Kong Council of Women's discussion was sexual harassment – a topic which here, as elsewhere, has recently received a much needed awareness boost. The need for continuing education was emphasised by a so-called humorous male columnist on International Women's Day. Writing of the Queen's visit to Australia and Prime Minister Keating's hands-on approach he commented, 'a passionate hug might have done her the world of good'. This echoed the story told by a sister in one of our discussion groups, of how a man with whom she had had an argument at a dinner party told her in parting to 'go and get yourself raped' – the male solution to uppity women.

Perhaps the most moving event of the weekend was that on Sunday afternoon organised by women workers to publicise discrimination in the workplace. This includes not just unequal pay, sexual harassment, and the most blatantly sexist job advertisements you can imagine; many employers also bar women over 30.

Hong Kong used to concentrate on manufacturing. Increasingly, the demand for 'cheap labour' has sent factories to China and the service industries now predominate here. But women who have lost their factory jobs are finding it difficult to get replacement work. One marcher, aged 33 and experienced, told how it took a year to get a job in a doctor's clinic because most doctors want women 25 or under. Department stores and hotels similarly discriminate.

All the grass roots women's groups joined the march to Government House, including those sheltering at Harmony House – the refuge for battered wives; they wore masks to conceal their identity.

However hard the lives of many women, we swung effortlessly up the hill. It was a marvellous weekend of shoulder to shoulder – a solidarity on which we all intend to build.

DANCING ON THE MOON   *April 1992*

I discovered the dry cleaning collector in the hall when I went to open the door to greet the photocopier repairer. I took advantage of my opportunities: there were suits to be cleaned to go to Beijing; but what else?

'Can you think of anything?' I asked Petty ironing in the kitchen doorway. I was sure she would have no idea; I was stalling for time as I dragged my mind from the computer to domestic chores – one of the perennial problems of working at home.

'Your b---,' she replied after a moment. After the third repetition of the word, I took her into the bedroom to show me. It is always very awkward, isn't it, when someone's English or accent, or your faculties, are not quite up to communication? She took up from our bed the large white polar bear named Gorbo in those halcyon days of Gorbachev's preeminence. 'Look how dirty,' she said.

I cannot deny it. Like anything white in a big dirty city, Gorbo's once pristine belly is a sticky grey. The thought of the cleaning man being confronted with this image was too good to miss, no matter how badly jokes travel across cultures.

Petty and I took Gorbo out and I explained the joke, while I added that my mother-in-law's twin bear has been in the washing machine and come up smiling. Our visitor was, not surprisingly, bemused.

When you talk about cultural clash, however, you must be careful of the dangers of generalisation. Petty, as I have hinted before, is not run-of-the-mill. While I could not be sisterly, let alone demonstrative, with Danny her predecessor, Petty is warm-hearted, loving, womanly wise, sentimental and imaginative. Danny disparaged all our possessions, or lack of them, from our antique rugs to our non-existent television set. For Petty, our things are as precious as her own, particularly Gorbo.

This has introduced a slight problem which is totally insoluble. We came back from Christmas in England to find Gorbo with one of my winter scarves round his neck and, by him on the bed, a handmade Christmas tree stuck with red and silver hearts. Later I was presented with a photograph of Gorbo and Christmas tree in our bedroom surrounded by Petty's three children. Bedrooms are private places; and insurance companies are fussy about the security of flats when one spends time abroad. But I could never ask Petty not to bring the children in when we are away.

The main reason, apart from the obvious one of not hurting her feelings, is the size of her own flat. One day she told me that the whole of it would fit into our bedroom. There live not just Petty, her husband and three children, but two grown-up children by her husband's earlier marriage. As if that is not bad enough, we were discussing breakfast one day, and Petty told me that she and her children eat four slices of bread for breakfast – a rather un-Chinese diet.

'Brown or white?' I asked, getting all healthy and interfering.

'They don't like brown,' she replied shamefacedly.

'Perhaps if you started to eat brown, they'd eventually follow your example.'

'But, you see, our flat is rather small. There isn't enough space to keep a brown and a white loaf together.'

Petty speaks very little English. These conversations are cobbled together and often take time to disentangle. But sometimes neither language nor lack of material privilege is a hindrance to Petty's expressiveness.

She has just ordered a ladder, so that she can clean our ceiling fans ready for the summer onslaught of heat. Usually Derek cleans them because he is tall. But Petty knows he has had a slipped disc and wants to save him the task. Following the Gorbo incident, we were in full flood of sisterly communication. In a moment of language idiocy, I chirped, 'You'll be able to dance on the ceiling.'

She answered, her face alight, her chubby body ready to take flight, 'And can I dancing on the moon?'

THE GOVERNOR'S LADY   *May 1992*

Lady Lavender. That's what they'll call the wife of Hong Kong's 28th Governor. The news media, perhaps to give the consort of a knight her own standing, will accord her the courtesy title of an Earl's daughter.*

What else can Lavender Patten, practising barrister, wife of a politician turned Governor of a fading colony, mother of three daughters, expect?

It will probably take her a while to be comfortable here. In spite of two large, well-run houses and a gracious style of life, she will feel disoriented for some months. She will not be able to show it, of course, for 'Face' is everything. And in many ways she will be cocooned from the noise and crowds that normal mortals find difficult to acclimatise to.

If she will be protected from the human sea surging through the buildings and streets, the intrusiveness of building works will be worse for her, living in the middle of Central, than for most others. In fact, Government House, which in 1855, when it was first occupied, had a glorious view across the whole harbour and the hills of China, is now horribly hemmed in; there you cannot even enjoy, from a distance, the fine modern buildings.

Lavender Patten's predecessor, Natasha Wilson, obviously took a vow when she arrived never to regret, in public, this deprivation. But losing your view – the freedom of your spirit to soar over a beautiful land or seascape that you know is there – and listening to the jack hammers that hasten it, can be demoralising. Of course, there are many people in Hong Kong without a view, many who live in cramped conditions, many without a home at all. And, in the end, the opportunities for being useful to those in need will be what helps the new Governor's wife to settle.

She will be asked to be patron of this, that, and the other cause. And once she has made the difficult choices, the rewards will begin to compensate for all that she has left behind in terms of career and community involvement. But she is likely to cause offence by accepting some invitations to lend her patronage, and refusing others, and all her skills will be required to limit the damage. Then there is exactly what is expected of a patron, particularly when her chosen cause finds itself having to campaign, and expects its patron to get her hands dirty behind the scenes.

---

* It was assumed that Chris Patten would, on taking up the governorship, be offered and accept a knighthood; he did not. He has, though, now taken a peerage.

There are bound to be misunderstandings and backbiting which may surface in the press and cause distress to a public figure who cannot answer back in public. For Lavender Patten will be one of those public figures of whom everything is expected; and yet, really, she has no public standing. She cannot call a press conference to put her point of view, or initiate a course of action to prove a point.

She will be accused of being the power behind the throne, of not being cooperative, oh, a dozen shortcomings. She will not be able to win. Still, she has been in a similar position before and must already have developed the necessary thickness of skin. The secret will be, in spite of that, to remain sensitive to the fascinating experiences that Hong Kong will offer.

At least the Governor's wife today can be totally occupied and thus, all being well, fulfilled. For the first 50 years of the Colony, the first lady, if she could cope with the climate and ill health, was only a gracious hostess. By 1907, and the arrival of Flora Shaw Lugard, the possibilities for community involvement began to expand. Lady Lugard, although her health was poor, achieved much behind the scenes here, and her successors have followed her lead. The names of institutions throughout the Colony bear witness to their dedication.

If, during sleepless nights, Lavender Patten wonders if she was right to say, 'Let's go!' I hope five years from now, she will be glad she did.

HOME SWEET HOME   *June 1992*

'Don't you feel resentful when you come to our big flat and then go home to your flat?' I asked Petty when it emerged that seven of them live in a flat the size of our main bedroom. It was rude to put her on the spot like that, but she answered cheerfully, as she finished ironing a shirt, 'We are trying to move to something bigger.'

Hong Kong's housing problem is not easy and no one can say that the post-war government has not tried to tackle it. But there seem to be no easy solutions in a free market economy. At various stages of the Colony's history, and at times of trouble in China, people have flooded in. The first time was in 1841 when the British took the island as spoils of war. The population jumped again in the early 1850s when the Taiping Rebellion exploded in Southern China; in 1911 at the time of the first revolution; in the 'Thirties when the Japanese moved brutally through China; in 1949 when the People's Republic was established; and in 1967 at the time of the Cultural Revolution.

Refugees have meant a proliferation of boat communities and squatter settlements with all the attendant risks. In December 1953 the settlement at Shek Kip Mei went up in flames; overnight 53,000 people became homeless. The authorities really moved then and started a concerted policy of urban renewal and public housing. To the outside observer it looks impressive, even with the problems of high rise housing that have dogged other societies. But how effective does it seem to those for whom Hong Kong is their permanent home?

I recently asked my English class at the Women's Centre to tell me what they like most and least about Hong Kong. Christina is 37 and last year gave up her job as a clerical assistant in the police force to look after her two young daughters; her husband is a paramedic.

I quote Christina's views at some length because she wrote from the heart when she told me, 'One thing I like least is the living environment. In Hong Kong there is a very big gap between the rich people and the poor people.'

The wealthy man can live in a very big house with very good and beautiful scenery. The poor people not only facing the inflation but also facing the bad living environment.

Some poor family just living in a small hut. Their poor children have to share a bed with their sisters or brothers. There is no recreational facilities for the children to play and no suitable space for them to study too.

In the early time, Hong Kong Housing Authority has carried out a series of plan that people can buy back the house which they are still living now, but they are not able to afford a house.

The price which is scheduled by the HK Housing Authority is higher than they need. On the other hand the structure of the house is very bad. Some parts are broken and leaked.

There are other problems too, particularly concerning flats for sale on the open market. Speculation has been rife, with Triad (gangster) involvement. They would take over queues waiting to buy; so the property developers introduced a ballot system. Now the Triads are intimidating those successful in the ballot to re-sell.

Last year, in the road where we live, an ugly skinny little brown block of flats six floors high went up where before there had been a gracious mansion. Before the block was occupied, it was knocked down. Now the site next door is vacant and the two sites are obviously going to be redeveloped together.

Someone is on to a good thing; indeed, many of the mansions in Jardine's Lookout have been pulled down this year and blocks are beginning to go up. No wonder. Our flat, bought by Derek's institution when we arrived five years ago, cost them £250,000 ($HK3.2 million) now it's worth £650,000 ($HK9 million)!

Christina is lucky: she lives in the fire station married quarters. But what happens when her husband retires? And how will Petty ever get the home of her dreams?

WHAT THE GOVERNOR LEFT OUT   *October 1992*

The day Hong Kong has been waiting for arrived at last. The Governor, Chris Patten, made his speech setting out Government policy for the next five years. And it was all very interesting, quite controversial, and generally impressive to listen to. But where was mention of women's specific concerns? Where was a promise to look at the need for a Women's Commission, or the extension of CEDAW to Hong Kong?

Some weeks ago, our group, AWARE, wrote to the Governor asking him to tackle these matters in his policy address. He replied that he was waiting for the report of an inter-governmental working party on sex discrimination at work. But, as we responded in our turn, that working party's terms of reference are too narrow. More important, the heart of those involved is not in the questions they are asking. That is because their heart is not in any possible solutions. Political will is lacking.

Emily Lau, the only directly elected woman member of the Legislative Council (Legco), has this year chaired a Legco working party on the feasibility of a Women's Commission. But she has drawn back from the issue since the new Governor arrived, even though Legco voted in principle for a Commission. Her main concern at the time of her election was not the Woman Question but Democracy.

The Governor and, by implication herself, she advised us, has more important things to think about at this time.

Only the many women's groups have stayed loyal to the issue through this period leading up to the Governor's policy address. But even we have not been as vociferous as we might have been, as those with other concerns have been. And that is for the same reason that the Governor's tinkering with the democratic process will, in its implementation, also fail to include women. Women here are not politically assertive. They have been brought up to believe that their place is in the home, with their mouths shut on public matters. In recent years many have made their way in the workforce but still they have kept their mouths shut on issues such as sexual harassment and unequal pay. Those women who do get involved in politics, whether on the broad stage, or as members of women's groups campaigning for social reform, are the exception.

So, when the Governor tells us that he has managed to increase the democratic element by, for example, making District Boards and Municipal Councils elected, rather than appointed, where does that leave women? Probably with fewer members than before. There has been increasing representation of community-minded women through appointment to those bodies, undemocratic though that was. And it should be said that appointed women here are seldom those who make a difference to other women's lives, but at least it gets people used to the idea of women in politics.

Now that they are to be elected, women will hesitate to put themselves forward, and their sisters, let alone men, will hesitate to vote for them when they do. So, when people say that there are more important things to think about at the moment than a Women's Commission and the broad spread of women's issues which it would address and harmonise, I disagree. Within the scope of a Women's Commission would be a commitment to raising women's political consciousness, and thus their involvement at all levels.

Another 'democratic' reform put forward by the Governor is that all working people will now have an extra vote for 'Functional' or special interest Legco members. Needless to say, this will not include housewives. A Women's Commission would monitor such proposals, and not allow them to slip through.

The only specific mention of women in the Governor's array of social and political reforms was the setting up of three Well Women Clinics. Good; but it is not even a start.

THE CLASSMATES   *October 1992*

'Would you like to come to my English classes?' I asked. I had been feeling guilty for months that I spent so much time teaching other women English while Petty, who does for us with such dedication, was paying for lessons which did not seem ideal.

I had sensed recently that she did not have as many cleaning jobs as previously; it was worth asking if she was free on Tuesdays and willing. She jumped at the idea, even though it meant travelling to uncharted territory in Kowloon; she is an Island woman.

In assuaging my guilt, I was adding to a burden already heavy, however invigorated I feel after a lesson spent with the Classmates. Now, Petty would come to me on Tuesday mornings to clean, stay on to lunch, and travel with me over to the Women's Centre on the other side. Time when I needed to be alone as a break between preparation and teaching would have to be spent getting lunch and socialising; it was the least I could do, but I regretted that aspect.

I should have known Petty better. The first lunchtime as, distracted, I got out a tin of tuna fish and asked her if she liked it, she replied, 'I'm a vegetarian, and I've already eaten some noodles I brought with me.' Then she sat in a corner and studied the previous lesson. But we still had the journey together, and I had a 'flu-ridden throat. At the end of her second working morning before a lesson, Petty told me that she was leaving now and would see me at the Women's Centre in time for the lesson. I took the gift of solitude she handed me with both hands, for I still had 'flu.

I had suggested to Petty that she should not tell the other women that she cleans for us, nor that she is not paying for the lessons; (they pay the Women's Centre $300 for 12 lessons). I wonder if, as a result of her special status, she feels that she owes the Centre something or if, after one lesson, she already felt at home. I arrived at the Centre that second day to find her hard at work addressing envelopes. I noticed too that, whereas she had made no concessions the first time as far as dress was concerned, now she was rather charmingly colour-coordinated.

During the lesson, as I monitored a conversation about jobs before marriage, I heard her telling of how she had gone into a toy factory very young. It was done casually with the emphasis on the English words for the fluffy animals she had made. And yet I knew that her mother had disappeared when she was ten, and that she had had responsibility for bringing up her siblings. I have a debt to

Petty, then, quite apart from the love that she brings to keeping us clean and tidy. So I rejoice in her responsiveness to this initiative.

There is a bit more to it than that. The day Petty started lessons at the Women's Centre, I arrived to find a previous Classmate, Tam Man Ngai, sitting at a desk in the inner office. She had just been taken on as a full time secretary. Tam Man Ngai was a clerk in an electronics factory before marriage. In class she used to sit next to Janet, mother of six daughters and former factory worker. Janet is enthusiastic about, but a bit bamboozled by, the English language.

Every time I asked her a question which she could not answer, Tam Man Ngai, a younger, childless woman, would kindly prompt her. Good or bad for Janet I don't know, but it showed quickness and caringness, for saving loss of face is an essential ingredient in friendship.

Whenever my teaching is not quite up to scratch, or the Classmates not as quick as I expect, I am consoled, therefore, by Tam Man Ngai's new job. It may just be that a year of women-centred English lessons have given her that edge of confidence to get out of the house, not just to earn, but to be involved with women's issues.

And Petty, who is intelligent, caring, and highly motivated, may find that she, too, can think beyond washing our floors and ironing our shirts. As for Janet, Anita, who was a 'mother' in a children's home before marriage, now sits next to her and prompts her.

WRITING ABOUT CLARA*   *November 1992*

There was a time, over a hundred years ago, when a certain class of Hong Kong citizen was neither European nor Chinese, and unhappily caught in that divide. Since the turn of the century, however, and the rise and rise of men such as the comprador Ho Tung (later Sir Robert) financier and public benefactor, Eurasian families have formed an increasingly respected, prosperous and homogeneous part of society.

It was, therefore, with some interest that I agreed to write a 3,000 word entry for a five-volume encyclopaedia of Chinese women on

---

* This piece also appeared in my book *Chinese Footprints: Exploring Women's History in China, Hong Kong and Macau* (Hong Kong, Roundhouse Publications, Asia, 1996)

Clara Ho Tung, the matriarch. To call her the matriarch though is to simplify a rather more complicated story.

Eurasians were usually the product of a union between a European merchant attached to one of the trading houses that were responsible both for Hong Kong's birth and its subsequent prosperity, and a Chinese mother. The father was usually in the Colony without a wife; he did not marry the Chinese woman who bore his children, though they might have a comfortable relationship over several years. Historically, such a woman is known as a 'protected' woman, and she might be well kept and left well-provided for when her protector went Home, died or married a European woman.

Both Ho Tung and Clara Cheung were the children of first generation Eurasians, but their marriage and much, though not all, of their subsequent life followed Chinese custom.

Ho Tung married first Clara's cousin Margaret. But she was unable to have children, so he took a concubine, who also appeared childless. Then, in 1895, he married a second wife, Clara, who was, unusually, a 'level' wife, equal in every way, though giving precedence to her cousin.

The reason for Clara's encyclopaedia entry is not as matriarch of the Eurasian community but her legacy as a Buddhist philanthropist. You cannot, however, separate the public from the private. Clara had ten children, several of whom are still alive in their eighties. And the next and subsequent generations are flourishing. It is my communications with Clara's children, survivors of a bygone age, which have prompted me to write this footnote.

Her son Robbie was a Kuomintang general and at 86 writes me precise and elegant letters which exude a faint whiff of bitterness that his natural mother, Clara, misunderstood him and that, moving in with his other mother, Margaret, he became closer to her instead.

Jean Gittins, now 84, who married into another rising Eurasian family, thus uniting two powerful clans, and who was widowed during the war, now lives in Australia. She and I have become friends by post. Her warm, handwritten letters are the opposite of Robbie's impeccably typed ones.[*]

I met Dr Irene Cheng, no. 4 daughter, yesterday. For some years she has been writing her autobiography, following an earlier

---

[*] Jean Gittins died in 1995, three years after this was written.

biography of her mother. She had arrived in Hong Kong a couple of days earlier from California with suitcases full of computer discs and hard copies of manuscript. She had come to work with her publisher but she fitted me into her heavy schedule to go over my own little manuscript for a final checking with the doyenne of the family, since her eldest sister Victoria died earlier this year aged 95. My meeting with Victoria's gentle daughter Vera, and instructions received from Vera's powerful brother, Lo Tak-shing, belong to the story of another generation.

Irene's 'editor' at Hong Kong University Press both preceded and followed me in meetings with her. After her second meeting she left, tactfully saying that she would give Irene more time to prepare her manuscript. This was not the first time over the years that such a scene had been played out.[*]

I understand the problem. When I arrived in the bare hostel room at Robert Black College, my 88-year-old informant was hunched arthritically between two single beds spread with chapters, lading and teeming them from one pile to another. She broke off to talk to me – not to listen much for she is rather deaf. She had stayed up late reading and making suggestions for me which neither she nor I could now decipher. But meeting her (and later application to the notes she had made) was worth the effort.

Clara's real life as no. 2 wife, and that of the co-wife who outlived her, will never be written, though I have some inklings about the line it should take. An observer recorded Clara saying in 1920, 'I hope in the next generation there won't be any secondary wives. I would hate to have any of my girls live the way I've had to.'

I retain a memory of Irene, stately and sprightly still, and rather the Grande Dame, not quite Chinese, though fluent in Cantonese to her *amah*, not quite English, though fluent in English to me. It adds a warm note to the writing of a biographical entry of her illustrious mother.

A HYMN TO JULIE   *November 1992*

Julie has gone but her melody lingers on, and many women hum it as they heave their burdens through the crowded streets of Hong

---

[*] The manuscript was published as *Intercultural Reminiscences* (Hong Kong, Chinese University of Hong Kong, 1997). So far as I know, Irene is still alive, aged 101 (2005).

Kong. There are two Vietnamese women in Canada who sing it too. If that sounds a rather overblown way of hymning a friend and sister who has, as expatriates do all the time, left Hong Kong, let me explain.

I first met Julie, an English law teacher married to a Canadian, when she came to teach in the same law department as Derek two and a half years ago. Later, when we set up AWARE, our 'radical' women's group, Julie joined that too. And, when the established Women's Centre, to which our new group became affiliated, asked us to set up a Women's Free Legal Advice Clinic, Julie took on the task.

In the meantime, because Derek's law school also has its progressive patches, there were people there involved with the problems of the Vietnamese Boat People. Among those accepted as refugees, rather than rejected as economic migrants, were My and Mai. They had left Vietnam by boat in 1989 when My was 17 and Mai a year older. Since then they had lived in a camp in Hong Kong, waiting. Eventually, their family history guaranteed them safety from being sent back, and they had an 'aunt and uncle' in New Zealand which, therefore, accepted them, subject to various procedures.

Until these details were finalised, My and Mai stayed with Julie, by then expecting her second child. Then, New Zealand fell through and, in that devastating moment, Julie's Canadian in-laws made the necessary application in Canada for the two Vietnamese 'orphans' to join them. A few months later, Julie had her baby. A day later, I saw her for the last time before leaving for England on holiday; and she left for Canada for good before my return. My and Mai now live with Julie and her family, go to school and try, as they enter womanhood, to start enjoying life fully again in a totally new, though loving environment.

And what of the Free Legal Advice Clinic that Julie set up? That has gone from strength to strength. 180 women have passed through its tender hands in less than a year, and I know a little bit about their sad domestic histories. Not only does AWARE keep a motherly eye on the enterprise, but Derek is one of those lawyers who gives up a Tuesday evening to listen to and advise the women.

Yesterday evening, two women came out from talking to him with their faces puffed and blotchy. I think it might have been because his new interpreter, a former student of both his and Julie's, held their hand throughout their ordeal of self revelation. So well set up is the system, though, that a social worker is on hand, if need be, to take over from the lawyer and deal with other aspects of their 'case'; some of them, for example, may need to go to Harmony House, the refuge for battered wives set up in the early eighties when it was still denied that domestic violence existed in Hong Kong.

And yesterday evening was special too because Lavender Patten, the Governor's wife, came to the Women's Centre. She learnt of the Centre's history, work and aspirations, and she was briefed by AWARE on women's concerns more generally. But, as a family lawyer, her main interest was in the Legal Advice Clinic and we hope her visit can help to publicise it, so that more women know about it, and more lawyers volunteer their services. Perhaps, too, her interest will generate funds so that the Clinic can employ a much-needed, part time coordinator.

In time, Julie's name may become only a faint memory in Hong Kong, but many people of good will are ensuring that her efforts were not in vain. And, in their new home, My and Mai will make sure that she feels rewarded for her generous spirit.[*]

A CHINESE MARY POPPINS   *November 1992*

Two men were taking their birds for a walk on the MTR (Mass Transit Railway) yesterday. One carried two cages, each with an inmate, the other only one. They sat there, side by side on the shiny silver seat exchanging gossip, while their birds chirruped to a captive audience. All Heaven may well have been 'in a rage' at the sight of the caged birds, but it was more profitable to this observer to reflect that, as in most countries, you are likely to see everything on the underground if you travel on it often enough.

To see an elderly Chinese man pottering down the road in the sun holding up his caged bird almost as if it were a dog on a lead can raise a smile more readily than a frown, for he so obviously loves that bird.

I am not sure that women walking their birds are anything like as common. But there is one women's custom on the MTR that

[*] My and Mai settled in Canada and made new and successful lives for themselves.

makes me pretty cross. You will see an older woman, perhaps a grandmother, get on the tube with carrier bags in one hand and an 8-year-old boy holding the other. As someone gets up and leaves a space, you start to be thankful that she can sit down. But no: lovingly, she ushers the boy to it, and he sits there plumply, ruler of all he surveys, while she continues to sway tiredly and I grind my teeth.

But what do you make of this? The other day on the underground, I saw a mother with three children: a girl of 5, a boy of 6 and another of 7. The children were, uncommonly for Chinese children, boxing each other, the little girl lashing out with as much will as the boys. It seemed to be in play. Then the girl got bored and turned away. Immediately the two boys together punched her in the back. She turned round astounded and her little face crumpled into tears. The mother took no notice.

When there were seats free they sat down out of sight. Soon I heard the three of them chanting the alphabet in English, so I think they may have been Chinese on a visit from abroad. Their Western behaviour became more comprehensible. No doubt the little girl will learn that if she wants to be equal with the boys, she had better not turn her back on them during a fight!

But you can never be really sure about custom. I try and stop my mother talking to and touching adorable Chinese babies when she visits Hong Kong and travels on the MTR. Even a smile is likely to produce a grimace or a turned-away head – a white face is alien and such overtures from a stranger are not to be recommended. Recently, however, I was on the underground with Petty, on our way to the English class at the Women's Centre, when something happened that undermined all cultural pre-conceptions.

A European baby, pink skinned and white haired in a pushchair, was screaming at the hostile environment. I saw Petty rummaging in her shoulder bag and, the next thing I knew, she was striding down the train towards the child. Before the astonished gaze of its mother and her woman friend, Petty leant down and handed the child a small green plastic dragon. The child put the dragon straight into its mouth and stopped whingeing; the mother stuttered her thanks, and Petty bounded back to me.

'Where did you get the dragon?' I asked. It was the only half-sane remark that came to mind.

'Peter (her 10-year-old son) gets them with his hamburgers,' she explained. 'I had four but I've now given three of them to crying babies.'

So, never talk to strange Chinese children, no matter how appealing, on trains, but it is quite the done thing, it appears, to accept green dragons from a Chinese Mary Poppins.

A DAY IN THE LIFE OF A MAGISTRATES' COURT *December 1992*

I had finished reading my newspaper; the cold had begun to set my hands and feet in stone. I should not have come, after all, I thought. And yet, it had seemed a good idea. It was Derek's first time at Western Magistrates' Court as a duty lawyer, part of a scheme of 500 lawyers who, on a roster, give their defence services at less than market rates to whoever comes up before the bench that day without their own lawyer.

Derek had been given one brief the day before: the case of a Philippine woman who had overstayed her work visa by three years and two months. She would, I thought, just add that extra touch to a letter I wanted to write about foreign domestic workers.

We arrived to find the door to the duty lawyers room locked and Winnie, the staff member with the key, unable to unlock it. We sat outside: we had both given up a morning of pressing other work to be there. I could feel Derek's struggle: could he, as a big white man, offer to try to unlock the door? No. I offered to bring another hand to bear upon the matter. I unlocked the door; it was going to be an interesting and successful morning!

Then we sat inside. Derek's over-staying Filipina was taken from him; she had secured her own lawyer. Eventually he went to interview two Chinese illegal immigrants in the cells. I was not allowed to go. He came back calling one the Artful Dodger, the other Oliver Twist. They were mere boys. He was given more cases, then they were taken away. Everyone was busy and efficient except us. Should I go into Court and at least see what was going on? I started to get up.

At that moment, Harriet (not her real name) was ushered in. In all that Chineseness of Western Court, in a city where the vast majority of people are Chinese, there was this European woman charged with a misdemeanour without a lawyer, or even a companion. I sat there rigid as Harriet, in her black suit and frilly pink blouse, with red hair piled restlessly up in combs and a bit too much make up, sat down, gently guided by a Chinese male clerk.

She was respectful to Derek, calling him Sir, apologising, thanking, but her head was held high. She was charged with shoplifting from a supermarket. She intended to plead not guilty; Derek had only to ensure that her bail was extended until her trial.

She left and we went into No. 1 Court with its EIIR and a white magistrate sitting high above a pen full of Chinese lawyers, clerks, interpreters, and police. I saw Harriet in the public gallery and thought it discreet to keep my distance. But there was no room and she shuffled up for me. I had no choice then but to talk to her, engage with her, believe her story and offer to be there with her, a divorced woman alone through the shame of her situation, on the day of her trial.

All life, prosaically, unoriginally, was there in that court: the policewoman with the used, hard face; the neatly-dressed Chinese woman who, during a short break, wandered round in the official pen haranguing in English – quite mad; the row of neat Philippine women; another of macho young Chinese men in fashionable anoraks; the sad clusters of illegal immigrants pushed and pulled like dolls by the policeman in the dock; Helena, Derek's adviser, in her standard smart long jacket and short skirt, cool and competent; Harriet beside me, admiring my clothes, my earrings, anything to avoid thinking about what she was enduring.

'Were you told you had to stand with your hands tight behind you?' I asked, nodding towards a defendant doing just that. 'They look as if they're manacled.'

'Handcuffed,' she said at the same time. 'I wasn't'.

'You won't, will you?' I squeezed her hand and she smiled gratefully. She was called and bail was extended before I had even grasped that her name had been read out.

The Artful Dodger pleaded not guilty. His trial and Harriet's are still to come. Oliver Twist's main worry was, would he be given a toothbrush and toothpaste in prison? Derek managed to get his sentence, an almost mandatory 15 months, reduced to six. I sniffed quietly.

1993

THE BATTLE, BUT NOT THE WAR   *January 1993*

There is gloom and, in many circles, a sense of impending doom in Hong Kong. China and Britain are not speaking. The stockmarket – alleged indicator of the Colony's state of health – has plummeted, juddered, and plunged again. Many are choosing stability and prosperity over the Governor's too-late and puny but better-than-nothing democracy. Where will it all end?

And yet, for women, there is a gleam of light. And ironically, in it, evidence of an embryo democracy giving little cries of life. To recapitulate: two years ago, the British Government and Hong Kong's Governor replied firmly and negatively to women's call for a Women's Commission. Eighteen months ago, they were denying even the compromise of a working party to look into women's concerns.

For even longer, calls for the extension of CEDAW to Hong Kong were fobbed off: first, it was 'under consideration'; after June 1989 and the massacre in Peking, a Bill of Rights was proposed and women were told that CEDAW would not, therefore, be necessary. But business interests ensured that the Bill of Rights tackles only conflicts between citizen and government, not those between citizen and citizen, or private institutions such as employers. Equal pay in the public sector became law after campaigning 20 years ago; in the private sector it has seemed as far away as ever. CEDAW would require appropriate legislation.

Women did not give up campaigning. Then, a year ago, the newly elected and slightly more democratic Legislative Council (Legco) decided to set up a working party to look into the feasibility of a Women's Commission. And soon thereafter, the Government unexpectedly set up an inter-departmental working party to look into sex discrimination in employment and the extension of CEDAW.

In May 1992, Legco's working party asked their colleagues to endorse their approval of a Women's Commission. In July the new

Governor arrived; in October he left any mention of women out of his Policy Address. In reply to protests, he said he must await the report of the inter-departmental working party. The women who had talked to its members already knew what the outcome would be; they knew there was no political will, no inkling of the issues involved.

Then in November, there was a negative advance leak about the report and women's groups knew that they must give one last heave. Emily Lau, the only directly elected woman Legco member, was willing to introduce a Motion calling for the extension of CEDAW to Hong Kong.

The Government panicked and became vicious. The Secretary for Education and Manpower (sic), who chaired the working party, tabled an incomprehensible wrecking amendment about consulting the people. They issued a misleading anti-CEDAW paper to Legco members.

The night before the Motion, they issued a press release about their findings; we had to ferret out the full version of their report, absorb it and respond to it on the morning of the debate. They declared that there was not enough discrimination to take seriously; and no need for CEDAW.

Women's groups, galvanised, furious, knowing we had everything to lose, countered each weasel move. Our demonstration outside Legco for a final lobby and to greet our champion was impressive and heartwarming. We filled the public gallery.

The Secretary funked the encounter: he sent his deputy, a woman. They withdrew their amendment. How could they not? The Governor has protested too strongly about Legco being the Voice of the People regarding his constitutional reforms. The Government lost so much face, you almost had to feel sorry for them. Legco agreed without dissent to CEDAW.

Of course, we have only won the battle, not the war, but our spirits and determination are high.

AGONY AND ECSTASY   *January 1993*

A woman was mugged coming out of the tube station in the tourist area yesterday afternoon. I know because my mother was standing a foot or so away. It was not a tourist who had her bag stolen and her face slashed so that the sound of the attack and the blood that flowed remain food for nightmares, but an older Chinese woman. And it was not a man who did it, but a young Chinese woman.

We met Mummy later at the Cultural Centre and tried to reassure her that it was an isolated incident, that she should not now be afraid of travelling on the MTR. The concert we then heard was of such exquisiteness that I could not help reflecting on the narrow margin of experience separating the sublime from horror.

The programme was an attractive one even on paper: Stravinsky, Shostakovich and Rachmaninov. But it turned out to be a particularly memorable occasion. The pianist was Russian and his performance lived up to expectations; what was unusual was that both the solo trumpeter and the conductor were women.

The conductor was standing in for an international maestro and I thought, as the petite Chinese woman dressed in a black velvet trouser suit tapped quickly to the podium, 'Oh, poor little thing, fancy being landed with this!' But when it came to the last piece, Rachmaninov's rarely played Symphony No. 1, the emotions of the audience and the orchestra were pitched at such a level that I thought we might all burst with ecstasy.

There was this small figure, her short black hair swinging from behind like a shampoo advertisement, her stance that of a Spanish matador, the music in her head propelling her like a flamenco dancer. As the climax neared, she took the baton in both hands, as if to strengthen a backhand volley at Wimbledon. Applause from the audience burst upon her as the music had engulfed us, and she was called back again and again.

The American trumpet soloist in Shostakovich's first piano concerto, as if to make the experience less predictable, was slightly staid, not manic enough, nor even perky enough for the composer or the pianist. And we know how that Concerto can be played because two years ago, in a two-concert marathon at the Macau Music Festival, we heard it for the first time on an evening that vies in memorableness.

Until 15 years ago Hong Kong and Macau, a ferry ride apart, were notorious as a cultural desert. Now, we have so much choice from the international music scene (as well as good local musicians) that people can afford to be blasé. I had said to a woman barrister friend, 'We're booking for Christa Ludwig, how about you?'

'A bit over the hill for us,' she replied. I bridled, for a month before I had watched Svetlana Besmertsova – also 'a bit over the hill' – dance The Swan from Saint-Säen's Carnival of the Animals, dance it like no one else ever has, or ever could.

So, there was Christa Ludwig, one arm resting lightly on the grand piano, the moonlight shimmering on the red lacquer trellis behind her, and on the lake and water lilies that surround the Chinese pavilion in which the recital was held, and on her spun golden white halo of hair. She sang to each of us individually until our hearts were enticed from our bodies.

There were four of us and we had a quick and rather good supper before going on to the University of East Asia to hear the Shostakovich, conducted by the elderly and infirm but brilliant Sandor Vegh. The trumpet and the piano that night competed to thrill us by their laughter.

Living in Hong Kong it is possible, therefore, to experience the sublime, but there is, also, too much opportunity to grieve. For the day before the conductor Yip Wing-sie entranced us, a young Chinese nurse was killed by a stray bullet as a gang made their getaway from a jewellery raid. And a week earlier, on New Year's Eve, 20 young people were trampled and suffocated to death celebrating in the steep, slippery cobbled alley Lan Kwai Fong.

ASIAN WOMEN ARE NOT DOCILE   *February 1993*

Chinese New Year. That time when, unexpectedly, Hong Kong closes down; when tourists in search of shopping or exoticism should stay away; when hundreds of thousands of people leave for their families elsewhere or the sun.

The Governor left Government House at 4pm on Friday, New Year's Eve, for a holiday in Bali. He flew Cathay Pacific, the Colony's airline, child of one of its largest, and longest-established financial empires – Butterfield Swire. I tried to snap him as he drove through the portals stamped ER but a policewoman's hat got in the way. A few minutes earlier, I had photographed Sharon, a woman from Bombay. 'But I look awful,' she protested, pushing her hair back from her face.

'No you don't,' I assured her. 'You look radiant.' And it was true. In spite of her cold and her slightly red nose, and the fact that she had slept outside Government House since 1 o'clock that morning, she radiated that determined good looks and cheerfulness which the traveller associates with flight attendants on the long haul from Hong Kong to London.

Sharon's concern for her looks, the fact that she is a young woman whose face is her fortune, had misled Cathay Pacific management into believing that it could push her – and her sisters and brothers from ten Asian countries – around indefinitely. They thought that she would continue to smile and bend – bend gracefully over rows of seats, and to their own unreasonable demands.

But her training not only taught her to value her looks, to exploit her femininity: it also taught her to withstand tiredness and stress, to react capably to approaching trouble; it gave her strong nerves and stamina to withstand a two-week strike, much of it sleeping rough outside Government House.

A placard held by a member of the Association for the Advancement of Feminism encapsulated the myth, and the reality: 'Asian Women Are Not Docile'. The placard bearer, Tse Yuen-hing, and I climbed the hill to Government House several times to bring moral support to what, after a sudden downpour in the early hours of Saturday, became a well-run tent city. That moment of arrival, to chants of *Mgoi Sai* (thank you very much) or 'We Love You', or 'We Shall Win – YES', never failed to bring a lump to my throat.

But there was more than the need to express solidarity. Other unions and women's, students', church and community groups recognised that, if the Flight Attendants' Union (FAU) was broken by management, the future for all workers in Hong Kong would be threatened. And there came a moment, on the fourteenth day, when it seemed that the beautiful butterfly had been broken.

At 9.15pm we went to the picket line outside the Central Government Offices – to where the strikers had been shifted. We waited for them to come back from one of their mass meetings outside the Roman Catholic Cathedral. By 1.00am they still had not come, so we trailed home. The following morning we learnt that two strike leaders had resigned, and a thousand or so flight attendants had met the midnight deadline imposed by Cathay Pacific management for putting their names on the February duty roster.

But still 500 held out. They would not go back until management agreed that there should be no disciplinary action against strikers – the one clause that could not be agreed, that had prolonged the strike day after day. The apparent collapse was horrible; but the determination of the rump kept a feeble hope alive in the pit of our hearts.

Then Legco Members, who had blown hot and cold for days because of Legco's ambivalent status, rallied. They voted to set up a watchdog body to monitor the return to work and ensure that strikers were not victimised. Somehow, by this formula, everyone managed to retain some face.

What the future holds for trade unionism in Hong Kong is uncertain. But at least Sharon can look in the mirror and look herself in the face. As for next Chinese New Year, do we boycott Cathay Pacific, or do we fly hoping to see the warm smile of Sharon and her sisters?

NUDE MODEL, ROLE MODEL   *April 1993*

Nancy Chu Woo makes little distinction between the shape of luscious green, red or yellow peppers and the nude female form. Paintings of both hang near each other in her exhibition and, when describing them technically, her hands make the same movements in the air. Indeed, at that moment, she also emphasises their similarities in words.

Her paintings are suffused by nature, earth, sky, water and the seasons, real life, but the spirit behind them is determinedly non-representational. She has something to say, and she has worked many years to refine her technique the better to express herself. She is no dilettante.

On this occasion, she was talking mainly to a group interested in her technique and she was impressively articulate about it. I bided my time and then asked what she felt about being a role model for women. Momentarily she was taken aback by the change in subject. I explained briefly that I teach English to Chinese working class housewives and that I use a magazine page colour photograph of her beside one of her paintings in my teaching:

> 'Do you remember who this is?' I ask, as I pin the picture up yet again.
> 'Nancy Woo,' they chorus obediently.
> 'What does she do?'
> 'What do you think of her? Is she beautiful, attractive?'
> 'What do you think she's feeling?'

'What do you think of Nancy Woo's painting?'
'What do you feel about it?'
'What do you think about a woman being an artist?'

I am teaching them the words 'feeling' and 'thinking'. But I am also hoping that they will express their opinions about the painting, Nancy Woo, women and themselves.

At my question to Nancy Woo, the professional artist becomes a woman talking to women about the problems of being a woman painter, in the world, in Hong Kong. Her lovely face which has been animated by the excitement of explaining her work technically, becomes lively with the mischief of swapping notes on womanhood.

She continues to move gracefully on the spot in her fashionably tailored 'artist's tunic' over black leggings. 'I don't get back ache bending over large canvases on the floor,' she explains, 'because I'm good about doing back exercises every day.' Then, 'Let's go and have some tea,' she suggests to those of us who are left.

Studying at Cornell University was not easy. As a young woman she was expected to be filling in time before she got married, not flogging herself to be a good painter. As a married woman in Hong Kong, it is assumed by the uninitiated, and hoped for by male artists, that she is merely dabbling in painting.

But she wins out in the end: she takes advantage of the financial security of a middle class marriage to paint what she likes, how she likes. And because she works sometimes 18 hours a day, seven days a week, and is highly ambitious to communicate through selling her work, she is successful. 'Women painters do well in Hong Kong now,' she chuckles.

She is one of those Hong Kong women who get ahead no matter what the obstacles. The sort of woman that makes people say, 'Hong Kong women aren't discriminated against, they don't need any help.' Fortunately, behind that bright, almost brittle, facade is a woman who treats her nude models as human beings, and takes trouble, through part time teaching at Hong Kong University, to help those climbing up behind her.

It is good to find that I chose well with this role model and I return to the classroom inspired. The next step, now that the Classmates have had their first meal in an Indian restaurant, and have signed up to see the Birmingham Ballet dance *Romeo and*

Juliet, is to invite Nancy Woo to come with a roll of paper under her arm and a paint brush between her teeth and talk to them, in English, of course.

THE MADNESS OF SPRING   *April 1993*

I saw three strange things out walking today. The first was a brilliant clump of lavender-in-the sky – a jacaranda tree in flower. When I was a child living in Kenya, it was nothing to see an avenue of jacaranda in full bloom; though it is a memory that refreshes my spirit. And, sometimes when you fly into Sydney, the mixture of jacaranda trees and swimming pools is most distinctive.

I'm not trying to suggest that Hong Kong's own flora is not a delight – though 150 years ago the island was described as 'a barren rock'. At this time of year, as I've described before, a walk round Jardine's Lookout is a most satisfying experience. The azaleas may be over by a month, but the mustard wattles are just coming into flower, the bougainvillea are dazzling, and the flame trees are flaunting a delicate tracery of green leaves preparatory to bursting into flame. We already have our money on the table: a dollar for the first to see the first hint of orange down in the valley, where it starts.

But jacaranda is not a part of our landscape. What is going on? Well might I ask as I came across Dino being fondled by a Chinese construction worker. That Dino is eminently inviting and available for fondling is not in dispute. He started out as a white labrador puppy 18 months ago. Now, in every appropriate place, he has become suffused with apricot.

What is more, while I talk to most of the dogs guarding the grand mansions, he is the only one I touch. Soon after we met, he demanded it and, with only a moment's hesitation, I gave way. Now, not only do I caress him when he comes bounding to the gate, thrusting his wet nose at me, but I throw one of his several tennis balls for him too, through the bars, and we then share a laugh as he teases me with it.

It is also true that a few months ago I caught a Chinese woman fondling him through the bars while her husband sat in the car alongside, and we exchanged pleasantries about what a beautiful and loving dog he is. But a construction worker from the building site next door? Everyone knows what the Chinese feel about dogs:

for the rich they guard their property, and act as a status symbol. For others, the Australian Minister for Foreign Affairs summed it up when the Pattens' dog, Soda, went missing by suggesting – in private, I'm sure – that Deng Shao Ping had eaten it.

The British, of course, love dogs, and this is a British colony. During the period when Soda was absent without leave, one had to ring friends up in advance to say, 'We're not going to be discussing Soda, are we?' But there was this man, Dino's head held lovingly in his hands. I came up alongside, which was not pleasant as the man was smoking. '*Hou leng,*' I suggested tentatively.

'*Hou leng,*' (very beautiful) he responded. I gave Dino a cursory stroke and went on my way. After all, he got there first. I looked back, and there he was, fondling Dino.

Further on I saw a woman cementing marble tiles to the outside wall of a mansion that has been under construction for at least two years. I was flabbergasted. Women in the construction industry are extremely rare, because they are unlucky. I remember seeing women carrying baskets of rubble when they were clearing that site; that is allowed and they wear Hakka hats with wide straw brims and black protective cloth flaps hanging down.

It is also done for wives to help their husbands with the caissons that form part of the foundations. She lets him down into the deepening hole by rope and is responsible for his safety. In spite of the care the women obviously take, accidents are rather too common. In the technical colleges, too, women students are increasingly registering in the construction courses, and women in charge on a site could eventually become common enough. But this woman was entirely out of place.

Then I looked closer at the pony tail and cut away black and white striped tee shirt. The figure was breastless, and there was a suspicion of a beard. Everything has not gone mad this spring, after all.

FORGING LINKS AT THE WOMEN'S CENTRE   *June 1993*

I bumped into Jennifer as I approached the City Polytechnic. I had come from my English class at the Women's Centre to meet Derek at his workplace. She had come from preparing for exams that will enhance her position as a social worker. She was on her way to supervise the lawyers (such as Derek) at the Free Legal Advice Clinic at the Women's Centre.

It was still a coincidence, for I rarely go to the Polytechnic which is miles away from where we live. What is more, I had just been explaining the meaning of 'coincidence' to the Classmates. This interweaving of women and their concerns is constantly uplifting and links have been forged even more strongly recently by meetings I have at the Centre after my teaching.

In a few weeks we are expecting 18 cadres from the Mainland – senior members of the All-China Women's Federation – to visit Hong Kong as part of a Women in Development Project. I, and thus AWARE, became involved because a year ago I met the Canadian woman involved in Beijing and she had kept my card in a safe place. The Women's Centre, to which AWARE is affiliated, was roped in firstly to add respectability, but now we have a strong organising team.

I have quickly become close to three members of the Women's Centre Executive Committee, middle class Chinese women whom I previously did not know well in any sense. And they have proved to me that the sort of derogatory remarks that abound in the press about *tai tai* (Ladies Who Lunch) are way off beam where they, at least, are concerned.

They meet regularly at the Women's Centre, for it is now a considerable set up to direct. In the two years I have been teaching there, education has expanded, so that it is on its way to becoming a women's college. There are classes now not only in English and Mandarin, but in health and nutrition, and a working group on CEDAW. What is more, so strong a link are the Classmates forging that several of them have cooking and massage classes together outside the Centre.

These friendships are marvellous. If only my Petty was still involved. In a way she is. 'How's Peggy?' asked Anna, a Classmate, as we took the underground together away from the Centre. I had to reply that Pet could not come any more because her work did not allow it. That was only partly true. Pet had organised her work so that she could come to lessons, but it meant doing one of her cleaning jobs on Tuesday evening, and arriving home late.

After her third English lesson, her husband pushed her against the door for being late, and she stopped coming. Some months later, when she found out about his mistress, she talked to me about divorce. I suggested she ring Linda, the social worker who runs the Women's Centre, and Linda arranged for her to attend the Legal Clinic.

Discussing divorce with a lawyer must have brought home to Petty the enormity of what she planned, for Linda told me she thought Petty had had second thoughts. She stopped talking to me about divorce and the wretchedness of her daughter answering a telephone call from her husband's mistress.

The next thing I knew, it was Petty's birthday and she brought me photographs of the birthday cake her husband had produced. A few days later, it was her Chinese birthday and her husband arrived with an expensive gold chain with a small pendant. I looked closely at the pendant, brought for my admiration, and asked, 'Who's that figure?'

'That's Kuan Yin,' Peggy explained.

'Do you realise its significance?' I asked. He can't say anything about his behaviour, because he would lose face, so he gives you a gold pendant of the Goddess of Mercy!'

A DIFFERENT KIND OF GOLD PAVING   *July 1993*

'It's a heartless city, no doubt about that,' said a young expatriate who had spent six weeks living in Chungking Mansions. That seedy rabbit warren of shops, Indian restaurants and hostels for backpackers and other indigent visitors is right in the heart of Hong Kong's gleaming tourist area Tsim Sha Tsui.

A week after that radio interview, not necessarily connected, there was a newspaper exposé of Chungking Mansions. It was revealed as a hotbed of sleaze, degradation even, typical of a greedy, uncaring metropolis. The unemployed or the adventurous come here from all over the world expecting the streets to be paved with gold. They are somewhat gilded, but mainly if you are Hong Kong Chinese, hard working, determined, and lucky.

People, mostly men, on contract from Britain, and other foreigners who have valued expertise and get contracts and work permits before they come, can also do well. But if you turn up as Neelam did the other day – a Pakistani woman fleeing the constraints of family and society – you could come unstuck in Chungking Mansions. Some unsuspecting tourists do, even if it is only escaping from one of the regular fires. Some women, we now learn, are brought over specifically to be prostitutes there.

Innocently, Neelam went from the airport to Chungking Mansions, known worldwide for its cheap hostel rooms. Fortunately, a friend of us both in Pakistan had given her my telephone number. And that let Neelam into a network of friendship and mutual help the full depth and strength of which no one, least of all me, could have suspected.

Neelam rang me out of the blue and I arranged to have lunch with her. By that evening, the network had begun to hum. An AWARE sister gave me the telephone number of Robyn, the chairperson of WIPS (Women in Publishing). Robyn rang dozens of WIPS members about possible work. Polly, Robyn's colleague, moved Neelam into her one room flat, and we put her on the waiting list for a room at the Helena May Club, founded in 1916 for women like Neelam. At the Hong Kong Council of Women AGM that evening, Robyn networked further.

After a week, the advice that guests and fish start to smell after seven days had me on the telephone again. As luck would have it, Janet, an American anthropologist from a Canadian university, had just arrived for her usual summer of research. She had rented a university flat, and was delighted to have someone to share the outgoings. Janet tucked Neelam under her wing socially, too, and took her to Macau, the nearest foreign place, in the hopes, unsuccessfully, of extending her three month tourist visa.

But, in spite of all Robyn's endeavours, and Neelam's own efforts, work proved frustratingly elusive. Two weeks computer programming were well paid, but temporary. Two jobs were offered, but withdrawn because Neelam didn't have a work permit. The Helena May cannot take her until she has a job. She cannot get a work permit without skills which local Chinese do not have. No one answers her job application letters.

She cannot go back to Pakistan. Her father and her society will not forgive her; and then there is her own determination to be independent, to lead her own life. What struck me most forcefully about the reasons for her flight from Pakistan was her wonder at seeing Asian women walking alone, heads high, and by the thousand in the streets of Hong Kong.

So, with no prospect of a job here, with accommodation only for a finite period, and dwindling funds, Neelam will probably have to move on. But where? In Canada, the Immigration and Refugee Board has recently been given guidelines which allow it to admit women seeking refuge from sex discrimination and persecution. Janet will sponsor Neelam. But how do we find out how to apply? The High Commission here says they've never heard of the scheme.

Julie, the AWARE sister who founded the Free Legal Advice Clinic at the Women's Centre, now lives in Canada. A request for information was soon winging its way across the fax wires. However miraculous those wires might be, they are nothing to the strands of our human network. You're wrong, Young Man: Hong Kong is not heartless. But neither are its streets paved with gold.*

WHO WEARS THE PANTS?   *September 1993*

I have to tell you about this wife and husband who were sitting across the breakfast table from each other. The radio was tuned to 'Hong Kong Today'. Thegovernorchrispatten (as he is always called) had been recorded at a business occasion discussing corruption in a way that might not harm the Sino-British talks. '…And our business men and women …' he reassured.

The wife spluttered into her pawpaw. 'Business men *and women*,' she repeated triumphantly. 'I know it's only a little thing but how many times, in public and private print, have I nagged against the use of "businessmen" as a generic term? He is educable!'

The husband grinned wryly. 'I think it's more likely that the new phrase is attempting to prove something else: that there are plenty of women involved in business, and no need for equal pay and anti-discrimination legislation.' The timing was important. The Hong Kong Government recently released a Green Paper entitled 'Equal Opportunities for Women and Men'.

The first draft title had read '… Men and Women'. Reversing the order was the only impact women's groups had on the drafting of the document, in spite of the endless hours we spent, yet again, on meetings and submissions. And even these are weasel words, for we are rather more concerned with real equality than with equal opportunities.

---

*   Neelam has had many adventures since; perhaps one day she will write about them. She is now married and settled abroad.

In retrospect, seeing the nature of the document that has been produced, we were foolishly cooperative in its research and drafting stages. Our cooperation almost proved counter-productive to our cause, as those who solicited it no doubt intended. But we pulled out just in time, refusing to respond to the pathetic draft points when they were shown to us as a great favour. We are not, therefore, party to the final version which is released on a mostly unsuspecting public for comment by the end of December.

I can hardly go through the whole sorry report with you, but let me give you one example of the use of language that, however superficial an indicator it might seem, sums up attitudes and intention. Under 'employment' the authors write, 'It has also been claimed that employers tend to reject female job applicants in certain occupations and positions, thus resulting in occupational segregation.'

'Claimed'! Isn't that a word you use to put down the arguments of your opponent? This is supposed to be a neutral government document, though the Legislative Council's Women's Affairs sub-committee had suggested to the bureaucrats – vainly – that they start from the premise that there is discrimination, and proceed from there to find solutions.

Let me give you one small example of how things are for women in Hong Kong; again it is at first sight superficial, mere words. The Governor has just appointed Anson Chan to be Chief Secretary. Marvellous! The first Chinese, and the first woman in this position. But at the press conference that followed the announcement Anson Chan, a highly intelligent, capable, and personable woman, uttered these immortal words to reassure those who might think that a few privileged women in high places might forget themselves and encourage other women to do the same: 'My husband wears the pants very much in the family.'

Whatever the truth of her words, her need to say them is why we have an *appointed* woman Chief Secretary, an *appointed* woman senior member of the Governor's Executive Council (cabinet), and only one *directly elected* woman Legco member.

What worries me about the Green Paper in the short term is that the efforts of women's groups to combat such attitudes in Hong Kong society are being sidetracked by the need to respond to it. The immediate and related issue that requires their energies is elections in 1994 and 1995. How can we quickly obtain the impetus and resources to ensure that women participate fully at all levels? By the setting up of a Women's Commission, *now*.

After all, Legco has voted for a Women's Commission. And Legco is the body the Governor says he will rely on to approve the political package being negotiated with China.

SHEREE AND CO. *October 1993*

Derek and Sheree hardly see each other any more; once they were inseparable. Happily, the parting has been entirely amicable.

Sheree was Derek's secretary. He was a raw recruit in Hong Kong, but a big cheese in colonial and academic terms. She was a young woman at the start of her career, slightly shy and inexperienced, hiding her ambition. Soon she was indispensable to him. In a Hong Kong institution that indispensability is pronounced, even for a secretary; for many layers are entirely Chinese, and impenetrable culturally and linguistically. Hierarchies and administrative regulations – usually of British antecedence – are more byzantine than in Byzantium.

Sheree was my first entrée to a certain type of Hong Kong Chinese woman: educated and English-speaking to a certain level, modest, always neat, and fashionable in the Chinese secretarial way (cream tights – never bare legs – low heels, wet-permed hair, cardigans against the permanent air conditioning).

One feature is not at first obvious. For many Chinese in Hong Kong Education is everything – a continuing process that allows ambition to flourish and be rewarded. When Sheree got her first diploma in business management, taken, of course, at the same time as full time employment, Derek and I stood by her at the award ceremony; her parents could not take the afternoon off. A year or so later, Sheree asked the institution for advancement, fully supported by Derek. She was turned down.

The unthinkable happened: she gave in her notice and decamped to a rival establishment. How could she? We asked each other in bewilderment. How could any other secretarial job be so fulfilling, any other boss be more kindly, more sensitive and encouraging? It was a lesson to us in Hong Kong upward mobility. But was it really? Within three months Sheree was back as Derek's secretary. She had missed something in the air, or the big general office with all her work-sisters, or even her boss.

Then she got married, a ceremony we missed because we were in England. In Hong Kong marriage dates are not moveable – some dates are lucky and no other will do. We winced, waiting for her to leave, or to get pregnant and leave, as is too often the way. She stayed on, gaining further diplomas as she did so. When the gates of the Open Learning Institute (OLI) opened, she was one of the 7,000 applicants for 400 places. She was unsuccessful. She started teaching short-hand typing at the YMCA.

Rosanna, Derek's moody, high-flying, highly-educated adminis- trative assistant went to fry more enticing fish in a fast-localising sea; it had become infra dig to work with an expatriate. Sheree decided that she wanted that ultimate job. It was a big step up, apparently outside her league, and the powers that be dismissed her with a wave of the hand; she didn't even have a degree. Eliza came and went. Sheree applied again. She and Derek persisted; insisted that she be considered. She got the job.

Now she ran a sizeable ship; once again she had abandoned Derek, but in a good cause, for instead of running his personal office, she ran his wider fiefdom. And she soon justified every confidence he and she had had in her. In her place as Derek's secretary came Alice, nervous as a kitten for six months, finally coming into her own – as competent a secretary as Sheree had ever been, conscientious, humorous, strict.

Meanwhile, unbeknown to me, Sheree had at last got a place at the OLI and started a degree in business management. Thus she ran the wider domain, a household, and her higher studies – that slip of a girl we had first met six years earlier.

When the management structure was re-arranged, Derek moved upwards to be Dean of the new Faculty. Alice went with him, Sheree stayed behind, and Emily arrived to be administrative assistant of the new, smaller, more select ship. At first we wondered about Emily: was she exactly right? But with Alice pushing from behind, Derek pulling from in front, and her own determination, she, too, soon proved as indispensable a part of the team.

By now, Sheree's own team in the original general office – where they eat instant noodles at lunchtime and then fall asleep on their arms – was constantly expanding. And she and a new secretary – Wendy – had to look after Dhirendra, Derek's replacement as Head of Department. 'Does Dhirendra fully appreciate Sheree's worth?' I've just asked Derek as I write.

'Oh yes,' he replied. 'The question is, does she fully appreciate Dhirendra's. The power in the Department is fairly well acknowledged!'

I bump into Sheree, but only very occasionally; I rarely go to the office at all, and now she is neither in Derek's inner nor outer office. When Derek takes his crew out to lunch it is Alice, Emily and Cora, not Sheree; the presents to be searched for every leave are no longer for her.

But recently we have all come together for a special occasion: Cora's wedding. Last Saturday, on a lovely sunny autumn day, all the generations that keep and have kept Derek on the straight and narrow for six and a half years – Sheree and Alice and Emily – clustered with us around Cora in her flouncy cream ballgown. The photographs should be historic.

So there is a loyalty and friendship between them and Derek in the wider scheme of things; but, within, a close and fast sisterhood between these special, extraordinary, ordinary young women of Hong Kong.

STORIES FOR EVA   *October 1993*

I'm so excited about a development in my English teaching at the Women's Centre! It started at our end of term lunch, and has just begun to bear identifiable fruit. A few mornings before, there was a piece in the local paper about two schoolgirls who had won a prize for reading a novel in English and writing a report on it. I photocopied the piece and added to it homework instructions for the forthcoming summer holiday break. The Classmates were to do the same for me.

Our lunch was convivial and fun, and defences lowered even further than during lessons. Trust and confidence have been an integral part of the women-centred teaching I devised when I first started five terms ago, but a social occasion naturally enhances it.

Eva, sitting beside me, confided how important the lessons are to her. I gently drew from her an ambition: to use the English classes, which she has quite recently joined, to further her education. Tracy, sitting the other side of her, nodded in agreement. What made this confession all the more poignant was the family background that emerged. Eva has a brother who read Economics at the University of Hong Kong; another is doing Computer Studies in Japan; a third is studying Civil Engineering in the United States.

Her father expected her to leave school and start work in his Chinese medicine shop before she finished secondary school. She begged to be allowed to stay on and was allowed to do so for a while, but there was no question of tertiary education. She cried for weeks. Thereafter, Eva became, as I taught her in her first lesson, and as she has since remembered with relish, a 'dogsbody'. She spits the word out. Then she got married, and had children.

At the end of our lunch, I handed out the holiday work and noticed that smiles drooped a little. I realised then that to read a novel in English was beyond their ability. It had occurred to me before that I should write them a novel to fit their needs. Now the idea resurfaced. But as I travelled back to the Island, another idea began to intrude; and by the time I got home it was fully fledged.

I sat down and wrote a letter to 60 well-educated, professional Hong Kong Chinese women. I told them about the lack of suitable literature, and about Eva. I asked each of them to write 1,000 words about anything at all, as long as it was written simply.

Our contributors are replying in drips and drabs. I have been gratified at how warmly they have responded. They have really understood what it is about, been pleased to be asked, and to do their best.

There is more work involved for me than I had expected. Inevitably, I have had to rewrite the pieces. Only I know the Classmates' capacity, and I work out what they need from each piece as I come to prepare it for use. I also devise questions and a list of useful vocabulary, grammar and pronunciation.

I gave out the first piece just before the Mid-Autumn Festival. It was about that celebration, as remembered by Betty Wei, the Shanghai historian, when she was a child in Nanjing. I explained to the Classmates that Betty had written it specially for them. I watched them read it through for the first time, sitting in pairs. I knew immediately that we were onto something.

The following lesson, I read it through to them; they read it through for me. We discussed everything to do with it. 'Tell me what else you know about Nanjing – other than its famous duck,' I asked. 'I know two things.' Within a few minutes I had four pieces of information. They had looked it up. They were interested, engaged.

Now, at the end of each lesson I hand out the story for the next week. I explain who wrote it, and they go off to prepare it. For the first time, HOMEWORK has become a pleasure. Eventually, the Classmates will have their own book, written specially for them. I think we'll call it *Stories for Eva*.

JUST A HOUSEWIFE   *November 1993*

When the doorbell rang yesterday I was in the middle of a sentence, racing against time to prepare the latest story for the Classmates. It was one about vision and ideals for a better Hong Kong by appointed Legco Member Christine Loh. Outside stood our next door neighbour, a Korean woman long-established in Hong Kong but with whom I have only a slight acquaintance, partly because of a language problem.

When the family moved in a couple of years ago, she gave us, without consultation, an impeccable front door mat to match theirs. Now Madame was pointing at our door mat. 'I have asked our *amah*, Lourdes, to clean yours when she cleans ours,' she said. 'But she obviously forgets.' I smiled politely and she continued, 'I also discussed it with your maid once when you were away.'

'Really,' I replied, still smiling politely.

'Yes, you see, it really must be kept clean.'

'Of course,' I replied. 'Goodbye.' I came back and recounted the story, with embellishments, to Pet.

I notice this morning that neither Pet nor Lourdes has managed, or even attempted, to get the white specks from under the impractical surface of the mat. I wonder if Madame will speak to the men who deliver our groceries or our vegetables? But I shall leave the matter in her capable hands.

To be honest, I have housewife acquaintances with more pressing things on their minds, and it is to them that I devote my attention.

Wynnie Wing-yee Cosgrove calls herself a domestic manager and, as she told us in the story she wrote for the Classmates and which we discussed last week, she is the only manager she knows without a business card.

Wynnie lived a quite ordinary life in Hong Kong until she was in her mid twenties. Apart, that is, from losing an eye in an accident on the way to kindergarten when she was five. As a result, her parents encouraged her to be sporty though, as she says, the loss did not hold her back academically. She ended up with a university degree and a good job with a radio station.

Something happened in 1988 to change her life. Hong Kong did very badly at the Seoul Olympics and its Chinese athletes were both maligned and satirised in the press. Wynnie decided then and there to become a world class runner. With the help of her New Zealand husband, an experienced sportsman, she has since had considerable marathon success. She wears Hong Kong's colours proudly and looks forward to the next Olympics.

'Please let me know if I can do any other things to help with your association,' she wrote in the letter that accompanied her piece for the Classmates.

Dear Wynnie, if you only knew how much you have already done for your fellow housewives, how your story enthused and inspired them.

Unfortunately, Grace was not there that day. Indeed, Grace has not been to class for 18 months, but she came yesterday, just to say hello to me. She brought with her the little boy who I thought was the cause of her staying away. He used to hate her coming and grizzled and tugged at her throughout the lessons. He seems quite grown up now and I hoped that Grace might come back to class.

'I can't,' she said, ducking her head. She looked weary, the bloom and vitality I remember quite faded.

'Why not?' I pressed her mercilessly.

'My husband won't allow me.' My widening eyes urged her on. 'He says women who come to the Women's Centre learn to leave their husbands. His mother left his father and him when he was little to go off with another man.'

'Are you listening?' I asked Linda, the social worker.

'I already know,' she replied. 'And she's not the only one.'

It's at times like this that you have to question your role in raising the consciousness of women in their own worth. You question it, and you continue teaching in the same way.

But what is the answer for Grace? Must she continue for ever a doormat?

1994

January 1994

'I hope you didn't think I was snubbing you,' I said apologetically to Harriet on the telephone. I had sat near her at the Club and studiously avoided her eye. I didn't want her to have to explain to her companions how she knew me.

She laughed. 'I'm so shortsighted I didn't even see you. But thanks!'

Harriet and I knew each other really quite well for six months. Then one afternoon, she got out of the taxi we were sharing. We said a fond goodbye and off she set. A postcard from France was all I had received from her since. And I understood. I was part of something she must forget.

I've mentioned her before. She was one of Derek's clients when he was duty lawyer; he got her bail extended. She was charged with shoplifting from a supermarket: a bottle of wine and two yoghurts. Derek's dealings with her ended then. But, against my better judgement, I had sat next to her and heard her story. She felt too humiliated to tell any of her friends, and she was divorced. She was facing the nightmare alone.

'Would you like me to come with you next time? I asked. She jumped at my offer.

There was no sign of Harriet at the Duty Lawyers' office on the appointed day. 'But it isn't today,' the clerk said. I was taken aback. I had heard the magistrate quite clearly.

A few minutes later, Harriet came puffing in. 'I thought we were meeting downstairs,' she explained. I was not the only one mistaken. Some formality had been omitted; no one had told her of the change. It was the last time the Duty Lawyer system let her down, but there were to be many more delays and excursions.

Harriet had been all keyed up for that day. The thought of further delay appalled her. There was one advantage. The next time we met at court, she had copied my plain black skirt and jacket; her red hair was tied demurely back. She had a new duty lawyer now.

103

He felt she should play the health card. She had, indeed, a medical condition which, handled properly by her lawyer, might get her off. But I could see her baulking. She believed she was not guilty.

She was quite clear that she had taken the bottle of wine into the supermarket; she was on her way to leave it at a friend's house for a party she did not wish to attend. A close friend had just died. She accepted that the yoghurts, put carelessly into her trolley, had fallen into the open mouth of the capacious holdall that is her trade mark. She had forgotten them when she paid the bill; but she had not stolen them.

The avuncular, British magistrate at one of Harriet's subsequent appearances suggested, tactfully, that he would consider the extenuating circumstance of bulimia. 'I hope you don't mind my suggesting it,' he said kindly. 'But I have had several expatriate ladies with the problem.'

'No, thank you,' replied Harriet firmly. The case was adjourned.

She prevaricated about approaching her doctor. I did not nag her for I was in complete sympathy with her need to prove her innocence. But her lawyer was visibly irritated. Without a medical excuse, he did not feel she had a chance.

After many months of adjournments for one reason or another, Harriet had a new duty lawyer, a young Englishwoman. She understood. And there was a case. Put simply, the supermarket alleged that Harriet unzipped her bag to put the yoghurt and wine inside, and zipped it up again. The zip on the bag had long been broken, as the magistrate could see.

Thus it was that, finally, the bulimia magistrate, without a letter from Harriet's doctor, found her not guilty. And thus we three women put our arms about each other and shared a taxi back to town.

'I wrote you a soppy letter that evening,' Harriet told me last week on the telephone. 'But I didn't post it; it's still here on the mantelpiece. I'll write you another one.'

'I want that one,' I insisted. 'It's mine!' She laughed. We may never be in touch again.

HUNTING THE COUCAL   *March 1994*

'Bode watching?' enquired the middle-aged Chinese man pleasantly as he passed me.

'Yes,' I replied, smiling to return his greeting.

I knew why he had said 'bode' instead of 'bird'. It had nothing to do with his English, which I suspect is good. Our brief interchange epitomised how for 150 years our two cultures have adjusted as far as necessary, and as far as possible, to each other.

I had stood aside instinctively from the narrow path to look at birds that might or might not be there because I did not wish to be treated as if I were not there. That might mean being jostled or having my space otherwise invaded in a way that, even after seven years, is still unsettling.

It has nothing to do with my being a woman, or an expatriate; more to do with Hong Kong being one of the most crowded places on earth. There is no room in the streets or lifts, nor even in over-crowded housing, for individuals to be too sensitive about their body space.

The stranger, on the other hand, being a 'gentleman', was over-anxious to give me two messages – thus he came to make a slip of the tongue. Not only did he notice that I was there, he also acknowledged it. What is more, while he may have been walking purposely from A to B, as Chinese prefer, he was accepting that I was probably just going for a walk, even looking out for birds.

And he was right. That little-frequented short cut from one part of Jardine's Lookout to another is a tropical haven. The air is heavy with moisture and heat there, even on a dull, cool winter day. The undergrowth is thick and lush, many of the leaves oversized. There is always a sprinkling of vivid red flowers, the sound of running water, something stirring in the undergrowth. Here, I quite often see a squirrel. I might just see or hear a coucal (crow pheasant). I always walk through it hopeful and prepared, my eyes darting hither and yon.

The unexpected stranger in my path had distracted me. As I turned back, however, I saw the low black undercarriage and wide wing span of a large bird skimming overhead. My heart jumped. Is it or isn't it? It had almost reached a thicket, there to disappear, when it tilted slightly and I saw the glorious cinnabar upper wings of the coucal.

How can I get so excited about the glimpse of one coucal? And yet I always do, partly because it is so rare, partly because it is so beautiful. Living on the fringe of an urban jungle we don't see much wildlife; but we do see just enough for each occasion to be special and memorable.

We hunt coucals with our eyes and ears throughout the year, never quite knowing at what season they appear. Sometimes we will be woken at dawn by the sound of someone blowing into the neck of a bottle. We'll leap from the bed, rush to the window and strain our eyes at the mass of foliage spreading like a green sea floors below. If we're lucky, we'll spot a pair as they glide from one secret place to another, with those irresistible flashes of blue black and cinnabar.

Once or twice, we have watched one of these beauties flaunting itself for some minutes on the trampoline of creepers that veils the slopes of a nearby hill. The excitement and pleasure is almost too much to bear.

More common cabarets are provided by the white (sometimes dirty) cockatoos. They say that the flock of 12 we see were released from the Botanical Gardens to save them from the Japanese when Hong Kong was invaded in December 1941, that they still wear their tags. I find it hard to believe.

Once, just after Chinese New Year, the cockatoos raided the cumquat tree – with its small, egg-shaped and lucky citrus fruit – on a balcony beneath. They sat on the rail in a row, sulphur yellow crests erect, each holding a cumquat up to its beak, nibbling like monkeys, and carelessly discarding the orange skins.

I see a squirrel once in ten walks. Sometimes, a lithe dark grey shape in the tree above catches my eye and I laugh as the fluffy, dandelion clock tail flashes from branch to branch.

Recently, I heard a frantic screeching and chattering. It took much effort to pinpoint the sound. But why was a snake thrashing around in a tree? Very primeval. Then I realised that it was a squirrel lashing the branch again and again with its usually feathery tail furled like a leather whip, and screeching with each frenzied thwack. I believe it was courting!

With such overt sexual goings-on, no wonder the Chinese gentleman and I observe the proprieties as our paths cross in that steamy vale.

A CRICKETING WIFE   *March 1994*

When you become a cricketing wife, you quickly imbibe essential courtesies. You don't, for example, greet a player returning to the pavilion with polite applause if he is out for a duck. Such observances make the difference between being a crass outsider and an almost acceptable appendage. You also develop sensitivities about how *you* are treated. And, last weekend, I came across the ultimate dismissive response from a male player to a female spectator.

As you know, if you need to move around during an over, you only do so between balls; you must never be distracting. Derek is an opening bowler. He takes his bowling seriously, and has done for 50 years or so. For 15 years I have too. Even now, he has a long run up. I match every step of that trundle with heartbeats of anticipation. At that very moment, as he took the leap preparatory to the ball leaving his hand, a padded player walked in front of me, a foot away.

I said nothing; we were guests in a foreign country – though the culprit was British. But I thought, as I sat back exasperated, either I am a non-person in front of whom, therefore, one can walk. Or, I am a mere woman. I won't mind if I am walked in front of because I haven't a clue what's going on.

We had gone all the way from Hong Kong to Singapore by cruise liner to play two games of cricket. Our team of 13 players and their spouses arrived somewhat the worse for wear after three days and four nights of 'relaxation'. Singapore, after the cold, grey, bleak damp of Hong Kong's March, was hot, steamy, sunny and intermittently rather wet. When we thought we could not play the first afternoon because of a sodden outfield, we tucked into an unbeatable Sri Lankan curry.

The rain cleared, the hot sun worked, and some players had to trundle down the wicket rather weighed down. We lost both games. Whites became very soggy, mud-spattered and smelly. But it was all worth it, as playing cricket so often is.

I've faithfully followed Derek's cricket passion that fails to diminish with age through several exotic climes now. In Papua New Guinea I even used to keep score. In Hong Kong I carefully evade that responsibility. I regard my purpose as twofold. Firstly, I support my husband's teams.

One season he played at least four games against Hong Kong University for four different teams: City Polytechnic (where he teaches law); Legal Eagles; Oxford and Cambridge; and the Hong Kong Cricket Club Casuals with whom we went to Singapore.

My most anguished game was two days before we sailed. Derek played with the Casuals against City Polytechnic. 'Who do I support?' I wailed.

A philosopher from the City Polytechnic advised, 'You hope Derek plays brilliantly, and that we win!'

My second function, through thick and thin, is to monitor, sympathise with or exalt over Derek's every run up, ball bowled, catch or dropped catch, boundary or run out, block or swoosh, wicket or failure to get to the ball.

'What's the betting,' I said to Victoria, as her husband Paul bowled a good ball and fumbled the catch that would have made an unforgettable memory, 'that all Paul will be able to talk about when he comes off is that missed opportunity?'

Paul walked towards us. 'How could I have …?' he started, pain turning to bewilderment as we collapsed in laughter.

For Derek, playing cricket is a joy beyond compare. But what do I get, apart from wifely satisfaction? It is the only time in my whole hectic life when I do nothing at all. The white on green, preferably with a blue sky; perhaps palm trees or bougainvillea in the background; silence except for the sound of leather on willow; all work an indefinable magic. I relax a hundredfold – my mind and my body. It's worth a lot.

A DEVIL OF A DAY   *April 1994*

It is very hard to be impartial when you are a lay devil. When I go as Derek's assistant to the magistrates' court, all his clients are innocent, as far as I'm concerned. And the wife there with the child in her arms is not a cynical ploy to influence the duty lawyer or the magistrate, but a genuine victim who needs my moral support.

I wrote those first lines sitting in the room where Derek was to interview his client. He had asked for the handcuffs to be removed, and the police to stay at one end of the room, so that there was privacy for the heroin addict facing sentence today. The several police officers in their impeccable uniforms lounged on chairs smoking. The 'client' sat hunched, pale, the back of his filthy sandshoes trodden down, his ankles splodged with pigment deficiency.

We waited for a report to be got that should have been ready. I started to write. Derek's voice saying my name suddenly cut across my thoughts. I looked up. Four young women – girls, under 18; 15, perhaps – had been brought in, accompanied by policewomen. They sat in a row on a bench and their handcuffs were taken off. The keys did not work at the first turn. They grimaced, and rubbed their wrists when the cuffs were removed. I could see the red-blue bracelet mark.

Interview over, we moved to court No. 5. Our man was brought in, handcuffed to two others. They had been sitting beside me. I had not realised their close, so close, connection before. The middle man was elderly, gaunt, hair uncombed, mouth open; the third, young and pockmarked.

We sat in court, desultory conversation in Cantonese bandied between the police lawyer, the police officers, the clerks, and the interpreter. The accused sat silent.

The magistrate comes in, male, Chinese. We've had him before. He has a manner which suggests an aversion to silver-tongued, tall, Western professors of law who insist on winning cases. Derek asks for a suspended sentence, a last chance for his client, an addict for 20 years who now has the offer of a room of his own and a job, to take a grip on his life. The magistrate knows the addict too well; he gives him two months in prison.

The young man of the trio now turns out also to be a client, as yet un-interviewed. The sentencing of the old man is delayed while papers are sought. The interview of the young man takes place where we have been sitting.

I move into the public area and a young woman moves beside me to overhear the interview; wife, sister? If I ask her, she may not understand and I will interrupt her listening. Wife, I think, she has a wedding ring. I shuffle up to allow her to hear and see better. She is soberly and smartly dressed in a blue silk blouse and silk trousers. Her face is set and anxious, her raised fingers pressed against the bench. I don't listen to the interview. I will hear Derek distil it when he puts the case for leniency. But I hear the duty lawyer adviser say that the client is 18. He has been on drugs. 'Would your triad friends leave you alone?' I hear Derek ask.

'Yes.' The woman has closed her eyes.

I tap Derek on the shoulder. 'Who is this woman? What family support does he have?'

'Thanks.' The adviser goes to talk to her. She is his mother.

That is why I come with Derek, not just out of human interest, not just to write stories. Later, I track down his missing briefcase to the interview room where he left it among the accused.

The mother is sitting there now thinking, How did this happen? Where did I go wrong? She is a respectable woman, seemingly far too young to have a son of 18.

A young man with a fashionable haircut has arrived in the public gallery out of breath. The woman goes to sit beside him. Another son, obviously. He is also pockmarked. At some stage she has coped with two boys with smallpox. There is no father mentioned.

The charges are not about drugs but thefts. The boy has already pleaded guilty. Now, the magistrate asks him again, and I paraphrase, if he is ready to shop his mates. 'No.' He looks sly in the dock, unrepentant, in spite of his neat haircut, his navy blue tee shirt and clean white anorak. He has committed many offences on probation. And there is one robbery with violence with his 'confederates' and iron bars.

'You will take your medicine like a man,' says the magistrate in English. I don't know how it is translated to the boy. He is to be sent to training school – twelve to 21 months re-education inside; three years close supervision thereafter.

He had wanted the 'short (six months), sharp, shock' of a detention centre. His lawyer said he would be a model detainee. The police cannot wait to get the handcuffs back on him. His mother hurries out to have a quick last word with him as he passes.

In the lavatory afterwards, I asked the duty lawyer 'In-Charge' what the four young women were there for.

'Juveniles,' she responded. 'C and P.'

'C and P?'

'Care and Protection.'

'Prostitution …?

'That … running away from home …' She was more concerned to explain how the lavatory works. The flushing system does not. You fill a red bucket from a misshapen piece of plastic hose fixed to the tap in the basin outside, and pour it down the lavatory pan.

I did it, and thanked her for her advice.

Back at home, I wanted to discuss the case of the drug addict. How long would he actually serve in prison? Would he have treatment there for his addiction? Did he really have a job and room offer as he claimed? 'And I was interested to see,' I probed further, 'even though he's a street sleeper, that he seemed to speak a little English. I saw you talking together when the interpreter wasn't there. What did he say?'

'Oh, darling, do you really want to know?' asked my husband, his face changing shape. 'He just said, over and over again, "Help me!"'

PROUD MUMS   *October 1994*

Both Petty and Theresa have a new look. It says 'Relaxed Mum'.

Theresa has been particularly tense over the past few years. First it was a threat by her landlords to evict her from her little flower stall outside the supermarket complex at the bottom of our road. I wrote to the managing director of the supermarket chain on her behalf. Whether or not my letter was instrumental, she is still there and expanded. Then there was her ambition to open a second stall outside the new rival supermarket on the other side. I wrote a letter of support. Her application failed.

The reward for my help is getting half-dead flowers more cheaply than Theresa's less-favoured customers. But, as so often when you do favours, I have been more subject to her moods than have customers who still need to be courted. Perhaps I'm regarded as 'family' for whom an effort to be sweet is unnecessary. I should be flattered!

Then there was the perennial problem of Johnny and George's schooling. Derek's position in a tertiary institution empowered him, in Theresa's eyes, to pull strings for the boys throughout the secondary school system. She got quite grouchy when I tried gently to explain that he could do nothing.

Then George became bolshie and refused to confide in his mother about his future. Her eyes were full of hurt and she took it out on me when I went to buy flowers and asked how things were. Finally, she insisted that George come to see Derek to discuss possibilities.

He arrived one Saturday morning with two mates, his younger brother and a bouquet of leftovers. The young men wore rather dirty Doc Martens and plonked themselves down. I served jasmine tea and biscuits and gracefully retired.

George speaks little English but I think he must have been encouraged by Derek's avuncular ministrations to his self-esteem.

Recently Theresa informed me, her face aglow, that he had been accepted for a cookery course run by the Jockey Club.

Then it was Johnny's turn. He has always been more lively, his English better. Theresa really thought he was going to do well for the family, and no doubt George always sensed that.

Johnny had applied for a post-secondary course too. Theresa was dumbfounded when he was not accepted in the first batch. 'The second batch will be informed on 23 September,' she told me a little warily. Passing by a week or so later, I had to decide. Should I say something and be told coldy that he had failed? By asking, would I make her lose face? Or should I say nothing and be thought of as uncaring? Johnny had not been taken in the second batch either.

But last time I bought tired orchids, she burst out, 'One of those accepted has fallen out. Johnny had a telephone call. He's already started his motor mechanics' course.' At last there was general rejoicing. Her boys are settled on respectable career paths.

Sally, Petty's elder twin daughter, has been settled for a while in a bank. Helen, who had an operation for deafness that held her down for a year, left school and became an assistant in a leather goods shop. She has been taking typing lessons in the evening and now has a job as a clerk. The girls are still 'lazy', but they are not working in factories as their mother did, and they are not cleaning other people's lavatories, as Petty is now. That is the ultimate goal of a Hong Kong mother.

Then there is Peter Bear, the apple of his mother's eye. He was due to go to secondary school. It was Petty's brother's old school, and he is a white collar worker. I was roped in to write a letter of recommendation. For some reason I never fathomed, Peter was not accepted but he has, instead, gone to a school with which Petty is perfectly satisfied. He started a couple of weeks ago and is happy.

I don't know if our efforts had any effect on the future of Theresa and Petty's families. But I feel closer to my two friends and share their relief.

THE FACE OF JUSTICE   *October 1994*

'What a cow!' I said to the officer of the duty lawyer scheme as we came out of court. It was hardly discreet for the 'devil' of the duty lawyer to speak thus of the magistrate. But I felt strongly.

It had started well. Our client was accused of obstructing the police. Not only did his statement seem logically to rebut that charge but the man himself, a mature, single parent truck driver who lived with and looked after his elderly parents and children, was mild and plausible.

Then we got into court. Our duty lawyer officer was a woman, so were the police prosecutor, the interpreter, and the clerk; and so was the magistrate. I expected to see an example of women running the show with competence and humanity.

During an adjournment break, the interpreter endeared herself to us. This was not easy because of our strong feelings against the proceedings being in English, to the bewilderment of the vast majority of defendants who understand only Cantonese. She is taking an external law degree on top of her full time job and delighted in the opportunity to discuss her prospects with someone from a law school, and to obtain a precious business card.

The police prosecutor was reasonable and friendly; the atmosphere in court was relaxed. Even the defendant's parents seemed reassured: their son's lawyer, though tall, fair and non-Cantonese speaking, and therefore slightly alien, seemed friendly and helpful. His devil beamed sympathy. The elderly pair sat there, clean-scrubbed and best-dressed. Frequently, mum slipped out – she was obviously having bladder trouble, and it was very cold in court.

Then the Chinese magistrate appeared. She was carefully-coiffed, carefully made up, verging on the glamorous. There was a case before ours. She laid into the young defendant. Fair enough: he had not reported to his probation officer; he was still apparently on drugs; he was no doubt a bad lot. But the magistrate screwed up her pretty face and her voice was petulantly hectoring to match. And when our case came on, she treated the English duty lawyer, old enough to be her father, and quite wise in the ways of the law and the world, similarly.

She certainly seemed uninterested in his best efforts to defend his client. From her exalted height, there were lots of 'tsks' and sighs and impatient eye movements, second guessing interruptions and almost a tapping of her pencil.

Was it her cold I wondered? A cold can make you feel out of sorts. But I don't think so. I think it was another problem – one that often bothers me with inexperienced professional women. It is a phenomenon for which they are not entirely to blame. It is just as much society's fault with its view of professional women, particularly if they are fairly young and rather comely.

I noticed it personally and most strongly with my GP in London. I once heard a patient call her 'nurse' and then I understood why she was always putting on the authority in a way which inevitably made the situation worse.

So our magistrate, to prove that she was fully powerful, found our mild-mannered client guilty. He had been stung by the traffic policeman's first words – 'F... your mother' – into the bolshiness expected of him.

He earns $8,000 (£750) a month. On that he keeps himself, three children and his parents. She fined him $2,500 (£200). What is more, during the case she did not look or listen, let alone think. She had made up her mind from the start. That I detected simply from her body language – more potent than English or Chinese.

The magistrate, her own authority always under threat, could not bring herself to disbelieve the clean cut young policeman, and therefore to consider that he may have abused his power.

CLASH OF THE TITANS   *December 1994*

You could be forgiven for thinking that the magistrates' courts are run by women. Or is it that women are sent to the back of beyond? In the courts on Hong Kong Island, accessible to the homes of most middle class magistrates, most of the magistrates are men. At Kwun Tong, which the coiner of the phrase 'concrete jungle' obviously had in mind, and which is out on a limb on Kowloon side, we appeared before three women yesterday.

Once the women have daily made their way there, other less practical, more obviously ideological issues arise. Because of how Derek's work load was managed, I was able to watch an expatriate woman magistrate handle a case which the Chinese woman defence lawyer suggested to her was beyond her ken.

As I settled in court, a Chinese woman witness was leaving the stand. And it was only during an adjournment that I debriefed the defence lawyer and understood some of the ramifications. The woman, a prosecution witness, was the natural mother of the seven year old child in question. She had given testimony of how her elder daughter had brought the victim to her; how she had found bruising on her body and taken her to the doctor; how he had then found five horrible marks on her legs – marks made by a bamboo cane.

Before the court, accused of cruelty to a child, was the father. The bruises were not at issue; the prosecution had decided to concentrate on the cane marks, recorded for posterity by the doctor, together with his testimony.

It transpired that the victim's mother was the father's mistress, by whom he had had two daughters. And they had once lived together. But at the time of the caning, which was admitted, both daughters lived with the father and his wife and their three older children.

The victim has epilepsy and is, by all accounts, very naughty. She is prescribed medication and, according to the defence, it has to be taken after food. (Though the doctor told the Court food was preferable, not essential.)

On that day, she refused to eat the food to enable her to take the medicine and was, thus, caned ten times on her legs, five of the lashes leaving shocking lacerations.

Defence counsel was a woman of some spirit and considerable self-esteem. 'Your Worship and I both have children like Yu-ling,' she declaimed, swinging her long black hair. 'But I must ask you not to be influenced by that in judging my client.'

The magistrate gazed back benignly from under her short, fair curly hair.

'You must judge these cane marks objectively,' continued defence counsel, and the magistrate's often mobile face continued to restrain itself. 'Different cultures have different ways of controlling a child. For Chinese people this is a common type of cane to correct children.' The defendant had not caned his child wilfully, as the law demanded for a conviction, but for good reasons, for her own good.

The magistrate only allowed her face to tighten when the Defence changed tack and scavenged for technical points: the prosecution had not proved that the girl was under 16; had not proved the father who inflicted the marks was the man in the dock. The magistrate then accused the younger woman defence counsel of misleading the Court.

During another adjournment, defence counsel whinged about only doing her duty for her client, and feared the worst, because the magistrate could not be objective. But if her client was sent to prison, she would have ample grounds for appeal.

But the magistrate was experienced in the ways of cheeky barristers. And she could calculate the force needed to inflict the wounds she had seen. She found the defendant guilty and remanded him in custody for two weeks pending reports. But how about bail? Defence counsel's tone and body language said much. She suspected she had been thwarted as far as an appeal was concerned.

'I've thought about this for a very long time,' replied the magistrate immovably. There was a pause then she added, 'But I can tell you that I may consider a non-custodial sentence.' She almost hid her satisfaction at out-manoeuvring defence counsel by the sentence, as well as confirming, by finding the accused guilty of the charge, that there is such a thing as universal human rights.

How members of that Chinese family will now relate to one another remains to be seen. At least the youngest may in future be physically inviolate.

1995

I was scrambling eggs for lunch, and eating them at the kitchen table. Petty was in the kitchen too, ironing my silk vests. This is our lunchtime ritual on Tuesdays and Thursdays, the only chance we have to talk.

I asked her if she had bought new clothes for Chinese New Year, as is customary. She had: trousers, a top and jacket, and shoes. She couldn't remember the predominant colour, she would look. I told her that Mummy and I had, for the first time, been to the Jade Market on Saturday. She warned me against fakes. We discussed jewellery. 'I can't wear rings,' Pet said, 'because my hands are always in water.'

'How about round your neck?'

'Well, my husband gave me a gold necklace once.'

'I remember.' We had both been surprised; it was the only human thing he had done in recent memory – an attempt to mollify her when he suspected she was finding it hard to continue with him. She was gently pleased at the time.

Then Pet said, refilling the steam iron with water, 'I've got a new room in North Point.'

I wondered what she meant. I have written before of the small public housing flat she shares with the rest of the family in Aberdeen. They moved a year or so ago into one with an extra room – a red letter day. 'You mean,' I ventured uncertainly, 'a different flat from your one in Aberdeen?'

She nodded. 'Yes. We moved there last Saturday: Peter, Helen, Sally and me. Not my husband.'

'You've left your husband?' I could feel my eyes get big and round.

She nodded again, her face alight with mischief and satisfaction. 'It costs $3,300 a month,' she added.

'Just one room? All of you in just one room.' She nodded no less delightedly.

'Well … You told me you were saving up "running away money" but I didn't expect it so soon.' I had thought more in terms of ten years!

'You know you asked me what I had done over Christmas,' she said. 'Well, we spent the time getting things ready. On Saturday when my husband came home we'd gone.'

'What did you feel that day,' I asked her curiously, though I knew what she'd say, even the words she'd use.

'I felt free.' She lifted her head proudly, and the iron off my silk vest.

She explained that her husband was shattered by her departure; he hadn't eaten since. Not knowing where she'd gone, he had got in touch with her brother and begged her to come back, to give him one more chance. 'But I've given him many one more chances,' she replied. Then he wrote a letter and took it to Peter Bear's school and gave it to him to give to his mother. In it he begged, again, for a final chance.

'Well?' I asked.

There was a silence. She always has to search for the English words; I can actually watch the process as she turns the pages of her mental dictionary. She usually manages to convey her meaning to me, often in a remarkably apt, poetic, or philosophical way.

'I'm going back after work tomorrow. I'm only taking Peter. I'm giving him one more chance.'

I nodded in agreement. 'Perhaps it's only fair.' Then I asked, because she seemed ready to discuss the issue, 'How about the other woman? Why does he want you back? Why can't he live with her?'

'She's married to someone else, a neighbour. He denies he has another woman.'

'But you know he does.'

'Yes.'

'So what does he want you back for, just to do his washing and cleaning and cooking?'

'He says he didn't know what he had until he'd lost it.'

'Do you still love him, did you ever love him?'

'I can't bear the sound of his voice. I can't bear the sight of him.'

'Well, if you decide you must leave finally, and then that you want a divorce, remember Linda at the Women's Centre, she can advise you about things.' Pet nodded, and I continued, 'Divorce should be easy, just a question of paper, but you know if you need a lawyer, Derek will do it for you?'

'Thank you.'

'Are you sure you're all right for money?'

'I'm sure, thank you.' Another smile as she remembered the freedom that is hers for the asking.

So now I sit here writing, remembering her looks and inflexions and knowing that this evening she will leave the one room haven in North Point, where the twins will stay. I worry about her going back, for many reasons, for her safety, for her peace of mind. But I think she's wise and just in her responses. I'll try not to ring her at her old home to see that she's all right.

SO FAR SO GOOD   *February 1995*

Petty's twin daughters are still living in the one room in North Point. They don't bother to use the shared kitchen but eat out – hamburgers, pizzas, and coke. From time to time, they go home for a meal and eat proper Chinese home cooking. Petty is still back with her husband. 'Quite good,' she replied to my question the first time I saw her after she agreed to return. Over Lunar New Year, she had a sore hand and her husband took over domestic chores. He washed up and cleaned. The twins came for supper and they were a proper family, the first time for a long time.

Petty is nearly always cheerful. She was even when she was, unknown to me, in the process of leaving her husband. But there is a difference now. She has started wearing interesting and unusual colour combinations to work – the sort a fashion-conscious woman might wear, even though they are her cleaning clothes. They are a noticeable innovation, as if she has smartened herself up.

Yesterday was her husband's birthday, she told me; he was 45. The twins came to supper. 'Did you give him a present?' I asked. I didn't fully understand the answer but it was something to do with an old watch he wanted. She would give it to him if he could find it.

'He gave me a present,' she ventured. We were in a taxi by this time. I was going to teach at the Women's Centre and giving her a lift to catch her bus home.

You will come back to classes when you're ready, won't you?' I had asked tentatively.

'Yes,' she replied.

It wasn't just the better relations with her husband that prompted me to say that. I had asked her what she was going to do with her afternoon.

'Read,' she replied. I was quite taken aback. This is a woman who left school at 13 to work in a factory to keep her brothers and sisters abandoned by their mother. A woman, though, who has somehow not only learnt to speak some English, but also to read and write it. Her husband reads and writes in no language.

I'm not quite sure what she was going to read, not a novel, something to improve herself, in Chinese. But she is also working on the English stories that I have been keeping her supplied with each time I have taken them to the Classmates. This was the first time I have heard her say she was going to do something for herself.

Now, in the taxi, I asked her, 'What did he give you?'

'A gold ring. And a gold bracelet,' she replied.

'How nice. How nice that he should give you a present on his birthday.'

'Well, you see, I sold my other jewellery,' she explained.

'What do you mean? That gold necklace he gave you?' That was his last present, I think, when some intuition prompted him momentarily to make an effort with his marriage.

'Yes. You see, he told me he had no money, so I sold my jewellery, and gave him the money. And that's when I moved out.' In reply to my wordless response, she continued, 'He thought I'd moved out because he had no money. But it was because he hit the girls. We were all in danger. We couldn't stay.'

'Does he understand now?'

'Half.' She grimaced.

'Perhaps he'll learn a little more, slowly.'

He goes to work – as a van driver for a construction company – at the same time as Petty now, and he's home by 5.30pm. I gather that's unprecedented; previously he was out until all hours.

I rang the other evening, not to check up on Petty's safety. For the first time I talked to him – except that he couldn't understand a word. I thought he sounded awfully rough and gruff. But for the moment Petty seems to have half tamed him. She is calling the shots. I admire the way she has worked it out for herself and is now working it through back in her home. Her book learning may be limited. But that does not affect how her brain takes advantage of her instincts.

HOWZAT!   *March 1995*

When a man is asked about his cricket in Hong Kong, it means the pet insect he keeps and pits against those of his friends. And when you see an antique cricket box for sale, you give a start of surprise and realise it is not what you thought. And, whereas little girls in England keep hamsters, and in Africa they might keep a chameleon as a pet (as I did), in China, traditionally, they kept silkworms in a box and fed them on mulberry leaves.

I was struck by the differences between the use of leisure, pleasure and exercise when I saw an elderly woman swinging back and forth between stands of bamboo stems as if they were upright parallel bars. She was holding on to them because she is old and unsteady. But her grandmother might have done the same thing at 20 because her feet were bound. Certainly, physical exercise in the Western sense would have been beyond her contemplation.

Attitude to exercise is particular, as anyone who looks out of their window at 6.30 in the morning in China or Hong Kong can vouch. Harmony and alignment are the name of the game, not a pounding heart and sweat. Indeed, the senior bamboo swinger was performing beyond the boundary of a cricket field where expatriates of all colours (but no Chinese) were frantically hitting, throwing, bowling and catching balls. In another corner, three men sat on stools with their back to the pitch watching their birds in cages suspended on low branches of a fir tree. A Chinese lad was jogging round the boundary, but he was quite unusual.

Recently, I noted a similar contrast in Macau. Unable to sleep, we rose at 6am to go for a walk. On the driveway leading past our hotel in an otherwise traditional Chinese area, fifty or so mostly older, mostly women residents practised *tai chi*. However certain you may feel that your own brisk walk is supremely healthy, the sight of this getting of harmony by friendly, sprightly people is always pleasing.

That scene is replicated even in more sophisticated settings. At our block of flats, if you go into the kitchen overlooking the courtyard at dawn, and just before the security guards change shifts, you can see Mutt and Jeff in their uniforms doing *tai chi*. Jeff is fairly adept, Mutt follows him one beat behind, all uncoordinated. A few minutes later, a string of older women and men take to the railings around the fishpond as if at the barre at ballet school.

You see the same in any park in Beijing, or other urban or rural setting. But the exercise I enjoyed watching as much in Beijing was ballroom dancing on one of the terraces of the Summer Palace. In this enchanted spot, once razed by British troops, Beijing couples waltz round and round to the strains of the *Blue Danube* blaring from a tape deck. And it seems to give them great pleasure if you join in.

I wouldn't presume to expatiate about *tai chi* or *chi gung*. They are different but related forms of body movement that fit into the traditional Chinese culture, with *feng shui* (or geomancy), the union of the elements and their relationship with space, and with Chinese herbal medicine. But I do remember a quotation that I feel catches an aspect of the difference in attitude towards leisure, pleasure and exercise. An American woman wrote, as she travelled through Chinese Turkestan in the 1930s by traditional means, 'Most Chinese are completely unable to understand anyone enjoying travel for its own sake. They look upon it as a necessary hardship and usually do it very badly.'

And yet there is a Chinese man who lives in our block who seems to combine something of both Chinese and Western approaches to mind over matter. He had a stroke some years ago and we have watched him since then. At first he came out every morning and afternoon in a wheel chair. Then came a walking frame, inch by inch; then a tripod walking stick or the arm of a nurse.

Now, whatever the weather, he brings his tripod stick down but stands it up in the middle of the pavement. Then he leaves it and sets off, slowly, slowly, but with all the perseverance and bravery of any sportsperson or traveller to the furthest reaches.

AND MAY THE BEST PERSON WIN?   *March 1995*

They have always said in Britain that if you tie a blue ribbon round the neck of a pig, Conservatives will vote for it. Certainly, I always vote there for the political party I prefer, whoever the candidate.

But here things have not been so easy for me since I've passed the seven year mark of residence that allows me to vote.

Yesterday, we had the municipal elections for Urban and Rural Council members. These councillors are concerned with refuse collection and potholes, trees and noise and, historically, they have usually been independents. Since the Legislative Council (Legco) elections in 1991, however, voting has become increasingly polarised. For the first time, then, political parties were to the fore. Some of the candidates were being elected directly, and the Liberal Democrats, now the Democratic Party, almost swept the board. There were still appointed members of Legco then, and indirectly elected ones, but the democratically-elected newcomers were an attractive, vociferous and powerful force.

Then, and still in Legco, the confusingly-named Liberal Party, the voice of big business, was the Democrats' main opposition; now, increasingly, outside Legco it is the Democratic Alliance for the Betterment of Hong Kong (DAB), one that prefers accommodation with China to confrontation.

Yesterday, which Party won – simplistically, pro-democracy or pro-China – was, therefore, of some significance.

The best candidate in my voting area appeared to be the one representing the Democratic Party. But for me, there was an added element – the Woman Question. More than anything, I wanted to vote for a woman.

The last interchange with my English class went thus, after exhorting them to vote. Me: 'If there is a woman candidate and a man candidate of equal worth standing, which do you vote for?'

And the Darlings chorused, as if in kindergarten, their faces alight with mischief and solidarity, 'THE WOMAN.'

The day after tomorrow is International Women's Day. On that day in 1908, working women in New York demonstrated for the vote, and in many places in the world women have suffered to get it. For several reasons, therefore, my vote yesterday was precious to me. For days I had been accumulating campaign literature. There were four candiates, two women, two men. At first sight I thought, objectively, what a pity, four apparently good people standing against each other, what a waste, particularly of women power.

I needed to reject John Tse, the Democrat and good man candidate, because he was not a woman. So I looked and looked at the two women candidates. One, Ada Wong, a lawyer, was an independent but a former Liberal Party member – and therefore unacceptable to me. What is more, she was attempting to trade on her father's position in the Chinese community – another negative. (Her mother *might* have been acceptable!) And she was supported by some people I don't respect, as well as by some that I do. In the latter group was Elsie Elliot Tu, a big plus as you will see, but not enough.

The other woman candidate has the same given name as me, a weak-limbed plus! And she has apparently done good work in the community in the name of the Democrats whom she has now left. (And they were no longer supporting her.) But Susanna Yeung, a public hospital manager, started her electoral address, 'Being a good Catholic I always believe in serving people.' Did that mean others don't? More important, where does she stand on women's choice in how they plan their families? She could only have my vote if at the polling station she could answer that question to my entire satisfaction.

The fourth candidate was managing director of a fur company, which Susanna Yeung, not he, disclosed.

It was obvious that John Tse was the best candidate but there was still an apparently insurmountable barrier to voting for him, and it was not his sex. It was the Democratic Party's behaviour towards Elsie Tu.

Elsie has been a local councillor since 1962, since the days when that was the Chinese population's only means of democratic expression. And in those days only the educated and the propertied Chinese had the local vote – incidentally excluding nearly all women.

I described Elsie when she became a Legco member in 1991: born in England, arriving in Hong Kong as a missionary, she served the poor and disenfranchised. Over the years she has worked tirelessly for the rights of women, as well as serving as a role model. Selflessly she campaigned, too, against corruption in the police, and earned the disapprobation of the establishment. Because of her commitment to the people of Hong Kong, she decided some months ago that the Governor's 'democracy package', which has caused so much trouble with China, is misguided, destructive even.

Fighting for the people of Hong Kong, she, the original democrat, has thus been labelled the arch pro-China candidate. As such, defeating her was seen as essential by the Democrats. To that end, they put up against the 81-year-old one of their strongest members, backed by their full machinery. The DAB stepped in to help Elsie, thus adding glue to the pro-China label. The campaign must have been a nightmare for her.

How could I vote for a man who is on the executive committee of a political party which could hurt and humiliate such a woman for their own ends?

I walked to the polling station intensely troubled. I determined to exercise my right to vote, but to spoil my ballot paper, writing on it why I did not put a tick against the name of the best candidate. Then I read again John Tse's credentials. He, too, has campaigned tirelessly, though only relatively young, for the equality of the sexes, and for the rights of indigenous women in the New Territories. Together with work for unpopular but essential community services, he founded The Movement Against Discrimination (MAD). I had been with him on many a demonstration.

At the polling station there was no Roman Catholic candidate to answer my question, and none of her helpers had a clue what I was talking about. John Tse's helpers were mostly from Derek's institution where he also works. They were chastened and at a loss for words when called upon to account for their party's behaviour towards Elsie Tu. They would pass on our message; we were not the first voters to confront them.

So, in the end, I voted for John Tse. I remembered what Petty had said when I discussed this matter with her in 1991. 'I'll vote for the woman if she's the best candidate.' Tse was the best candidate; we had to help to get him elected. We had made our point about Elsie.

Theresa voted for John Tse too. I was surprised about that because she wants to be left in peace to get on with her business, before and after 1997. Her reason was that John Tse, with his doctorate and lectureship in sociology, is 'knowledgeable' – everything she wants for her own sons.

But, ironically, or deservedly, John Tse lost. A woman candidate has won – Ada Wong, whom her Catholic rival Susanna Yeung branded 'pro-China', and whom I have branded 'big business'. I had a hunch she would.

First, as spoilt professional expatriates, we live in an area of very rich Chinese people. They don't want the boat rocked by the Democrats and are assiduously pursuing their business interests in

China. Secondly, Ada alone took the trouble weeks ago to plaster her face and name over the walls and railings of the squatter settlements that lie nestling and hidden in the valley beneath our high rise.

Doubly ironic because, elsewhere, the Democrats have been the most successful party. And treble irony: where the Democratic Party has failed to capitalise on its general popularity is in the New Territories. There over the past few months they have campaigned, with independent women legislators (appointed and elected), to change the inheritance and electoral law on behalf of women. The New Territories men have not forgotten or forgiven.

Many will not easily forgive the Democratic Party for another reason: Elsie lost her seat.

TENDER LOVING CARE   *June 1995*

'How is Derek?' Petty asked. I was especially touched because she does not often ring me. If she does it is about something important. That being so, she usually puts her brother on the line because she has more confidence in his English than hers. I brought her up to date on the progress of Derek's high fever and accompanying temperature, told her that it seemed to be falling and thanked her for her concern.

She had arrived the day before to clean and iron expecting me to be in the full flurry of packing to go to Sri Lanka for ten days. Instead I was anxious and distracted, ready to leave for the hospital. I had no time for anything but to tell her that Derek was rather ill and off I set for the Matilda and a bedside vigil.

Now she added quietly, 'I went to the temple yesterday afternoon to pray for him.' I was overwhelmed by the gesture. So was Derek when I told him. And, happy atheists though we are, we could not help remembering that the previous afternoon had been a turning point. The headache then had been so bad that they had given him a pethidine injection. It worked in 20 minutes. Then, too, his doctor had changed him to different antibiotics. In a few hours that seemed to start the eventual recovery. So it was not only Petty's intercession that had helped, but also the scientific skill of a first rate doctor.

On top of that there is the Matilda itself. Perched on the side of the Peak, with stunning views in all directions, it swirled in mist during Derek's stay. But the bleakness outside the window was more than made up for by the extraordinary nursing care he received.

The Matilda, built in memory of Matilda Sharp who died here in 1893, is very much part of Hong Kong's history. She was a quirky sort of woman whose nineteenth century letters home give a strong impression of the life of expatriate women in the colony over 35 years. She was just as likely to complain of the weather and tell her family what she was wearing, as give details of the Christmas party she had thrown for the wives of ordinary soldiers. Their lives were very much less comfortable than hers.

The Matilda was opened in 1907 and its first nurses provided the colony with the gossip it craved. Its first matron, Edith Smith, was sister of the first medical superintendent. Dedicated, and slightly self-righteous, apparently, she went off and married the chief manager of the Hong Kong and Shanghai Bank. For all I know, the nurses' quarters are still a hotbed of love affairs, but it does not affect their work. Every day, birth announcements in the newspaper thank them effusively. Now we know why.

Petty arrived this morning to find Derek home from hospital and grateful to her for her concern, and her visit to the temple. 'Which temple was it?' I asked. 'Was it the one in Aberdeen (where she lives)?'

'No,' she replied. 'It's in Tsuen Wan.'

Tsuen Wan is a dormitory town in the New Territories, at the far end of the underground system, as far away as you can get from where Petty lives. The temple there is special, she told us; it is dedicated to the Dragon Mother (*Lon Mou*). And Petty stood there, in a spurt of inspired English, regaling us with the myth that surrounds the Dragon Mother.

Later she took me aside and explained that she had made a payment at the temple to learn what was wrong with Derek. She was told that someone wished him ill and that, to allow him to recover, a further payment would be needed. Unhesitatingly she handed over part of the wages that I had just given her to save him.

What it really goes to show is that, whatever one's beliefs, expressions of love are the best possible companion to science in the healing process.

INTRODUCING TOSH   *June 1995*

Your hairdresser is usually a gossip exchange. But when you are exploring another culture you see her as a provider – you are not so concerned about your part in the enterprise. My only objection to Tosh in full flight is that she stops cutting my hair. Getting my hair cut becomes something of a marathon. I try not to have an urgent appointment straight after a session.

Today Tosh started telling me about Elyse who had just spent $900 at the fortune tellers. '$900! You'd think if she was spending that sort of money it would be on something to make her happy,' Tosh said, scissors suspended, making eye contact in the mirror.

Elyse is in her thirties. The fortune teller told her that she had missed her opportunity to get married at 30. 'Will you have another opportunity?' asked Tosh who is 34 and unmarried.

'Yes,' Elyse had replied, 'when I'm 40. But he says I'm going to die at 42.' This had not improved Elyse's day. And Tosh was shocked at the waste of money.

Tosh does not have money to throw about. She was sent to school in the United States when she was 15. This was the sort of investment that Hong Kong parents make in their children. And by Hong Kong people, I'm not talking of families who have been here for generations. Tosh's parents came from North China as migrants, or refugees. They still don't speak English, or Cantonese, only Mandarin and their dialect.

In California, Tosh's fees and board were paid for; everything else she earned herself. And she put herself through College, gaining a diploma in hairdressing. At 24, she was faced with a momentous decision: did she stay in California earning a living, leading a life of relative freedom and, thus, sacrifice her Hong Kong visa? Or did she come back to Hong Kong and move in with her aging parents. She is an only child and filial piety, or family responsibility, comes first.

Tosh, her parents now 72 and 76 years old, and two much loved cats live in one room half the size of half the tiny hair-dressing salon where she is an employee. Tosh sleeps on the top bunk, her mother underneath; her father sleeps on the sofa bed. They share a communal 'bathroom' and kitchen with another family. The lavatory was a hole in the ground but has been redesigned (by the public housing authority, I think) to accommodate an operation Tosh had to her leg. I expressed concern. 'Oh, we're quite lucky,' said Tosh cheerfully. 'Our neighbours are five to that one room.'

From concern my expression changed to guilt. 'I know,' said Tosh laughing, and waving the scissors. 'I noticed your address! The only thing I feel guilty about,' she continued, 'is that I didn't study to become a doctor or a lawyer, so that I could earn real money to keep my parents more comfortably.'

Tosh's parents spend a lot of time ill at home or in hospital. She is often running from home to hospital to the salon in the morning, and the reverse in the evening. 'They looked after me when I was young,' Tosh explains. 'Now I look after them. I just wish I could tell my father I love him. I have never been able to do it.' The closest father and daughter came to admitting their feelings was over a pair of trainers. Tosh, for all her traditional Chinese ways, is a rather modern woman. She is thickset, her hair en brosse, coloured pale orange. She wears long shorts and trainers.

Her mother questioned the hair; her father the trainers. She extolled the virtues of the shoes. She offered to buy him a pair to prove her point. He demurred. When he had sore feet, she bought him some trainers. He wore them every day and felt miles better. She asked him at Chinese New Year what he would like for a present. He looked at her slightly shamefaced and said, 'Could I have a new pair of trainers?'

You learn a lot at the hairdressers about life, and love, Chinese style, universal style.

LETTER FROM HUAIROU (UN Women's Forum, Beijing)
September 1995

The evening after the United Nations Women's Forum ended in Huairou, I was sitting in a French restaurant in Beijing. A trio was playing the tune 'Misty' and it occurred to me that those were the best moments of the Forum – the ones that made me feel 'misty', slightly tearful.

My group of activists from Hong Kong didn't arrive until Monday, 4 September, half way through the Forum. Many thousands of women were already at home there, in spite of days of rain and mud and intrusive male security. Cecilia and I felt a little lost as we wandered round the 40 hectare site, up and down weeping willow avenues and steps, in and out of tents, past half-finished buildings, consulting our map, trying to get our bearings.

In the main thoroughfare, behind two buses with a security camera on top, we came upon a demonstration – hundreds of women dressed in black and white sitting on the ground. They held candles and posters detailing military violence against women in many parts of the world. It was a surprise because we had been told that demonstrations could only be held in the 'parade ground'. I never did find that designated space but I came upon many demos, or they came across me, as they snaked round the Forum site.

As we stood there, spectators, new girls, a member of another Hong Kong group got up, took us by the hand, led us into the seated ranks of women and we were welcomed. Then, at a signal, everyone jumped up and we ululated. It was my first experience of 'mistiness' that week.

The second came that evening when we attended a concert by April Light. Who were they? Women, of course. What would they play? On came 18 players, one singer and a conductor. The women, all from the Nordic countries, carried jazz instruments and proceeded to play their own compositions and arrangements with a verve, muscularity, and musicality that was intensely moving.

Wandering round the tented village at lunchtime on Tuesday after a seminar, I heard a voice say my name and, turning round, found my friend from Pakistan, Cassandra Balchin, baby on hip. Neither of us had known the other would be there; among 25,000 or so women we had discovered each other. We bought a rather ordinary Chinese lunch in an environmentally-unfriendly styrofoam box, procured two chairs, found some sparse, newly-planted grass for the baby and, ignoring the drizzle, whiled away an hour or two.

On Wednesday one of my seminars – one of the 5,000 events in ten days – was Women in Politics. The organisers didn't turn up. This was quite common and frustrating, but often something special happened. The audience took the initiative and we created a lively, spontaneous workshop. There were politicians there and at least two passed the door, heard interesting sounds, strayed in and took their turn. Each story – from Japan, Sweden, the USA, India, Argentina and Uganda – told of fighting, and winning, seats against heavy odds with the help of women volunteers and the new woman vote.

I, and hundreds of others, missed out on an event that might have been 'misty'. Hillary Clinton came to address the Forum, but no one had thought to make sure there was enough room for us all. There was a scrummage of umbrellas outside the hall but even

Betty Friedan was left out in the cold, as an arty farty photograph I took from behind her showed.*

On Friday morning, a workshop called 'Burmese Women's Struggle for Democracy and Human Rights' was an obvious 'misty' candidate when they showed the video of Aung San Suu Kyi's address to the main Government Conference. The braveness of that woman shining from the television monitor was overwhelming.

Later that morning, I kicked puddles and felt low and tired and cold. A workshop had been cancelled and I had barely an hour before leaving. Then, across the section of the 'area' tents – the Arab world, Latin America and the Caribbean, the Pacific Islands – a voice boomed out. It extolled the women of Papua New Guinea and I recognised the voice. It was that of Nahau Rooney, former Member of Parliament and Minister for Justice whom I had known during our five year stay in Papua New Guinea. And I went to the tent and joined the Pacific Islands workshop and, when it was ended, threw my arms round Nahau.

And that was what the Forum was all about – the memorable, 'misty', moments that inspired women to continue their work, the sad and happy struggle for equality.

DEMOCRACY FOR WOMEN?   *September 1995*

Many people in Hong Kong are jubilant following this week's elections for the Legislative Council, our last before 1997. And that is in spite of China's threat to disband this Legco when it resumes sovereignty. The jubilation is partly a response to the threat – for Hong Kong has thumbed its nose at the future. The Democratic Party, and independents who are 'democratic', have done well; but how democratic has the election really been?

The Democratic Party fielded not a single woman candidate, and one million housewives were disenfranchised by the new functional constituencies – part of the Governor's 'democratic' package that has so angered China. Housewives were not deemed to be 'active in the labour market', and therefore not given a privileged second vote. But now that the results are declared, how have women fared?

Between the previous elections in 1991 and these, there were eight women members of Legco. One was directly elected, Emily

* Betty died on 4 February 2006 (b. 4 February 1921)

Lau; another, Elsie Tu, indirectly (through the earlier-established functional constituency system); five were appointed; and one, Chief Secretary Anson Chan, was an Official.

This time, out of 16 women candidates (of a total of 138), seven women have been elected. There will be no Official Members. Outspoken Emily Lau has romped home again with the highest direct election majority – exceeding even that of the popular leader Martin Lee. Elsie Tu, aged 82, has gone down fighting.

Three women previously appointed have stood for election and won – one in a geographical constituency, two in functional ones: the independent Christine Loh, and two Liberals, Selina Chow and Miriam Lau.

It is rather ironic that the Liberal Party, which is the conservative party of big business, fielded three women candidates. That party has not overtly supported the women's cause and does not make a noise about democracy.

Two independent women have done very well in functional constituencies. Elizabeth (Libby) Wong, a former top civil servant, easily came first out of five candidates in the ragbag constituency that represents everything from civil servants to street sweepers and hawkers (and includes freelance writers). Margaret Ng, a barrister (and well-known political commentator), did unexpectedly well against an experienced male solicitor in the legal constituency.

The seventh woman is a dark horse. She is a trade unionist who did well last time but failed to win, probably because of too recent memories of June 1989 and the Tiananmen Square massacre. She belongs to the 'pro-China' Democratic Alliance for the Betterment of Hong Kong whose leaders were defeated this time. China's threat, repeated on election eve, may have had something to do with that.

The English-language press is trumpeting the wins of democrats and independents – though there is no analysis of women candidates or the woman vote. The very real success of Chan Yuen-han has, however, raised no comment. As a trade unionist, she is someone to watch. One of the issues which recent anti-discrimination legislation has failed to address is discrimination against women on the grounds of age in the workplace.

Both Christine Loh and Libby Wong have promised to re-introduce a withdrawn private member's bill to extend equal opportunities across the board introduced earlier in 1995 by appointed member Anna Wu (who has not stood for election).[†] There is still plenty of work to be done here. When Christine was appointed in 1991, she was interested in democracy, accountability of government, and transparency. Quite quickly, she allowed herself to be educated on women's issues and has fought bravely for them since then. She has earned her spurs.

Lawyer Margaret Ng is determinedly against separating women's concerns from men's. Libby Wong is experienced in the ways of government and big-hearted, if relatively inexperienced, on the Woman Question. It's easy to tell that she's inexperienced. Very tired, after hours of waiting up for her result, she twice said that she was firmly behind the call for a fully directly-elected Legco; or, as she inadvertently put it, 'one man, one vote'!

CLASSMATES ON PARADE[‡]   *September 1995*

First lesson of the year: I should have a totally new group of 'Classmates'. That would make life practical and easy. I'd start again from scratch. But it's never like that. This year Ada at the Women's Centre tells me the day before that its six new, eleven old. Luckily, I'm already mentally prepared.

By the time the lesson is ten minutes old there are five new and 14 old, and the old team is raring to go. Some of them have already been with me a year, some two terms, some only one. One Classmate has been in and out for at least three years. That's the way it always is. How can I object when the atmosphere in the class is so good – friendships forged, trust built up, jokes and memories shared, some English learnt?

The five new ones sit expectantly at the front. They are made to stand up in front of the whiteboard and introduce themselves, including their English name and their age.

Linda is a retired primary school teacher aged 72; Wendy an assistant nurse, 42. Suzanne and Peggy stand up together; they are

---

† I have elaborated on Anna Wu's bill in the epilogue.
‡ This piece was previously published in *Stories for Eva: A Reader for Chinese Women Learning English* (Hong Kong, Hong Kong Language Fund, 1997)

sisters. Before they married, one was a typist in a shipping company, the other a factory worker.

'Guess which is older,' says Suzanne boldly – a good start. Happily, most of the Classmates guess it is her.

Amy is a receptionist in a hair salon. She has been given an afternoon a week off to improve her English. We now have an unusual number of Classmates in full time employment. Three of them are nurses in clinics. Many years they are all housewives.

The time comes for the old Classmates to introduce themselves to the new. They have to give their ages as well. We want no self-consciousness about age. This is where we start the fight against pigeon-holing and ageism. I'm 50. Cynthia is the baby at 34.

Connie L says she is 39. Theresa, who would have liked to be an actress but is rather deaf, makes one of her usual outrageous interventions in Cantonese. Laughter erupts.

'Come on, what did you say? It's not fair; I can't understand.' My usual routine. More laughter.

Teresina, a former teacher, explains, 'Last year Connie said she was 39 as well!'

'Is that true?' I go back to last year's register. 'It's true.' More laughter. Connie blushes, loses face, tries to extricate herself. I hurry on.

Suddenly, a large cockroach is spotted. The reaction is predictable but Eva, long-established Classmate, full of dreams and aspirations, moves towards it. I know, she wants to catch it and put it in a box so she can encourage her two exquisite daughters in their biology studies. After it has run the full gauntlet of the class, Bonnie, a nurse, squashes it flat. Newcomer Amy walks calmly the length of the room with a tissue. Deftly she gathers up the corpse and disposes of it.

The last lesson of the term is always a celebration, rather than work. Over the past year or so we have been taking it in turn to invite the class home. At decision time last term, Teresina called out, 'Yours'.

They were intrigued when I said that I would also invite a few contributors of the stories we use as lessons. In the end, only Christine came – Christine Loh, appointed Legislative Councillor, and by then candidate in September's elections. It was generous of her; there were no votes in it.

I had expected 15 Classmates and prepared accordingly. In the end, we were 27, including some old, old Classmates recruited on the grapevine, and six children. They criticised the way I cooked the rice. 'Haven't you got a rice cooker?' How could I explain that we like our rice with the grains separate, instead of like pudding, as they serve it? While I slaved in the kitchen, trying to keep them out, Christine held friendly court, in Cantonese. Now, at this beginning of the new term, I debrief them on what they discussed with her.

She told them she must win the election; she explained about women in the New Territories and the campaign to get them inheritance and voting rights. 'Will you stay after 1997?' Theresa asked. Earlier, in class, she had been critical of Christine's Cantonese. (She was educated abroad in English – a sensitive point electorally.) Theresa explains to me now Christine's response. I don't quite understand: something to do with human rights. Christine asked them about their English lessons and jokingly offered to substitute for me. She should be careful about offers made in jest!

Brought up to date, I wheel out one of Christine's campaign posters and we discuss the recent elections (Christine won). All but four of the Classmates voted. They wanted the democrats to win; or it was their duty as citizens. Newcomer Wendy admits that she didn't; she wasn't interested.

'Perhaps we can help you to be interested,' I reply pleasantly.

'Brainwash,' calls out old hand Eva from the back. Lots more laughter. Which of us is responsible for her impeccable vocabulary!

HISTORY ONLY HALF REPEATS ITSELF   *October 1995*

'How's your father?' I asked Petty as she was leaving today. Last Tuesday as I set off for the Women's Centre she came with me in the taxi. She was on her way to see him in a Western hospital the other side of the island, a flask of Chinese medicine in her knapsack.

'He's lazy,' she replied, pulling a face. This Chinese use of the English word 'lazy' always intrigues me. The last time I heard it was, as coincidence would have it, in the same hospital, Queen Mary's, now housing Petty's father. Florence, the public relations officer, had accused herself of being lazy as she showed me round in the footsteps of one of my historical characters. I taxed her with what exactly she meant because the Classmates often use the word about themselves. Not taking initiatives in her life was how she explained it. Now I taxed Petty. It seemed such an odd word to use about a 78-year-old father confined to hospital since August.

'He won't walk,' she said. 'He won't get up from his chair at all and use his ankle. Before he was in hospital he used to sit and sit, and his knee has become useless. He lay on his back until he took the Chinese medicine my brother gave him. Then he sat up. But he won't walk. He's lazy. He's always been lazy.' All this was teased out, of course, and is interpreted. For obvious reasons, Petty never speaks in paragraphs, as she searches painstakingly for each word.

Ever anxious to find a reason why someone might behave in a peculiar manner, I start probing with Petty her father's psyche. I know he lives alone and that when he's at home she often takes him soup and other good things to eat. I know she despairs because, as usual, he mixes her home-made soup with any other rubbish in the saucepan and that he keeps this mixture going day after day.

I wonder if he isn't lonely. 'No, of course not. He chooses to live alone. When I take his grandchildren round, he doesn't want to see them.'

I psychoanalyse him further! 'Do you think,' I venture hesitantly, 'that it all has to do with your mother leaving home, without a word, when you were all little? She never even got in touch again. That must have affected him.'

This really gets her going. Her own departure is delayed; indeed, so late does it become that she shares my taxi again and continues the story. 'That's not true,' she bursts out. 'Mother couldn't write (because she was illiterate) but she sent a photograph of herself with an address on the back of the envelope. 'But father did nothing. And we didn't find the photograph until ten years later. We went to the address but it was all too late.'

I had always assumed that Petty's mother left because she was feckless, or had a lover. Now the extent of the emotional abuse she suffered from her husband, her mother-in-law, and her husband's sister emerges. She obviously hoped, by her departure, to prompt her husband to come looking for her and treat her better thereafter.

After she left, her husband let slide the little business they shared – a shop selling daily hardware and clothing necessities. Money became scarce in the household. Petty's elder two brothers – before universal education – were taken away from school to help in the shop. Petty, aged 10, looked after her younger brother and sister, and all the household chores. At 13 she went to work in a factory. Their father tried to take the youngest children away from school, so the oldest paid his wages direct towards their education. The youngest brother now has a good job in a bank.

The youngest sister has never married and was, says Petty, 'crazy'.

'Was that because your mother left home?' I asked.

'No, it's because she was spoilt. She had a terrible cough when she was little, what we call "a hundred coughs". To stop her crying, so she wouldn't cough, mother used to give her everything she wanted. Later she demanded everything from us too.' The definitition of crazy was that she got involved with an Indian religion and expected to be kept by the family. But she now has a job as a sales assistant.

When I hear all these details of Petty's family, I understand more clearly her deep concern for her own children and their education. And I understand how important it was that when she left home she took her children with her. And why she went back when her husband begged her to. Often history only half repeats itself.

ANOTHER LECTURE (A Radio Broadcast)   *November 1995*

When I arrived here nearly nine years ago, RTHK's programme 'Hong Kong Today' was also new. My work made me become a regular and appreciative listener. But almost from the first day, I started to keep a list, one that became so repetitious that I soon gave it up. I didn't stop making a mental note of the programme's fatal flaw, though, and I knew that one day I would have to act. Something happened last week that made me recognise that moment had come.

A panel of experts had been assembled to discuss business ethics. I came in late and noted the interviewer deftly calling on each expert: 'Professor Donleavy, what do you think? Dr Ethridge, let's have your opinion.' And then, 'Catherine, do you agree with Professor Donleavy?' Catherine, it emerged, is a senior officer with the ICAC (Independent Commission Against Corruption) and she was not appearing incognito.

Soon, I was so incensed that I rang RTHK, spoke to a man attached to the programme, and asked that my complaint be passed on. But back on the radio, it was still professor, doctor and Catherine. Thus I came to ask if I could present my point of view.

There will be those of you listening who understood immediately what offended me; there will be some who are baffled; and there will be some who have an inkling but who are now muttering, 'Oh no, not another lecture on political correctness!'

Well, yes! Forgive me if I don't apologise.

The other day I heard an exchange something like this:
Interviewer: 'Mr Snooks, what do you think the man in the street will say?'

Snooks: (politely but firmly) 'Well, I think ordinary people are optimistic ...'

Interviewer: (cloth-eared as ever) 'Thank you for your views on the man in the street ...'

You'd think that after nine years of flogging that old cliché they could have moved on, even if it were not so gender-insensitive.

In news broadcast after interview, business*men* are doing something or other – flying off to Japan, complaining about this, promoting that. And no matter what's being done, 'he' is doing it. I stop listening to lecturers with constant 'he/him' on the first page.

Why am I so sensitive to this continuing flow of gender-bias? Is there any point in pursuing the issue? And what am I asking for? It's very often people with the most influence – broadcasters, journalists, lecturers, Legco members and those who speak for the Government – who commit these solicisms.

Not long ago, I chided the Governor, in public, for referring to 'business*men*' in an address on the economy. To be fair to him, he regretted his mistake immediately and agreed that I was not raising a trivial matter. I did not intend that he lose face but language is how we communicate, and it's not just words, it's attitude. The treatment of women unequally in language perpetuates lack of equal treatment more generally.

If it is business*men* who fly off (even when there are women among them), the glass ceiling that prevents women's advancement is reinforced. Words are like role models. And language can better be used as a tool to construct than a weapon to victimise.

Now, I'm not asking you to go round constantly inserting an awkward 'she' after a neat 'he'; though he/she or she/he is sometimes unavoidable. I feel perfectly comfortable, in spite of fussy grammarians, about using the plural pronoun 'they' with a singular subject and verb. But it often makes more sense to put the whole idea into the plural. Eschew the old fashioned 'The ordinary person he'; use instead 'ordinary people they …'. You'll find with practice that the word businesspeople comes naturally too.

When I told the business ethics story at a women's seminar, two senior women academics came up to me afterwards and told how male colleagues call each other doctor this, professor that, and, in the same breath use their first names. The women only flinch inside, as they are patted on the head, for what can they do about it without jeopardising a working relationship, or even their position.

I rang both Gabriel Donleavy and Catherine Chui after the programme in which they took part. Gabriel knew exactly what had bothered me. 'I did feel very slightly uncomfortable,' he said.

As for Catherine, she explained, 'I knew Gabriel and John before, so I didn't notice what the interviewer (whom I didn't know) called me.' She admitted, though, that she felt neutral about the matter.

Some women don't mind; nevertheless, they, as well as those who do mind, are affected by language that patronises and excludes. So much of progress has to do with awareness. Sometimes people are unaware until a matter is raised with them. Once you are aware of it, your insensitivity is less excusable.

1996

February 1996

Each story we discuss in the English class has the potential to strike a chord – preferably to start a discussion. If in the excitement Cantonese takes over, that's all right too, as long as someone translates the gist for me. Elsa Lo's 'Reflections on a German Fable' was suitably, though unobtrusively, provocative.

She started with how God talked to the first human and the first dog, donkey and monkey about how many years they wanted to live. The human later appropriated the sum total of all their lives – 75 years. Her version of the fable ended, 'That is why our life is as it is. The first thirty years are the sweetest period. The next fifteen years see hard work and constant nagging. From 45 to 65, life is a bit of a bore. In the last ten years, even children don't give you any respect.'

Elsa followed this account with the reflections of a Chinese housewife who was 'petrified' upon reaching the age of 30. Over the next four years – those originally allocated to the dog – she lived, in essence, a dog's life. But then she rallied and started educating herself, eventually studying Applied Computing. Thus, in her forties, she became, as she put it, proud to be 'among the world's full-time housewives free to cruise through cyberspace'.

Elsa's story came to me through the Open Learning Institute (OLI). I had approached Belinda in the public affairs department to ask for a story about the OLI. For some time we have been discussing in class the possibilities of further education. OLI is one of the options, but expensive and rather inaccessible. Through a story, I hoped to make it more transparent.

Belinda sent me Elsa's story as a stop gap and I took it at its face value until I came to write Elsa's biographical details. Belinda called her a colleague; she called herself a housewife. To my query, Elsa replied that she too worked in the public affairs office; she is in her late twenties, has a master's degree in communication and is particularly interested in children's literature and in the power of fables. To write her story, she had put herself 'in the shoes' of some of the graduates of the OLI; 'I wonder if this is all right?' she added.

It was fine with me, of course, and I put her explanation in her biographical details. But I did also add, as the last of the 15 questions I devised for discussion in class, 'Elsa is not a housewife graduate of the OLI; but she wrote as one. What do you think of this literary device?'

Well … The first question where Elsa came unstuck was 'Were you petrified when you turned 30? If so, why?' Most of the Classmates got the wrong end of the stick here. They thought I was asking what they would do if they were 30 again. Theresa said she would be a 'power woman'.

'What are you now (at 45)?' I asked.

'A small woman,' she flounced with dissatisfaction.

'It's not too late, you know.' My usual refrain.

When we had sorted out what the question really meant, and gone all round the class, no one was prepared to admit that, in passing 30, as they all had, they had given it any thought at all, let alone one of fear. So I tried 40. Connie was all right: as she laughingly admitted, she is perpetually 39. She's come on. Last year we caught her out at that game and she flushed and lost face.

Then I turned to Linda who is 72. 'And 70?'

'I only worry about being healthy,' she replied.

'I spend so much time looking after my children,' explained Bonnie, who works in a clinic, 'I don't have time to worry about age.'

The general feeling was that young Elsa, university educated, and working for the OLI, hadn't a clue about being a middle aged Chinese woman who might not have finished secondary school. And she shouldn't have presumed to put herself in their shoes. 'Also,' declared Theresa firmly, 'she must be writing about Western women.' So much for a literary device of the sort used by novelists throughout ages and cultures.

Only Celia was prepared to give Elsa credit. 'But look what she says here,' she urged. '"I should be the one and only person to decide the direction of my life." That's …'

'Inspirational?' I offered.

'Yes, inspirational.'

So we came on to computers. Talking to my physiotherapist recently, I'd learnt how a friend of hers has a son who used to be extrovert and a keen and a successful tennis player and who now spends all his time playing with his computer. He sidelines his mother as he does so. She is at her wit's end. I thought she might be typical, so I devised some questions such as, 'Have you got a home computer?' 'If so, what do you use it for?' 'Are you frightened by your children's relationship with computers?'

Here Elsa and I were on firmer ground. Out of 22 Classmates, probably 20 homes have a computer. Of the 20 computers, only two are useful aids to the family – both help their husbands in their work and use it as a word processor. One other, Theresa, uses it to play mahjong; another also plays games. The rest watch their children and husbands on the computer – even Eva who is up with and game for everything.

Then an argument ensued, almost the first ever, in English, between two schools of thought. Two women, Ivy and Nancy, have sons who spend all their time playing games on the computer. Bonnie's daughter has a gameboy which she is 'allowed' to play with; she has a computer which she studies with, no games. Bonnie was clear and firm about these rules. Ivy was flushed and bright-eyed about the impossibility of enforcement. Cynthia and Eva, when pressed, said that they were not in favour of such rules. That is not how one brings up a child. They have to be encouraged to study, not given orders.

But how about the alienation of the mothers? I re-routed the discussion. 'Don't you think you should know how to use the computer? If the Women's Centre were to organise classes, would you be interested?' Nearly every hand went up. And I couldn't fail to remember the reaction of Pet when I raised the subject of further education for the Classmates with her. 'What classes would you take?' I asked.

'Computer studies.'

'Why?'

'It's all about knowledge,' she replied. 'With that you can learn everything.'

Linda Wong, in-charge at the Women's Centre, hearing the saga, agreed that computer lessons would be a good idea. We're moving. Good story, Elsa. Well done!

GOODBYE YEAR OF THE PIG   *February 1996*

I've waited some months for Lunar New Year's Day to arrive. And I've done so with a certain amount of anxiety and, because of that, growing irritation, with myself, and with Petty. Little did I realise when Derek was ill last June and Pet went to the Temple of the Dragon's Mummy on his behalf what it would lead to.

She told me then that someone was trying to harm him and she took the necessary steps to protect him. But soon she added that he would remain in danger for the rest of the Year of the Pig. It was only very recently that I let slip that he was born in the Year of the Pig (1935 model). 'Ah,' she said, 'one is usually vulnerable in one's year.' Or words to that effect.

But that was not all. For dinner parties we burn red candles in brass candlesticks on the dining table. Red candles are not always available at a price I wish to pay. So, one day, when Pet had just cleaned the candle sticks, I started to unwrap two graceful white candles. 'No, No, not those,' Pet said quickly.

'Why not?'

'It's bad luck for Derek. We put white candles either side of the photograph of a dead person.'

'You may do that, Peggy,' I replied slightly sternly, not wishing to be rude but feeling firm. 'You're entitled to your customs. But it's not our way.'

'You're in Hong Kong now!' Pet shot back even more firmly.

'Well, you can buy the red candles,' I rejoined, unwilling to pursue the conversation.

The next dinner party came and went. No red candles. I used a small table lamp. Then my Christmas present was left in our letter box: 10 red candles costing £1 each – almost a morning's wage. What really made me cross, though, was my inability to ignore all this. I could patronise Pet by insincerely thanking her for going to the temple, and pay her back the considerable sum of money she had spent there. But the hem of my skirt was caught in the trap that has always lured Westerners living in the East. Indeed, in nineteenth century Hong Kong, Western women with time on their hands dabbled quite extensively in such things as the fortune tellings inscribed on temple sticks.

But I couldn't throw off the need to protect my husband from danger, however unacceptable intellectually I considered the fear.

He had fallen rather ill just before we were to leave on a cricket tour of Sri Lanka. The tour went well without its senior member. Left with two return tickets to Colombo and with an expensive Christmas family visit to England in the offing, we decided to use them. And our Sri Lankan team manager then set up a cricket component there specially for Derek. The security situation in Sri Lanka continued to deteriorate but we were enmeshed and went ahead with our ten day visit. At least Pet didn't put two and two together; my mother's anxiety was quite enough.

The first cricket match just outside Colombo went well, but I was adamant that we should not venture into the city itself. Instead we toured the island for hours and days on end (for a future book of mine) along narrow mountain passes avoiding mad drivers.

Our next match was in Galle. After lunch with the other team, I climbed into the minibus first, hitting my head as I did hard enough to fall to the ground. But my anxiety was about the intense heat and how it might affect the senior opening bowler. Half an hour into the game, the heavens opened. It never rains in Galle in January. After several restarts the game, on the Test ground in the lee of the Fort, had to be declared abandoned.

Soon after our return to Hong Kong, a bomb exploded in the financial and tourist centre of Colombo, killing and injuring many.

Back in Hong Kong, on the eve of Chinese New Year, the senior opening bowler got a ball to fly off the bat onto the batsman's chin. I spent two hours with the batsman in a nearby casualty department having six stitches put in. But what was going on back at the game, I wondered. Was the bowler all right?

I woke up on New Year's Day giving it a recognition I had never done before. At 9.30 Pet rang with a lame excuse for doing so. She wanted to see that he had made it safely through to the Year of the Rat.

YEAR OF THE RAT   *February 1996*

The news came out slowly, starting with the reply to an ordinary enough question. 'Did you watch the fireworks on Tuesday?' Pet took rather a long time to answer. 'No.' Pause. 'I had three taxi journeys to make. I was carrying things to North Point and I had to take a taxi.'

My little brain chewed on this. 'Your things?'

'Yes.'

'To North Point. From Aberdeen?

'Yes.' She wasn't going to help me. She continued ironing while I ate my soup.

Should I risk the question if she wasn't eager to tell me? Pause. 'You've left your husband again?'

'Yes.'

'Oh, Peggy, I'm so sorry.' I said. There had been clues. She rang rather early on Monday morning, the first day of Chinese New Year. Very odd thing to do. 'Why are you ringing me now?' I asked, puzzled.

'I've just woken up and I want to know if you want me to come to work tomorrow.'

'Of course not. I said I'd see you on Thursday. Tomorrow's a public holiday. You're supposed to be enjoying Lunar New Year, not ringing me.'

As soon as we'd hung up, I swapped notes with Derek who had answered the telephone and had a similar conversation. 'She wanted to see that you're all right,' I said, referring to the saga of Derek's health.

But, upon a few seconds' reflection, I wondered if she hadn't been crying. Her voice sounded thick and strange. What if she had rung because she needed an excuse to go out during the holiday period? What if she was in trouble?

I rang back within minutes. Her gruff husband answered and he took a while to gather who I was. He managed to convey that Pet wasn't there. Five minutes later,' he said.

I waited for her to ring back, and when she didn't, I did nothing. It seemed best. This morning when she arrived, I asked her how she was. 'Fine.' I admired her new padded anorak, so suitable for the freezing holiday and for today. Then I asked her why she had rung that day.

'Because you rang me.'

'But I rang you after you rang me.' We pursued this round in circles for a few minutes. Then it emerged that it was not the first time he had said I rang, when I hadn't. He has his own fish to fry. I let the subject drop. 'Anyway, did you have a happy holiday?'

'Very good. And Peter ate lots of hamburgers and fried potatoes and drank coca-cola.' I tut-tutted. And that was the end of the conversation until lunchtime.

'He's still begging me to give him one more chance,' Pet explained. 'But I said last time I went back that I wouldn't stay if he shouted. He's been shouting ever since. At me, at Peter, at everyone.'

'You've stuck it for a year,' I said. 'You can't do more.'

'But he knows where I am now,' she continued. 'He forced Helen to bring him to the room in North Point.'

There was a little sorting out to do here. It transpired that when Pet and Peter Bear moved back into the twins' room in North Point over the holiday, the girls had moved out and into their grandfather's room (flat) in the same complex in Aberdeen as Pet and her husband. Pet's father is still in the nursing home.

There their father had found the twins and persuaded Helen to take him to her mother. Quickly Sally had rung her mother to warn her, and Pet had the presence of mind to hide the telephone. They had always said the flat was without one. Thereafter, he'd made more than one sortie there.

'It's a pity he knows where you are.'

'Yes, but eventually he'll give up coming round.' She was still ironing methodically, looking at me somewhat mournfully from time to time. I made constant noises of commiseration. At least he wouldn't be able to pester her on the telephone.

Eventually I went to get the post and then to read it and ring Derek about the contents. 'And,' I added, 'Peggy's left her husband again. She's ironing here beside me.'

'I'm so sorry,' he replied.

'He's sad you're sad,' I called out to Pet.

'But I'm not,' she replied, at last smiling. 'I'm happy. And Peter's very happy. He's got a new television.'

STORIES WITHIN STORIES   *March 1996*

Writing these letters has turned me into a literary cannibal feeding on the lives of those who come near me. Commissioning 'stories' for the Classmates from professional Hong Kong women has compounded the habit, as this account illustrates only too well.

Irene is a young university lecturer working for a doctorate; she has a heavy workload. I have known her for several years; indeed, at one time we tried to recruit her into our tiny, select women's group. But she was too busy, or she preferred something more Chinese. But we stayed friends, meeting occasionally here and there, and I watched her grow in confidence in her work teaching a course on 'Women in the Third World'.

One day, we talked at greater depth than usual and the subject of her workload came up in relation to accommodation. I learned that she had taken on the senior tutorship of a residential hall in order to secure living quarters. She was about to share her new, one room university flat with her otherwise homeless mother and father. I remember being struck by what often lies behind Hong Kong's apparently middle class facade. Other, more senior university friends have large flats here and homes abroad. But many, like Irene, are first generation achievers still tied to Hong Kong's immigrant past.

When I asked Irene to write me a story, at first she said yes. A year later, when I sent her a reminder, she said she was too busy. She ducked her head as she said it and I forbore to mention my own workload, of which chasing up the stories, editing them and teaching the Classmates is only a small part. Thereafter, she slightly avoided my eye.

On 8 March, yesterday, we met at a women's lunch and out of the blue she blamed me for being too good to her: if only I would be less understanding, she would lash herself into writing a story. 'Go home tonight,' I replied with mock severity, 'and write me a letter. Write about International Women's Day, if you like.'

'Can I write about something more personal?'

'Of course. You can write about absolutely anything you like.'

This morning I received a fax. It told the story of six-year-old Irene living in Mongkok, the most crowded part of Hong Kong, of the world. She had a golden, adored teddy bear, Tung Tung. One day, for no reason that she could understand, her mother took the bear from her and gave it to another child. Years later, she confronted her mother with the cruel loss. Wet-eyed, her mother explained the family's situation at the time.

Her father, a textile worker, was facing unemployment. The other little girl's father might be able to help. In order to visit his wife and new daughter, Irene's mother needed a present, one she could not afford. She had to take Irene's teddy. Irene was devastated by the revelation, at the suffering of her mother. And when I read the story my tears dribbled onto the fax I sent her in response. Not only for her story, but also for the note that accompanied it:

> 'Thanks for your encouragement during our brief meeting yesterday. The story is here, finally. Please feel free to contact me as often as you wish from now on, since I will no longer be guilt-ridden each time I see you. I feel liberated!'

Irene seems to me liberated in more ways than one. Her story is of this time and this place, but it is also timeless. It is about International Women's Day.

A PERIOD OF MOURNING   *March 1996*

Once more Pet and I are sitting in the back of a taxi. She turns to me and says, 'My Father's dead.' I do a double take. She has said it so matter-of-factly that I feel sure I have misunderstood. She adds, 'He died a few days before Chinese New Year.' I put my hand across to hers and squeeze it in sympathy. This is very much not a thing a Westerner does to a Chinese woman, but she puts her other hand on top of mine to show she appreciates my gesture.

But I am flummoxed. Her father has been dead for over a month and she has not told me. She has left her husband, and much more besides in between, and now she quietly tells me her father is dead. I wonder somewhat tentatively why she has kept silent when we have discussed in detail her other trials. 'I couldn't tell you before,' she explains. 'It would have been unlucky.' It emerges that she cannot visit anyone at this time, and I realise that coming to clean for us has been a problem.

Now that she can talk to me about her father's death, I learn that six days before Chinese New Year he had a heart attack; he died in hospital three days later. She is keen to add that the nature of his bodily fluids in death prove that he was a good man. Somehow connected with that was that he bathed before he had breakfast and then a heart attack. She adds that she has known about his death for some time; it was foretold at the Dragon's Mummy Temple a couple of years ago.

I have ambivalent feelings about Pet's father. I have written to you about how her mother left home when Pet was ten. What I am in some ways more judgemental about is how he regarded Pet and her children. She explained on one of our taxi journeys, on her way to visit him, that her father discounted her children because she was his daughter, and doted on her brother's son because that was the male line. This revelation emerged from my innocent remark about how her father must be cheered up by visits from her children.

When I think what Pet has been through in the past month, and still come to clean and iron, hard-working and cheerful, I marvel anew at how tough women can be. You see, I have not yet told you the latest in the marital saga.

The telephone went a couple of weeks ago when Pet was here and I was pretty sure it was her husband. I wondered if she wanted to speak to him, so I was a bit non-committal. She took the receiver and had quite a long and intense conversation. 'Everything all right?' I asked when it was over.

She grimaced. 'He's just come out of hospital.' I looked questioningly and she began to tell me how she had borrowed a trolley from the marital home in Aberdeen when she moved out. She went round that week to return it at 4pm, knowing her husband came home at 6. But he was there. An argument ensued, during which he raised a chopper to her – no Chinese kitchen is without one; and few marital revenge injuries or killings are without one either. He proceeded to cut off the top of his little finger. This was to encourage Pet to come back to him.

It transpires that Pet's step-daughter has a long scar on her knee, and her step-son a scar on the back of his head from the attentions of their father's chopper. 'He rang me just now,' she continued, 'to tell me to come round this afternoon to clean the blood off the kitchen floor.'

'You're not going?' I said.

'Well, I said I would.'

'Do me a favour,' I pleaded. 'Ring Linda Wong (the social worker) at the Women's Centre and tell her everything.'

At the end of her conversation with Linda, Pet reported, 'She says I must not go near that flat under any circumstances.'

The next telephone conversation reported to me was about divorce. 'He rang me and said he wanted a divorce in a week. He said I know all about these things and could do it.' Then it was his birthday and she agreed to have a meal with him in a restaurant (I think with the rest of the family as well). He apologised profusely for his demands for a quick divorce. He didn't want one after all.

'That's been the story of our life together,' responded Pet severely. 'You order me to jump about, to do something impossible, and then change your mind. I've put up with it for twenty years.'

'I'll change. Really I will,' he promised.

'I'll watch you over the next three years to see if you keep that promise before I move back,' replied Pet.

THE RIGHT TO TALK   *April 1996*

'They've never had a chance to discuss their own sexuality, let alone homosexuality,' my adviser said. 'I don't see how you can use this story for a class – in English what's more. It's all right for the book, of course.'

I knew when I received the contribution that it was not a run of the mill story, that I couldn't just edit it and devise questions, and off we'd go. I'd have to take advice on how best to handle it. After all, there have been husbands who have stopped their wives coming to English classes – two cases that I know of for sure – because of what they might pick up there. We agreed that Linda W who runs the Women's Centre should decide how to proceed.

It seems a lot of fuss to make about a story introducing the subject of homosexuality among women but it has taken determination to build up a feeling of mutual trust in the class – a class which at least one woman attends for her third year.

As for the writer of the rather personal story, her motives are of the highest. At a time when the government has been circulating for public discussion its somewhat crass document on sexual orientation and discrimination, she is prepared to expose herself to public gaze. In the Chinese press, the subject of sexual orientation has been receiving prurient, rather than serious, discussion. She wanted, therefore, to make sure that the Classmates, at least, have a chance to understand the issues. 'Go ahead,' said Linda when I consulted her.

I gave the story out at the end of a lesson, as usual. I explained that it was an unusual subject, perhaps even awkward. But one which I hoped they would find interesting. I did not then mention Erica who had come to the class a few months earlier. She had heard me talking in public about the Classmates and explained that she ran similar consciousness-raising classes in England – could she come and talk to the Classmates? When it came to finalising details with her I swallowed a bit and suggested she might go easy on the sexual orientation of her own classes.

Erica came and talked about her mother's university degree, gained when she was an adult. Since further education was our main topic of conversation in class at the time, the session was a huge success, and they liked Erica. When she had gone, one of the Classmates ventured, 'Would "tomboy" be the right word to describe her?'

I said that was a word usually used for girls; 'butch' was more appropriate for women.

On the day of our lesson on sexual orientation, I arrived as usual at 2.15pm. Usually there were already a couple of Classmates there by then, but not that day. 2.20 came and went, and 2.25. I started to worry. At 2.29 they all trooped in together. Momentarily, I thought they were teasing me but I learnt, some time later, that most of them now usually lunch together.

Very recently we have started taking two lessons to a reading. The Classmates decide if the story is 'difficult' enough for this extra time. I was sure they would want this one over as soon as possible. 'One lesson, or two?' I asked.

'Two,' they chorused. And we were off.

It is true that they had never discussed their sexuality before, even if they had ever contemplated it. Indeed, it was difficult even to pinpoint the meaning of the term in English or Cantonese. I found myself using my hands in a vague, fluid sort of way. But soon we had the vocabulary neatly packaged: sexuality, sexual intercourse, heterosexuality, homosexuality, bisexuality, a crush.

Linda L, 73 years old and a recent widow, felt that we should define the meaning of love, and soon we were discussing incest and bestiality. 'How about the babies?' asked Eva of this latter activity.

'Have you ever discussed your sexuality with your husband?' I asked. Eva proudly claimed that she was able to tell her husband when she has a headache. I hadn't the heart to tell her that was a very early, rather old-fashioned form of communication. After all, it was obviously in advance of her classmates.

I brought up now the subject of Erica's sexual preference and they were much amused at their own naivete. They were flabbergasted that as many as 10 per cent of Hong Kong and China's population could be overtly, covertly or potentially gay. But they did accept that it was not a nefarious Western import. And they did see that discrimination was unacceptable, even if they did need a little convincing that AIDS was not confined to the gay community.

I had to leave punctually that day and was able wickedly to suggest from the doorway as I fled, leaving them to continue talking, 'Enjoy your sexuality!' Their warm laughter followed me.

My careful adviser feared that the Classmates would go home after the lesson and discuss it with their husbands, and have no secure base from which to talk, or argue. Hardly!

TUNG TUNG REVISITED   *May 1996*

'How many of you cried?' I asked the Classmates a week after I had given them the story of Tung Tung, the teddy bear who was given away. The body language reply said many things: don't tell us *you* cried, what on earth for? Why should we even be interested in a story of childhood poverty? Our families were there too.

It's a funny thing about the Classmates. I always assume that they will like best the stories about Chinese tradition, stories that they can identify with. In fact, I think the opposite is true. They like to learn about something new and different. Finally, sensing my disappointment, Eva said, 'My daughters cried.' Eva usually gives the stories to her two impeccable daughters to read. It's one of the joys of Eva – she fulfils so many of the points of Stories for Eva.

The lesson that day was just reading, vocabulary, grammar and pronunciation. Today we had comprehension and discussion. Two of the questions I had devised to go with the story became related in the answers they elicited. One was, Can you describe your favourite toy when you were six? The other, Have you ever lost a precious possession or pet in a similar way? Describe the experience.

Several Classmates said that they were too poor to have had toys at all; some described the toys they had made, such as little bags filled with rice with which they played five stones or jacks. But Linda, now 73, had been given something special when she was eight – a Japanese doll in a beautiful red and gold kimono and kept in a display box.

Then the Japanese invaded Manchuria – the Mukden Incident – on 18 September 1931. I knew of the anti-Japanese nationalist movement that built up in China over the following years. What

I had not realised was the strength of feeling in Hong Kong. Informally, a boycott of Japanese goods was implemented in the community and within families. Linda's brother took her beautiful and beloved Japanese doll and threw it on the fire.

Linda bowed her head as she finished her answer to the second question. Her toy, in answer to the first question, had been the grandest; her loss, lasting the longest time, hung palpably on the air in our classroom.

Eva set the scene for her answers. In her family of eight children, the boys had all the love and privileges. The girls were inescapably second best. One day, at market, Eva found a small wooden rabbit trampled into the mud. She picked it up and took it to her mother.

If it had been something for one of the boys, Eva explained, it would have been taken home and lovingly washed by her mother. On that day, her mother dusted down the rabbit and handed it to Eva with a 'There you are, you can have it.' For Eva it was a present from her mother, a gesture of love which turned the rabbit immediately into a treasure – one which she boasted about to her siblings, to prove that she, too, was loved.

Some time later, Eva got into an argument with a brother. He took her rabbit and cut off its brittle little paws. For days Eva tried to get at his toys to destroy them, but he was too clever for her. For a full year, she and a sister addressed not a word to him. 'What's your relationship like with him now?' I asked the 40 year old woman, not sure whether to laugh or cry.

She had been fierce in the telling of the story. Her screwed up face now said it all, 'Not so good!'

But, in the end, it was Connie – Connie who is perpetually 39 – who brought me closest to the brink. She held up her bare hand, 'I lost my wedding ring,' she said.

'But you can just ask you husband to get you another and put it back on your finger,' I said sympathetically but firmly.

A babble of voices competed to explain that was a joke: what Chinese husband cared about such trivial sentimentalities? Elizabeth held up her similarly bare left hand, and Kerrie did the same, explaining that hers had to be cut off following the birth of her daughter. But Connie just sat there, huge, silent tears seeping from under her half-closed eyelids.

And the tears come unbidden to my eyes as I write this story to send back to Irene, to show her how her story went down with the Classmates.[*]

BORN TO BLOSSOM UNSEEN?   *June 1996*

'You may need to get the Chinese characters of my name checked,' wrote Soong Moy. She has been an Australian for many years and lacks confidence in her 'Chinese writing'.

I turned, as usual, to Pet. She was cleaning the spare bathroom as I thrust Soong Moy's signature under her nose. 'What does that say?' I asked.

'Soong Moy,' replied Pet.

'Good,' I said, sketching in the background to the story. I then photocopied the characters and stuck them on Soong Moy's story which I was giving out to the Classmates today.

Five minutes later, Pet was at the door of the study apologising for disturbing me. 'Is that going on one of the stories?' she asked. She knows all about them, having briefly come to classes. And, anyway, I give her copies. 'Then, I think it would be better if I re-wrote it,' she said when I nodded. I gave her a piece of paper and, deftly, in perfect calligraphy, she wrote Soong Moy, in the top left hand corner of the page so that I could easily cut it out.

'How can you do that?' I asked, 'When you left school at 13 and went to work in a factory. Where did you learn to write so beautifully?' Most women of Pet's background lack proficiency in any written language.

'I don't know,' she replied smiling, pleased at my praise but not ignoring the thrust of my question.

'And you mended the clock, didn't you? I continued almost accusingly. One of our little alarm clocks packed it in a week or so ago. Derek fiddled with it for a while, found it had a hand swivelling loose, and left it on the bedside table with its back off, ready for an un-ceremonial chuck in the rubbish bin.

Pet smiled again. 'Yes.'

'You see, that's what bothers me,' I said, waving my hands about in frustration. 'You mend the unmendable clock; you write beautiful

---

[*]   By 2006, when Irene checked the pieces about her, she has an 'ever-growing collection of teddy bears' tended with 'loving care' by her parents.

calligraphy; you're a carpenter; you sew impeccably; you're highly intelligent, and you clean my lavatory. I can't bear it.'

'It's all right,' she soothed. Then she added, 'You know your book about Kuan Yin?'

We were standing by a pile of recently purchased books, ones that have not yet found a home. I fished out the book about Kuan Yin, the Chinese Goddess of Mercy (or Compassion). 'That's right,' said Pet. 'She's like the Dragon Mummy I told you about.' (The one she prayed to when Derek was ill this time last year.) 'When I'm cleaning your lavatory, I think about her, about things like not killing animals.' (Pet's a vegetarian.)

Yes,' I said. 'That's lovely. But, even so, cleaning lavatories is down here.' I put my flattened hand close to the ground. 'You should have a job up here.' I raised my hand level with my head.

I forbore to quote to her Gray's lines which come unbidden to my mind every time Pet does something like this: 'Full many a flower is born to blush unseen/And waste its sweetness on the desert air.' She would probably understand those lines if I wrote them down for her, and she could work them out. After all, the plants that I go away leaving half-dead – the poinsettia, the camellia and the African violet – flourish under her tutelage. (I do observe though that she does not remove the dead heads; and I don't want to interfere.)

I know she thinks of her lack of opportunity as unimportant. For her, the schooling and success of her son Peter – the boy who loves hamburgers – is what will reward her. (Her twin daughters, unfortunately, are 'lazy'; it's enough that they're not cleaning other people's lavatories.) But even so.

I have not given up the perhaps-naive dream that one day Pet will find an outlet for her remarkable talents. For the moment, it's something that she's left her no-good husband and is enjoying what she knows is her freedom. From freedom comes the possibility of progress.

MOURNING DOESN'T BECOME   *June 1996*

'You've had your hair cut,' I said to Tosh as I arrived to have mine done. Last time I went, she was not looking herself – her hair was no longer rather orange and it definitely needed the attention of a pair of scissors. Now, she was once again en brosse, perky and colourful. 'I'm so glad,' I continued. 'It means you're feeling better.' She had been rather down in the dumps last time, in keeping with her lack of coiffure.

'My father died on 15 May,' she finally replied, helping me into a gown. I collapsed in embarrassment at so misreading the signs, full of commiseration. 'It's all right,' she said, making eye contact in the mirror, and over the next 70 minutes that it took to give me a trim (no shampoo, no blow dry), she let down her hair, figuratively, of course.

Her 78-year-old father was dreadfully ill in November – in hospital for months with a collapsed lung. Tosh did her demanding job, looked after her mother at home, looked after her father in the hospital miles from home and work, and paid the bills. When I last had my hair cut, a couple of months ago, he was out of hospital and back at home but weak. She told me then that, in spite of his breathing problems, he insisted on having their two cats in the small one room flat.

'I know the cat fur doesn't help, but he loves them so,' explained Tosh.

It seems now that those few months of reprieve were among the happiest the family spent together. Then the other lung collapsed and he was back in hospital with Tosh keeping vigil. The medical staff were sanguine – all the machines keeping him alive read positive. But her father knew the moment that death set in, and told her so. She saw him through to the end, while her mother stayed firmly at home.

Her mother has taken his death badly; somehow she thought the reprieve was for ever and feels doubly betrayed. Tosh, for her part, seems to think it is time her mother climbed out of the abyss of her grief. 'But it's hardly more than a couple of weeks,' I said gently. 'She needs quite a bit more time than that to grieve.'

'Do you think so?' Tosh asked as if seriously considering that I might be right. 'Am I hurrying her too much?' Tosh wants her mother to attend the centre for the elderly in their public housing complex, to help take her out of herself. 'She could learn her ABC (in Chinese), so she could travel about Hong Kong by herself.'

But the new widow considers herself too old (73), ugly, poor, badly dressed, and she doesn't speak Cantonese; (she speaks Mandarin and her north China dialect). This loss of confidence leaves Tosh herself at a loss. Her mother won't go down to the Centre. She won't even use the front door of the flat. She doesn't want her solicitous neighbour asking questions. 'What's it to do with her?'

Meanwhile, on Tuesdays, Tosh's day off, they burn the fake money and elaborate paper household goods that it is Chinese custom to send to the netherworld with the deceased. Tomorrow it will be a big television set, with remote control. 'Last week it was two servants – paper servants,' Tosh said hurriedly, mistaking my look in the mirror.

'That's strange, isn't it,' I said. 'Did your father have servants in real life?' In my mind they are poor people.

'Oh yes,' replied Tosh. 'Before my parents left China they were really quite rich.'

What happens now to this widow who, for all her adult life, has subordinated herself to the interests of her husband? Her greatest achievement in recent months was to take the shuffling invalid out for the ritual of *yam cha* (late breakfast in a cafe). Now she has nothing to do, and no intellectual or social reserves to call on. She does not even water the plants; they have started to die.

And what about her 35-year-old daughter who has already sacrificed herself on the altar of filial piety? She has friends but even they tell her that she must not cut her hair for some months following her father's death. At least she has taken no notice of that.

THE LUCKY ONES   *September 1996*

Next year, two 70-year-old women will walk down the gangway at Heathrow Airport. Metaphorically they will be holding hands. Their tickets will have been bought for them in Hong Kong and they will have been put carefully on the plane there. They will be warmly met in England. They don't know each other intimately, but they like each other well enough. About four times a year they meet to play the national pastime, mahjong, The other two players at these sessions are the son of one and the daughter of the other. The younger players are married to each other; the two elderly women are mothers and mothers-in-law.

Next week, their two children emigrate to England. The mothers will continue living alone in Hong Kong. They are healthy and independent, both widows. One of them was originally a subsidiary wife, a status sometimes called a concubine. That doesn't matter much now. Both widows have other children in Hong Kong to provide the traditional support to the elderly of the Chinese family. If they had not, their two children would not be emigrating – or, if they did, their mothers would be going with them.

But times are changing here. Traditionally, when a woman married, she became part of her husband's family; her mother-in-law, rather than her mother, became the woman to whom she owed respect. Today, in many families, and in the family I am describing, widowed mothers – or even married parents – are treated turn and turn about, as in the West. Indeed, in some families, the wife's mother may be given preferential treatment where the wife is the primary support of her own mother.

For example, in the past the family dinner on Lunar New Year's Eve was the time when the whole family gathered at the husband's parents' home. Now it may be the wife's one year, and the husband's the next.

A less easy change is revealed in figures out today from Befriender's International, the umbrella organisation for local Samaritan groups. Suicides in Hong Kong have slightly increased – to 12 in 100,000. (This compares with 29 per 100,000 in Mainland China, and 42 in Hungary.) Based on this figure, elderly suicides here have increased to 37 per cent of the total.

The reasons for elderly suicides are many and various. One of the main causes is lack of a comprehensive welfare state so that, living in penury (if there is no family support), the elderly sick cannot afford medicine.

The new phenomenon is emigration leading up to July 1997 (now less than a year away). Many younger couples are emigrating with their children to Canada, Australia, the United States, the United Kingdom. There, re-settlement will be difficult enough for the two younger generations.

Often they are leaving their parents behind. Not only will they be too big a burden in their new and, perhaps, alien life but, just as important, the elderly may not want to leave the life and surroundings they are used to. But often, too, they are being left in homes for the elderly – an institution barely known even 15 years ago, and a Western one much disparaged by Chinese trumpeting traditional Chinese values and care for the elderly within the extended family.

The sense of abandonment and being institutionalised instead of in the bosom of the family may trigger suicide. But my friends who are off next week are leaving their mothers in the good hands of siblings.

When the new immigrants arrive in England they already have a home, and the husband already has an occupation he has carefully tailored to his new life. He also speaks and writes fluent English. His wife will be without a job, however, and, although she learnt English at school some years ago, it has grown rusty and she lacks confidence.

Still, her son is now at school in England and he has much matured in the year he has been there. He no longer kicks against what he used to see as her nagging. He has learnt to respect her since he left home. She has had to learn to loosen the reins – and she won't be able to pull them tight again when her 16-year-old comes home from boarding school.

So all three women will look forward to that day next year when the two mothers arrive in England for a visit. They are the lucky ones.

A MERE STATISTIC   *September 1996*

To think that Pet is a mere statistic – this woman who stands at the ironing board in my kitchen and is the flesh and blood of Hong Kong Chinese womanhood. Yes, Pet is working now towards her divorce, and her eyes sparkle as she says to me, 'It's good, I think.'

'Did you ring Linda at the Women's Centre?' I asked her the other day. Just before I went away for ten weeks I checked that she had the right telephone number and encouraged her to ring for advice.

'I rang and was put onto another social worker,' Pet explained. 'She told me that I have to live apart from my husband for two years. And,' she added, 'she rings me sometimes to see that I'm all right.' Bravo, Women's Centre is what I say.

Pet's husband has her new telephone number. 'It's easier that way,' she explains. 'Otherwise he bothers my brothers. He rings me trying to arrange family meals. He wants to see his son and daughters. I say to him, "If you want to see Peter and Sally and Helen, you ask them."' She's grown so wise about human affairs. '"It's up to them, not up to me."'

Fifteen-year-old Peter Bear is getting to be quite the little man. We could hardly believe it when we saw him the other day after a bit of a gap. We got off the plane after the 13-hour flight – weary, weary. The taxi drew up at Cavendish Heights. It can be pretty muggy in the evening in early September. We didn't know that the number 8 typhoon signal would be raised in a few hours.

This moment is always rather nerve-wracking. We've landed safely, will all be well in the flat after such a long absence? Up in the lift, no letters in the box, Pet must have come yesterday. Key in the front door. Suddenly it swings open and there are Pet and Peter, faces alight. Peter, burly, towering over Pet, shy with his English. She's hardly expected to be at work here at 7pm on a Sunday!

'How did you know we were coming then?' I asked some days later, expecting an admission of some sixth sense, which would not have surprised me.

'I didn't,' she said. 'I was just putting a clean bag in the rubbish bin when I looked out of the window and saw your taxi.'

She came to make sure that our vast expanse of parquet floor was as shiny as it could possibly be for our return, to take all the pipes away from our ingenious dehumidifier system, and to leave some food – tomatoes and avocado pears. (She doesn't realise they have to be ripe but she does know that we love them.) Then she went home to her one room flat with Peter Bear.

Now Sally is living there too. She has fallen out with her twin sister Helen who continues to live in Pet's late father's one room. It's something to do with a mutual dislike of each other's boyfriend, I believe. The twins have just had their twentieth birthday. Sally's boyfriend appears to be a gentleman, according to Pet. She used that word. But she suspects he is a fraud.

Helen's is a Mummy's boy. At 25, he still looks to his mother to organise his finances. I'm not sure that Pet is thrilled with either young man. But they'd be hard-pushed to beat her own man for unsatisfactoriness. Nine months down, just over a year to go and Pet can be divorced.

Statistics show that divorce is on the increase in Hong Kong. Eight thousand women rang the Caritas Family Service hotline last year about their marital problems. Sixty per cent needed counselling about their husbands' extra-marital affairs. Thirty per cent of callers wanted to know how to prevent these affairs; they want to put more life into their relationships. Women are prepared now to discuss their sex lives.

But 20 per cent asked about the marriage laws, and how to apply for legal and financial assistance. Not only is divorce becoming easier but it's also becoming more socially acceptable; and women now dare to be free. Each one of those statistical women is a person like Pet. Well, not quite like!

SOME CONSOLATION   *October 1996*

I've failed to learn Cantonese in the nine and a half years I've been in Hong Kong, and I feel unbearably guilty about it. I have tried. The first three months we were here, a tutor came to Derek's office twice a week for an hour and a half and we worked hard. I also listened to a tape while I washed the dishes.

Then we went to England on leave and when we came back six weeks later everything had gone – except the numbers one to ten, the expression for 'never mind' and 'hello' and 'thank you'.

We went to evening classes once a week for a term. Then we gave up. We were by then both so busy and Cantonese is fiendishly difficult to learn. Government servants brought out from England have traditionally studied the language full time for six months. Now, every time a Hong Kong person, knowing exactly what they are doing, asks in English 'How good is your Cantonese?' we cringe, flush and squirm.

I have one consolation and it is brought home to me every week when I go to the Women's Centre to take my English class: I am able to speak to Chinese women in Hong Kong about everything under the sun. This consolation for my major shortcoming is particularly warming at the moment. When I got back from England this summer, there was a letter waiting for me from the government-backed Language Fund. They have accepted my application for money to publish *Stories for Eva: A Reader for Chinese Women Learning English*.

It is exactly six years ago that I started my English class. And for three of those years I have been commissioning, editing, using as lessons, and fine tuning the stories. The Classmates' contribution and appreciation have been crucial. The book is truly theirs; indeed, I refer to it as 'our book' and it is dedicated to them.

When it came to the cover for the book, I remembered that some years ago, before we had the stories, I used to construct lessons round magazine photographs of people they might know. One of these was the artist Nancy Chu Woo – an earlier letter in this book was about Nancy and the Classmates. I had long ago written to Nancy asking her to write a story for the book. I had not really expected a response – she's a painter, after all. But now I wrote asking her if we could use one of her paintings on the front. The answer was yes. But which one?

I took a book of her paintings into class a couple of weeks ago to consult the Classmates about which one they would like. Nancy has three favourite subjects: impressionistic landscapes, feminine-looking fruit and vegetables, and nudes, either straightforward or impressionistic. I thought the Classmates might consent to a voluptuous vegetable or two. I was surprised and delighted when they agreed on two possibilities: a modernist painting in which I failed to find the nude, though its title made clear it was there, and a more obvious, if discreet one, called 'Walking in the Woods'.

Happily, the green vision of a naked woman walking, with her back to us, in the woods while she contemplates learning English and anything else she fancies is still in Nancy's studio and we may use it.

Then I had to decide what to put on the back cover, apart from the blurb. One possibility is a picture taken last July at the end of term party at our flat – the one legislator and story contributor Christine Loh attended. That would be nice, I think.

Then there was the picture of Anita, Anna and Patsy at a demo at least four years ago. I remember asking if any of the Classmates would like to demonstrate outside Legco in favour of setting up a Women's Commission. They agreed to come and I took a charming picture of them with their placards. We've since got a Commission, of sorts.

None of them has been to class for a while but I had Anna's telephone number and rang to ask if she minded if I used the photograph. I got the number of the other two from her – they are still friends – and also rang Anita (Patsy is out as I write). I was afraid they might be embarrassed about having such a public picture of themselves on our book but I need not have worried.

The thing which moved me most, however, and has prompted me to write this letter, is that they not only talked to me as if we were old friends but they did so in impeccable English.

TYPICALLY HERSELF   *October 1996*

Some of you may feel that I write about Pet rather a lot. Others may worry that, in writing about her at all, I am betraying her confidence. In my more historical writing, I have used her description of her grandmother as part of a case study on concubinage. Before I published it, I gave it to Pet to read – first to check the facts, secondly to alert her to my propensity to commit her words to paper.

I'm not sure that she has found time to read it, for she cannot simply skim through – there would be much thumbing of the dictionary, and she has other priorities. But at least she now knows what I get up to. And she continues to supply me with copy.

In writing about her I sometimes give the impression that I regard her as a symbol of eternal Hong Kong Chinese womanhood. And sometimes, I suppose, it must seem that I patronise her – because she has had little formal education and because she is, in my terms, superstitious.

One of her virtues is that she allows me to reject generalisation. When some Hong Kong woman has snitched my taxi from me, or barged at me unseeing out of a lift, I cannot say 'typical'. Because Pet, with her innate wisdom and integrity, is from the same mould.

For a few weeks now she has said 'no, thank you' when, every Tuesday, I ask her if she is going to share my taxi to Causeway Bay. Today, she said it again. Then she realised, perhaps from my face, that she had said it once too often. 'I don't want to come too near you with my throat,' she explained. And it all fell into place; and it was typical of her sensitivity.

Soon after we arrived back from England this autumn, she came with a bad throat infection. In spite of my concern, she has insisted on treating it with traditional remedies and, although she claims that it is getting better, I am not convinced. She brushes aside my attempts at (Western medicine) interference almost rudely. I would happily pay for her to go to our (first rate) doctor.

She seems to have come by this infection from the re-decoration in the room opposite hers. It has been going on for weeks and consists of spraying of some kind. The work people keep the door open while they spray and it goes straight into Pet's room, and down her throat. She has a very vulnerable throat; even the vapour of chillies in the atmosphere is hell for her. At the moment, I am washing the curry pans before she comes. That's the story of the throat and why she is trying to protect me – which is neither Chinese nor non-Chinese but concerned with proper social relations.

I have already explained that Pet is a vegetarian and opposed to any sort of killing. Why, she wouldn't even uproot the weeds that grew in the camellia pot while we were away. In the recent nationalist goings on concerning the Diaoyu Islands (which the Japanese also claim and call the Senaku), she has confirmed her commitment to non-violence. I showed her a picture of the Chinese and Taiwanese flags planted on the islands at dawn last week, the former flag by Hong Kong activists. I asked her opinion.

By means of the gesture of running her finger up her arm, she explained that the sticking of the Taiwanese flag there beside and at the same time as the Chinese one was laying the trail to a powder keg. Pretty sophisticated stuff for a Hong Kong person at the moment.

Then there are her views on the environment. Our gas cooker was almost on its last legs after nine and a half years. Recently, a gas man came to check its safety and, to my delight, fitted four new burners, saying as he did so, 'Most Hong Kong people have new cookers after four or five years.'

I fumed to Pet as I showed off the resuscitated cooker, 'In England I've had the same electric cooker since 1968. We don't change our equipment like you do here.'

'I've had mine since the twins were little,' Pet rejoined. And it is not just economic expediency: she made clear her aversion to today's throw-away culture.

She's shown herself to be unmistakably Chinese, however, in the way she approached a more trivial matter. Last week, she asked after Young Derek (my stepson) and his partner, Vivienne. She has not seen them since they stayed with us for three days two years ago. But she knows that they are now living in Hong Kong. 'They're fine,' I answered eagerly. 'And they were here on Sunday. In fact, they went swimming with us.'

'I know,' Pet replied calmly. 'And they used the spare bathroom.' I looked amazed at her powers of deduction. 'When I turned the taps on to clean the bath,' she explained smilingly but pointedly, 'the rain fell down on me.' Talk about coming at a complaint from round a long sweeping bend!

WHAT'S IN AN ACRONYM?   *October 1996*

'The JLG has finally agreed to CEDAW,' said Cecilia yesterday on the telephone. Even the women's movement has its acronyms and gobbledygook.

Cecilia is a sister in AWARE and chairperson of the Hong Kong Federation of Women's Centres (just about to open its second centre) to which we are affiliated. The JLG is the Joint Liaison Group, consisting of British and Chinese representatives who, since it was agreed in 1984 that Hong Kong should return to China, have held regular discussions – usually disagreeing.

CEDAW, as the initiated and those with a good memory will know, is the United Nations Convention for the Elimination of All Forms of Discrimination against Women. Hong Kong women have, for several years, been calling for the convention's extension to the Territory – since both Britain and China long ago ratified it.

I first became involved with CEDAW in 1991 when I stood up, knees trembling, at a lunch at the FCC (Foreign Correspondents' Club) and asked the Governor (Sir David Wilson) when the convention would come to Hong Kong. I had to keep looking down at my bit of paper to remember what the acronym stood for, and I was later taken to task by a male journalist, in print, for wasting the occasion with such trivia.

The Governor didn't know what it was about and his private secretary passed me a note saying he would look into it. Nothing seemed to come of anything then. And now, they say, it's finally to reach these shores. If there has been an article in the press, I've missed it.

A similar piece of news came my way a few weeks ago. Anne of BPW (Business and Professional Women) rang me on a Friday to say that the SDO (Sex Discrimination Ordinance) was to come into force on Monday (it had just been gazetted). Well, half into force: the employment provisions are still in abeyance, while a Code of Practice is finalised.

Anne wanted to know what club she could march into that excluded women. I couldn't bring to mind then the story of the KCC

(Kowloon Cricket Club) where women have always been excluded from membership because it was assumed that they should be. But there is nothing, they found, in the rules to say so.

Our EOC (Equal Opportunities Commission) (including, for the moment, women and the disabled), was set up (in name only) at the end of 1995. And, after much to-ing and fro-ing, Fanny Cheung was appointed to chair it in May this year. It has received nothing but criticism since, not only because there are too many men and too many employers on the 16-strong Commission.

A day or so after Fanny's appointment, the story of the year broke. The Lippo Group threatened to fine any woman $300 for wearing trousers to work. Presumably, the shortest mini skirt was all right, but to be penalised were, mostly, Chinese women who, traditionally, wore trousers as modest and daily dress. There was an awful row over this and, eventually, red-faced, Lippo backed down – with a statement from their Chair. But Fanny said not a word, and was roundly berated for her silence.

At that stage, the planned 60-strong office of the EOC consisted of Fanny and a desk, nothing more. But there was more to Fanny's failure to speak out than lack of a press officer or the full panoply of her Commission.

Fanny, deceptively small, slender and hesitant of speech, is easy to misread. I've known her, though not closely, for some years – ever since I was new in the women's movement here and brushed up against her at a conference. She was chairing a session and I was a stroppy member of the audience. Afterwards, I wrote her a conciliatory note and we have had, ever since I like to think, a healthy respect for each other's commitment, our different cultures and different temperaments.

When I was commissioning 'stories' for my English class at the Women's Centre (of which Fanny was then honorary president), she sent me one she had written some years ago and invited me to adapt it. On reading it, I understood her better than ever.

She came to feminism – and then to the struggle for women's rights – in the United States when she went there to study. And it was a slow and resistant transformation. But it was eventually complete and she has dedicated herself since, in her own way, to the women's cause. She set up, for example, the Gender Research Programme at the Chinese University where, until recently, she taught psychology and was Dean of Social Science, and was one of the instigators of the Women's Centre.

But there is a sentence towards the end of her story that is crucial to understanding how the EOC is being led. Fanny wrote, 'For my part, I assert myself much better through my unobtrusive tenacity.' Anyone who expects a lot of noise from the EOC is bound to be disappointed. So I, a noisy sort of an activist, quietly lift my glass to CEDAW – another battle won.

A SAFE HAVEN   *November 1996*

Tosh and I were chatting about this and that. As usual, her scissors were poised in the air. She has moved into a new public housing flat, a bigger one where her mother has her own room; and they have their own bathroom. Her mother is pleased and regaining her interest in life. The cats are settling down well. It's all so ironic when her father has recently died; he was never able to enjoy this greater comfort.

Suddenly, Tosh was contrasting the new flat with memories of her first home in Hong Kong – Rennies Mill. I pricked up my ears. Rennies Mill was, until a few months ago, a Kuomintang (KMT) squatter settlement on Kowloon side. It was there that those who fled China in front of the Communist advances of 1948/49 created their own enclave in the British colony.

There for nearly 50 years the KMT red and blue flag has flown more defiantly than almost anywhere else on the Double Tenth – 10 October – in support of the KMT, now based in Taiwan. And from there the last squatters have just been removed, much against their will, though compensated by the Hong Kong Government, ready for the return of the colony to China next June.

'You lived there throughout your childhood?' I asked.

'I was born there.'

'In a squatter hut, just with a midwife?'

'More like a tent, with a neighbour to help.' Still the scissors hung in the air, but I minded less. I urged Tosh on. I knew that her mother and father, originally from the North East, had left China since the war, now the whole story began to spill out.

Tosh's father was married at 15 to a 25-year-old woman. She was sold to his rich family as a daughter-in-law, a *mui tsai* – a young woman who would supply service to the family. The couple's first child (of three) was born two years later.

Meanwhile, the young husband was at school and there he grew friendly with Tosh's mother, a classmate. He wanted to take her as his wife. But his first wife objected. Her mother-in-law told her it had nothing to do with her – she would decide.

Tosh's mother also came from a rich mercantile family. It seems that the upper classes in the area had prospered under Japanese occupation. Tosh's parents, who have never learned Cantonese in Hong Kong, spoke Japanese.

Then came 1948 and the spread of Communist victories throughout China. One day, Tosh's parents decided to flee, some jewellery in their pockets and some gold bars. They dropped the gold bars as they ran, bullets zinging about them. The jewellery later proved almost valueless as they made their way down the length of China on foot ahead of the Communist forces.

In her childhood, when Tosh complained of the food put before her, her mother would remind her that for many months she and her father ate little more than roots pulled from the fields they passed. Finally, the couple reached Hong Kong and Rennies Mill. Eventually, her father, who had never had to work before he left home, got work humping goods around a textile mill. The work was intermittent, depending on what labour was required; a list was pinned up outside each day.

The community at Rennies Mill all mucked in and shared their resources. From time to time, a live chicken would be bought as a celebratory meal. Then, Tosh's mother, soft-hearted and practical, would delay its slaughter. She would gather up the eggs it had laid and hawk them at the nearby market.

Later, the family moved to an old house where its common facilities were used by six families. Tosh still has friends among the children with whom she shared everything then. But her parents' gracious home in China, and her half sister and brothers who had a separate house, she has never seen. Eventually they tracked their father down through the Red Cross but only for what money there might be; Tosh says they hated their father.

And Rennies Mill is no more. 'They pulled down the last huts on my birthday in August this year,' Tosh complained, at last snipping a bit of hair.

The flat she lives in now is very good compared to that. But I notice that she is wearing her baseball cap again. She hasn't got time or inclination to have her own hair cut. And her mother, now alone all day, let an itinerant salesman into the flat the other day. He simply flashed his identity card and took $200 from her for some device for cleaning the telephone. 'But I had the telephone cleaned last week, Mum,' wailed Tosh. 'And you might have been hurt.' Tosh's mum is slightly impervious to such warnings; she has been through more turbulent times. Oh, and she's not looking forward to 1997.

WANTING ANSON FOR NUTS IN MAY   *December 1996*

For months I smiled quietly to myself. Every time there was a news item about the new Chief Executive who will lead Hong Kong after the return to Chinese sovereignty, the newsrooms had to be careful. Normally, the male pronoun is used consistently and unthinkingly. You would think there were no women of authority in any sphere of Hong Kong endeavour; but they knew Anson Chan Fang On-sang was in the running for Chief Executive, so they always had to add, 'whoever he or she might be'.

What is more, Anson Chan was the most popular choice. In all the opinion polls, long before the list of possible candidates crystallised, she was well in the lead. In December 1995, when Tung Chee-hwa polled 0.2 per cent, and Sir TL Yang, 6.4 per cent, Anson Chan had 50.7 per cent. In May 1996, CH Tung had climbed from obscurity to 5.2 per cent because the President of China shook hands with him at a function in Beijing; TL Yang had progressed to 7.2 per cent – and Anson cruised along at 56.5 per cent. In August this year, CH Tung was streaking ahead with 10.4 per cent, TL Yang had slumped to 2.4 per cent and Anson Chan was 60.1 per cent.

Why was she so popular? Well, first of all, she was Chief Secretary – the top civil servant and the Governor's number two. She had climbed to that dizzy height – the first woman, the first Chinese – in 1993 and since then proved herself.

As far as the so-called pro-China lobby is concerned, she is in the Governor's pocket. And certainly she has supported him in public in a way which might be considered foolhardy for someone with an eye to the future. But she had two other things going for her. Her family came from China at the time of Liberation but, carefully, she began to return to her home place and tactfully to re-establish ties with the Chinese leadership. Then, you can't help but observe that she is a woman of integrity.

She may be a bit reactionary for my taste; she doesn't for example speak out, at least in public, on women's issues or other progressive concerns. But she's principled, strong and unafraid. She's loyal to the Governor because that's her job as the top civil servant, not because she's a toady, in spite of how it looks to those who denounce him. Hong Kong people saw her as able to provide continuity and an impartiality and, therefore, a security which no other candidate for Chief Executive could do.

But she obviously saw things differently. To stand for Chief Executive, she would have to resign first as Chief Secretary. If China really had decided who would be replacement 'governor', then she was unlikely to win, whatever the polls suggesting public opinion said. Even before that, she would have to win 50 votes from the selection committee to become a candidate. The Chief Executive was not being elected by universal suffrage. The person was being selected by a business-oriented electoral college of 400 who, in turn, were chosen by a small administrative office of the inevitably pro-China Preparatory Committee. To win the necessary votes would seem impossible.

And, if she were not chosen, at either hurdle, she would be left without any position at all. And Hong Kong would be left without a head of the Civil Service who could, at least in that capacity, provide continuity and security. So, instead, Anson Chan announced that she would not stand. But, without saying much, she was able to show herself indispensable as Chief Secretary, whoever became Chief Executive. Indeed, all the candidates felt the need to announce swiftly that they would keep Anson Chan on; it was their passport to acceptability by a sceptical Hong Kong populace.

I was intrigued by how this small woman with the large, slightly fixed but most attractive smile, the careful voice and hairdo, was able to organise herself round a situation that was so full of uncertainty and division. Even when it was clear that she was not a candidate, she continued to maintain a lead in the polls. In October, CH Tung was 14.7 per cent, TL Yang was 21.5, and Peter Woo, a newcomer, was 7.9 per cent. Anson Chan was 39 per cent.

Then the candidates formally announced themselves. The front-runners were CH Tung (businessman), TL Yang (now dropping his knighthood, former Chief Justice), Peter Woo (businessman) and Simon Li (former judge).

In my English class in late October, we had a rather political story which encouraged discussion about the forthcoming selection of the Chief Executive. 'Let's have an election ourselves,' I suggested. I wrote the four men's names on the board and added, 'Just for fun, let's put up Anson. I know she's not standing. But we can vote for her if we like.' So round the room we went, and this is the result: Tung = 6, Yang = 6, Woo = 0, Li = 0, Chan = 10.

CH Tung may have been chosen by the Selection Committee today by an overwhelming majority; and that might well provide some form of reassurance and hope for the future. But it won't harm his effectiveness to have announced immediately that he has asked Anson Chan to stay as his number two.

MUSICAL CHAIRS   *December 1996*

Musical chairs is a children's game, so it is rather hard to take seriously a political system that makes adults play it, and not even at a Christmas party.

A couple of days before Christmas, the members of the Provisional Legislature – the body that will replace the Legislative Council at midnight on 30 June 1997 – were selected. In the Legislative Council that sits until then, there are seven women councillors; in the new one there will be nine. But don't get excited about there being two more women. As Pet once said, 'I'll vote for a woman, [only] if she's a good woman.' And Pet wasn't even given a chance to vote on 22 December.

I need to explain how these nine women and their 51 male colleagues were selected. First of all, some months ago, 5,000 people put themselves forward to be on the Selection Committee. The electoral college that would result was intended, under the Basic Law which will govern the Special Administrative Region (SAR) of Hong Kong from 1 July 1997, to choose the Chief Executive.

Then it was decided to dispense with the services of the Legislative Council elected under the so-called 'Patten Reforms' in September 1995. Those elected then were no longer to ride on the 'Through Train' as had been envisaged by the Joint Declaration of Britain and

China when they agreed about Hong Kong's future. Instead, as a rebuff, a provisional legislature was to be set up for the transition period of, it is said, about a year. All being well, there will be new elections in 1998 which will conform to China's interpretation of the Basic Law, rather than Chris Patten's.

The 5,000 who applied to be on the selection committee for the Chief Executive and the Provisional Legislature, could be anyone who fancied their chances. They were whittled down to 409 by a small secretariat of the Preparatory Committee which has been doing what it's name suggests for some time.

Those 409 were further whittled down and another group – Hong Kong members of China's national parliament – automatically became eligible for the final 400. The 400 are supposed to be representative of Hong Kong people but they mostly belong to the business community, only about 10 per cent are women, and the Democratic Party and their allies – who won the largest number of seats in 1995 – boycotted what they saw as a charade. They chose, on principle, not to stand for the selection committee, nor to stand for selection by it. If they had stood, it should be said that they would probably not have been selected. They are branded 'subversive'.

These pages show that I was not a wholehearted supporter of Chris Patten's legislative reforms, not only because they too – through the expansion of the functional constituencies – favoured the business community. More importantly, they disenfranchised one million housewives.

It also has to be said that the selection earlier in the month of Tung Chee-hwa as Chief Executive by an electoral college of 400 gives a semblance of being preferable to the way British Governors of the colony have been chosen for over 150 years. Even if the final choice, at least in the twentieth century, was made by a British cabinet elected through universal suffrage, no Hong Kong people had a vote.

But the Provisional Legislature – that's another matter. You see, of the 120 people putting themselves forward for selection to 60 seats, many were also members of the Selection Committee and each Selection Committee member had 60 votes. One political commentator has rather nicely termed the proceedings a 'barter election'. I imagined the scene thus: 'You vote for me and my mates, mate, and I'll vote for you and your mates, mate.' Thus nine women were chosen of 14 who stood. Who are they?

Thirty-three Provisional Legco members are also members of the current legislature. Fair enough; there is an argument for pragmatism, as well as principle, in politics. One woman, Chan Yuen-han, a trade union representative, was elected by universal suffrage in 1995; Selina Chow and Miriam Lau were elected to functional constituencies, being appointed members for several years before that.

Of the other women, four were not new to politics; two I had never heard of. Maria Tam has previously been a Legco member, appointed by an earlier governor; and Rita Fan was an appointed Exco member as well as a Legco member. She fell out with Chris Patten soon after his arrival. Those two have worked hard on China's behalf since – they've earned spurs. But two women who were selected this week were defeated in the 1995 elections. One of them, 68-year old Peggy Lam hardly endeared herself to me by a remark she once made in Legco when she was an appointed member. She dismissed women's groups battling to secure the machinery to ensure rights for women as being 'tied to Emily Lau's apron strings'.

Twice democratically-elected Emily Lau, who lay in the road and was arrested during protests against the Provisional Legislature, and talked to the BBC World Service on her mobile telephone from the police station, is a brave and lovable woman. But our concerns were not her first concerns. Even if many of her concerns – such as human rights and the well-being of Hong Kong – were also ours.

I find it somewhat reprehensible that Peggy Lam should be defeated in a fair democratic fight by the far more capable and principled Christine Loh, and then put herself forward for non-democratic selection.

Then there is very dear Elsie Tu. She, too, lost at the last election, though the fight wasn't entirely fair. She too has put herself forward for selection, and been chosen. I've supported and defended Elsie through thick and thin. Even when the Classmates said she was too old to stand at the last election, I chided them. But I shan't be writing Elsie a letter of congratulation this time.

As for outspoken democrats, Christine Loh, Emily Lau and Libby Wong, we have to hope they'll have the chance to stand again for election in 1998, and win, and be safe in the meantime.

1997

Perhaps the true story can now be told – or a version of it, at least. It is the teller's truth only, and discretion among sisters is seemly. The Hong Kong Council of Women was wound up at the end of last month and any funds still remaining distributed to other women's groups. It is a historic moment because the Council was almost the longest established women's group here and has done some excellent work. But in the early spring of 1991 events took place which sowed the seeds of its eventual disintegration.

That January, if you remember, the Gulf War started. I wrote then of the demonstrations that took place weekly by a small group of anti-war protesters. At the same time, one of the organisers of the protest, Maria, who was also a Council of Women member, drew up an open letter in the form of a newspaper advertisement. Some Council members, including me, signed individually. In addition, as there was the requisite number of members to sanction a press statement, the Chair and Vice Chair, Linda and Cecilia, gave permission for the Council's name also to be used as a signatory.

All hell broke loose then for it transpired – contrary to assumptions – that some members of the Council were not only not pacifists but, as supporters of the United States and Israel's interests, actively backed the war.

There were exchanges of long, closely argued letters about the relationship between feminism and pacifism, as well as who said what to whom, and then a most unseemly, acrimonious meeting. As I write six years later I can almost feel again the flow of adrenalin. The upshot was that the Chair and Vice Chair of the Council and several of us ordinary members resigned.

For a few months previously, some of us had been working on a sub-committee of the Council on a project to involve more women in politics. The members of this sub-committee were among those feminist-pacifists who now found themselves without a home. The sub-committee, therefore, became the basis of a new women's group. We called it, initially, Women in Politics (WIP). Then a new member told us that she was a member of another new group called Women in Publishing (WIPS). Maria had recently come across a Singapore group called AWARE (Association of Women for Action and Research), so we hurriedly changed our name to that and established a very loose relationship with our Singapore sisters, placing ourselves in a regional and international context as well as a local one.

Meanwhile, the Hong Kong Council of Women was left somewhat bereft – with quite a large paper membership but with more than half its activists gone. It soldiered on but a haemorrhage of energy, ideas, commitment and membership had started which turned out to be unstaunchable. It was a great pity because the Council had a distinguished history. It was set up in Hong Kong in 1947 and affiliated to the International Council of Women in 1951. A book I bought in a second hand bookshop – *Women in a Changing World: The Dynamic Story of the International Council of Women since 1888* (1966) – gives a potted history of the Hong Kong chapter which includes such initiatives as the Family Planning Association.

But its most successful later campaign was that which resulted in 1971 in legislation to bring about the end of concubinage. At that time its leading lights were Chinese, including Ellen Li the first woman Legislative Councillor.

It still had a strong Chinese membership when it set up Harmony House, the refuge for abused women, in 1985, and in 1986 the Women's Centre where I have been teaching English since the creation of AWARE. But by the late 1980s, many Chinese members had left it to set up organisations such as AAF (Association for the Advancement of Feminism) less overtly middle-class, fully Chinese, more determinedly feminist.

In 1991, with the resignation of the Chair and Vice Chair, there was hardly a Chinese woman left on the Council and AWARE and the earlier splinters began to form a new more diffuse but more politically active and more consciously post-colonial women's movement, campaigning towards reforming legislation and a women's commission.

Organisations have their focus and, thus, their day. They are as strong or as fragile as their members and their ideas. The time and point of the Hong Kong Council of Women has been, and is now, sadly but naturally, gone. RIP 1947–1996.

A MOMENT INSIDE   *February 1997*

Almost exactly six years ago, we went to the collection of villages in the New Territories known as Lam Tsuen for a festival to drive away hungry ghosts (*Ta Tsui* or *Dajiao*) which takes place every ten years. We went on a formal 'outing', very much as outsiders, and I wrote to you about it (January 1991), contrasting East and West.

Yesterday, by coincidence, we went there as guests of a couple who live in one of the villages. It was so much of a coincidence that it was only after some hours that I realised I had been there before. Without the festival structures, such as the tin sheeting and bamboo opera house and fairground booths, the place was unrecognisable.

But going on an 'ordinary' day, and as individual guests, had, as is so often the way, its benefits. When I say it was an ordinary day, that is not strictly true because it was within the two week period of Lunar New Year, when all sorts of special activities take place; so we were doubly lucky.

Strictly speaking, we were not guests of real insiders; we were visiting an English couple who, on the retirement of one of them, Patrick, from the civil service, have decided to live in one of the three-storeyed villas which have proliferated in New Territories villages where the people used to live in traditional and rudimentary single-storey stone houses.

Patrick learned Cantonese and New Territories customs officially for his job, but has also become, over many years, a historian of the area. Aileen teaches, in English, in a Chinese school in the nearby conurbation. She speaks only limited social Cantonese and I forbore to ask how she feels about being ensconced in this totally Chinese community, without even a village shop. Patrick's Cantonese is fluent and idiomatic and he is already very much a part, an eccentric part, of the village scene. Thus he came to take us around it, and we came to have a unique experience.

The settlement is, in fact, three villages (near Tai Po) that lead one into the other. Patrick and Aileen live in Tong Sheung (village by the pond); then you walk through Chung Uk to get to Fong Ma Po – the village where the festival was held six years ago. And at the centre of Fong Ma Po is the Tin Hau temple dedicated to the Queen of the Sea. Beside it is a large spirit tree in which lives the local earth god. The funny thing is that, during the festival, the temple and the tree were a side attraction; and it was only yesterday that they made an impression on my consciousness.

We came first to the tree – a fine, spreading one on any day; but, at this time of the new year, magnificent. Instead of green leaves, flowers, nuts, seeds, it is festooned in multi-coloured paper favours. 'How on earth do they get them up there?' you swallow your question as you realise what's happening among the assembled crowd.

It all started fifty or so years ago, when an Aberdeen fisherman had a dream of this deity who promised him he would be healed if he worshipped him. After he was healed, he came to Lam Tsuen to discover the location of the god who had effected the cure, and worshipped him, as suggested by the villagers, by throwing a petition into the tree. Later, many people came from Aberdeen, having heard of this miraculous healing, and now they come from all over Hong Kong. There have been 10,000 visitors this year.

Under the tree is a shrine to the earth god; round the tree are stalls selling the paper offerings, raffia string, and oranges. You thread your string through the paper and round the orange and then you hurl it at the tree and hope that it will catch. Yesterday, there seemed to be many young women throwing – I was firmly told there was no significance, women and men participate equally. They did miss more often than not, but the pleasure when finally the colourful missile joined the others on the now resplendent tree warmed the hearts of all those willing their success.

Green and red papers signify the little people (imps?) who are causing you trouble; they will eventually rot away. The other colours – pink, yellow, white – are charms and offerings. The attraction of the earth god is that he is not remote from the people but approachable.

Some offerings never make the tree but lie getting soggy on the ground in the gentle rain that sometimes falls at this lunar period. And all through the villages are soggy dark pink banks of confetti – evidence that villagers have been letting off firecrackers. As I have earlier explained, this has been illegal since 1967 at the time of trouble across the border spilling into Hong Kong, for firecrackers sound too much like machine gun fire.

But firecrackers are smuggled in from China by boat and are let off in the villages hour after hour at new year. You finish your meal – to which all members of the family have come, often from other parts of the world – as close as possible to midnight on New Year's Eve; then you let off your firecrackers. They get rid of evil spirits – anyone who has been doing you harm.

When you're on the inside, as we were more or less yesterday, you can buy a packet of firecrackers getting crumpled in the stallholder's pocket and go to the open space in front of the temple, and light the fuse with an incense stick and, as soon as you possibly can, hurl it from you. Thus with a rattle of gunpowder – which the Chinese invented centuries ago – we are temporarily freed from the activities of our enemies!

This Tin Hau temple was built about 1730. It is particularly attractive and much in use, particularly at this time of year, with its offerings of suckling pigs, which will later be eaten by the family, and banging of the drum and beating the bell to attract the Goddess's attention to one's offerings and prayers. But the two things I couldn't help irreverently noticing were the very noisy extractor fan which sucks out some of the smoke wafting from the giant incense coils, and the village police station in one of the three small side halls of the temple. And that little room has been curiously empty these days of endless and illegal firecracker explosions. We felt delightfully wicked and, for a brief but memorable moment, participants rather than observers.

BEFORE THE WARM GLOW FADES   *March 1997*

If I've done nothing else in my life, at least I've done that. Everyone should have the chance to say those words. I'll write this experience down quickly, in case the warm glow fades before I can capture it on paper. *Stories for Eva* is finally between covers and has been well received. It looks as if it will continue to be useful after I've gone.

I've told you how the idea came about, and how I commissioned the stories and then prepared them and the teaching method for publication, and about the heartwarming reactions to the stories. But there is more to the earlier saga, and now to the later. I haven't told you, for example, how I was turned down by the Language Fund over two years ago. I asked for the money to publish the stories but other projects were considered more worthwhile.

I applied again, giving some thought to why I had failed previously. Perhaps the Fund, like commercial publishers, thought it important to look after the needs of the future generation, I suggested in my new application. But if there was an atmosphere of study at home, supplied by mother or grandmother, surely that was an added benefit? They gave me the money.

They said the book should be distributed free of charge, some to the organisation of my choice, some they would distribute to schools and teachers. They would provide the imprint; I should produce the goods. I rounded up an editor, a designer and, most important, a project manager, Polly. They had all been involved in one of my previous, more commercial books, and they were all to be paid. I hunted down a studio too – City University (as Derek's institution has now become); they would be paid too. But volunteer readers (for the accompanying cassettes) were added to the 62 volunteer authors.

The printed book was ready for our first lesson of 1997. The Classmates – including Eva – held it in their hands for the first time. I suppose the reaction that surprised and amused me most was their refusal to write all over it, as they had done for years on their photocopies. After two months, some still photocopy the story in their books to prepare for the lesson. I mock them. I promise them new ornamental copies. Linda, I'm glad to see, writes on hers in ink, and uses a highlighter too. But today I caught Theresa and Bonnie using an old photocopy of an earlier version I had given them months ago.

It's all very well for me to promise them new copies, in addition to those they've taken for women relatives and friends. But we've struck a big problem: we're too successful. That's because of the launch.

I wondered how we would do that; these things cost money and all the money, quite rightly, had gone into the production. Then Geeta, an AWARE member and one of the readers on the cassettes, sent me an article. It told of a new programme for women at the School of Continuing Studies, Chinese University. I couldn't believe there was such a thing. For years the Classmates have told me of their dreams for further education – for the education they missed out on as women before universal education in Hong Kong. I had, in a small, futile way, agitated for a Women's Afternoon College. Now someone else had seen the need and was doing something about it.

I rang Rosann Kao as soon as I read Geeta's fax. Within five minutes she had invited me to launch *Stories for Eva* at her three day exhibition to launch the next series in her programme of courses for women.

On 22 January we launched *Eva* under a notional umbrella organisation of Women Learning English Project (WELP). All the Classmates were there, and some contributors, and representatives of organisations who might be able to use it, and the press. The Women's Centre sent a basket of flowers, and so did Teresina. It was a right royal send off.

After it, we had our weekly lesson, attended by several old Classmates. The best moment was when Anita, whom I haven't seen for some time, questioned the title, *Stories for Eva*. It was just as she thought, Eva was always my favourite; why hadn't it been called *Stories for Anita*? She was only half teasing. So the teacher in me explained that Eve was original woman, the Classmate for all time. Anita was only half convinced, and not at all self-conscious about letting her feelings show.

It was quite a gruelling time for Eva actually because no one believed there was such a person and the press were only too delighted to find that there was, and to interview and photograph her.

The following day, there was a lovely picture of her and Linda, and another of me with several of the Classmates, including Linda – who winningly adds the older woman element. While that picture had been posed I had started to read a story, handed it over to Linda to continue, then tried to pass it on to Teresina. But she was too vain to wear her reading glasses for the picture, and so was Man-har!

There was a bit of a problem with the press publicity, though. I'm not quite sure what the Chinese text said but, whatever it was, 451 individual women (not counting organisations) rang or wrote in to the School asking for copies. That is a headache we are all still trying to sort out. The School started merely as the host but have opened a Pandora's box.

Because of Eva and her dreams for formal further education, which she tells in the last story – 'Story for Susanna' – the School is now doing research into how they can answer those needs.

Yesterday, Grace came from the School to our class at the Women's Centre, to talk to the Classmates and give them a questionnaire which has been specially designed. She listened too and, all being well, something may come of it. That's why I'm writing now, in case my dreams have been too ambitious, in case nothing comes of it all. At least at this moment I feel that I've achieved something. And it's a good feeling.

THE DAY THE SKY FELL DOWN   *April 1997*

Yesterday was my birthday; in two days' time it is the tenth anniversary of our arrival in Hong Kong for Derek to take up his post as head of a new law school; in two and a half months, Hong Kong will return to Chinese sovereignty. What exciting times we live in!

At 9.30am the telephone rang; it was Derek. 'I've just been sacked,' he said. 'With immediate effect and without cause given.' It was one hell of a birthday present! But at this culmination of months of strain and stress it was the funny little things that mattered.

The day before, a Sunday, the euphemistically-named Human Resources Office rang to ask Derek to appear at 9am the following day. And at 11am he was to meet the President – or vice-chancellor as he might be called elsewhere; or the Generalissimo or Gmo as we have come to call him. It was an interesting development: we assumed that the Gmo was at last going to take the necessary action: he was going to dismiss the Dean of the Law School – Derek's successor.

Just before going upstairs to the first appointment, my usually calm and collected husband rang me in panic. 'My zip's bust,' he said. I soothed him as best I could, but there was nothing to be done. He arrived at his meeting distracted.

'Will you resign?' the personnel officer asked him.

Derek found it difficult to comprehend the question. 'No, I see no reason to do so,' he replied.

'In that case you are dismissed. You are to leave the university immediately. You will be given three months' salary.'

All those dreams of ten years ago, of creating one of the best law schools in Asia, had become rather nightmarish over the past year. Now it is all over, as if one had been woken by a stab in the back – a wound which will no doubt remain numb for a while.

When Derek decided that a 60-year-old expatriate should give way to a younger Chinese Dean, as 1997 approached, he backed GG, a bright mainlander whom, for want of a better word, he had groomed for some years for the position. Since his arrival via North America, GG seemed to have had the law school's interests at heart.

Through his enthusiasm and connections, he had enabled ties to be made with Chinese law schools and government legal institutions that were invaluable for Hong Kong's future.

With him, we had often travelled in China creating and cementing those ties, attempting not just to promote the interests of the law school but to advance the cause of mutual understanding in areas of law more generally. On one occasion, one full of happy memories, we had even visited GG's family in a farming village north of Beijing. There, his mother and I had talked about the life of women in China, and Derek and his father had exchanged praise of the son who had pulled himself up from a peasant background to be a legal academic who should continue to go far in a much wider world.

And then, when a year or so ago GG married a charming and ambitious colleague, Derek was asked to stand in for his father at the ceremonies in Hong Kong. It was we who took him to the barred door of her family's flat – in the Chinese tradition; it was I who prompted him with the answers to the questions he had to answer to gain admittance and claim her as his bride. What is her favourite colour? In which city in the world does she most like to shop? 'Paris,' I hissed. That evening, at a grand reception, Derek and I, in *loco parentis*, circled the tables with the newly married couple, sharing toasts with the guests.

But we learned later that GG had been anxious to get rid of the *Gweilo* (Foreign Devil) almost from the moment he arrived; and it became easier to promote that policy when he succeeded as Dean and Derek retired to the boundary to help only when called upon.

Derek had no notion that there was a plot afoot, in spite of Pet's warning when he was ill that someone was trying to harm him! And in spite of rumbles of dissatisfaction in the law school with increasingly high-handed methods. It took a while to see a pattern of picking off the concocted opposition one by one, starting with the weakest.

There came a moment, though, when Derek had to take a stand over an issue of principle, a question of standards and integrity in the law school – one to do with the marking of exam papers, the old battle of truth against expediency. Then, the unseen net around him was pulled tight and, in due course, the Dean did not recommend that his contract be renewed. That was accepted by the Gmo, even though its arbitrariness was against the rules of the university. Already, then, against our hopes, our time in Hong Kong was running out; Derek's current contract was due, coincidentally, to expire on 30 June 1997 – the day of the handover to China.

Derek made one last effort to cleanse 'his' law school where many other issues of probity and integrity which needed attention were surfacing. He stepped up his agitation for a public inquiry. The Law School fractured and the storm raged in private and in public, with the most chilling propaganda being circulated about Derek. It was not an easy time. None of this had anything to do with 1997 itself: other bright mainland colleagues – seen as rivals – were also targeted. But the newly-arrived and inexperienced Gmo, with his American/Taiwanese background, was nervous; he obviously felt he knew which side his bread was buttered on. So, like all weak men, he took the easiest option. Yesterday he had Derek sacked without the need to give him a reason.

In retrospect, perhaps Derek should not have forgone his meeting with the Gmo at 11am – he might have been able to pin him down – even influence the future; but he has not found that previous meetings have had much point, and he was anxious to leave the campus as soon as possible (because of his broken zip). We learned later that GG has been removed as Dean but not sacked.

The previous head of the university had promised that that unusual clause in the contract – of dismissal without cause given – would never be used except in a case of grave misdemeanour. So the world must assume that Derek has committed some unspeakable offence. And this morning the Gmo on the radio hinted at that when the interviewer pursued the question. Many, happily, know better, though that does not necessarily help: Tung Chee-hwa, Chair of the University Council, and Chief Executive of Hong Kong designate, whom Derek had earlier approached for help, sat on his hands, preferring not to rock the boat.

We shall carefully consider what action to take now – such as suing for unfair dismissal – but we may be wise to turn our backs on this betrayal, to begin the healing process as soon as possible.[*]

---

[*] Although someone in the know told Derek that the University had put aside 5 million dollars (£450,000) in case Derek sued successfully, we decided against litigation, knowing what the costs are of all kinds, and Derek, I'm happy to say, suffered not at all and revels in the working life – writing, practising international commercial law and editing a learned journal – he has indulged in since in Oxford.

In the meantime, we shall make the best of our last precious weeks in Hong Kong, and we shall leave with our heads held high.

LOVE STORY   *May 1997*

When the definitive history of twentieth century Chinese literature comes to be written, a short paragraph may be devoted to the second Mrs Duanmu. Its last sentence will describe today's events.

Duanmu Hongliang's first wife was the Manchurian writer Xiao Hong who died in Japanese-occupied Hong Kong on 22 January 1942. Duanmu was by her side and he made arrangements to have her cremated in the Japanese crematorium. Then, taking her ashes, he divided them in two. One half he buried beside the sea at Repulse Bay, as Xiao Hong had requested, so that she had the mountain behind her and the open sea in front. Later, in 1957, those ashes were moved to the Star Cemetery in Canton (Guangzhou).

Duanmu took the second half back – through the war-torn streets of Hong Kong – to St Stephen's Girls College, then a temporary hospital, where Xiao Hong had died. With the help of a university student whose name has been lost, Duanmu dug a hole in the side of a hill under a big tree there and placed in it a funeral urn.

On his return to China, Duanmu discovered that, although he was a well-known writer, and became a more famous one, he was not regarded as a hero where Xiao Hong was concerned. He might remember the danger and anxiety surrounding her end and the disposal of her ashes, and the love he had felt the night he stopped his student helper from stamping down the earth too hard upon them; others immediately began mythologising Xiao Hong's life and death as victim – a brilliant writer made unhappy by Duanmu and others exploiting her vulnerability and talent.

Duanmu Hongliang married again – the second Mrs Duanmu. I met them both in Beijing in 1994 when I went to interview him for my writing on Xiao Hong. Mrs Duanmu stayed very much in the background then, unobtrusively keeping an eye on her elderly and ailing husband as he charmed my interpreter, Yu Jing, and me.

Yu Jing – a law student at Peking University – and I returned to the Duanmus' flat the following year. By then, I had finished my paper and, indeed, presented it at a literary symposium in Beijing. Yu Jing and I went through the paper with him, particularly the bits that mentioned him. He was grateful that there were no attacks on him, thrilled that I had written about Xiao Hong and taken my research into her life and death so seriously. He was in poor health on that second visit and his wife of 30 years or so had to play a more prominent role.

I monitored her face to see that we were not tiring him too much. The four of us bade each other fond farewell – we were by then old friends. And it was farewell. The month my book (*Chinese Footprints*) was published containing all the material on Xiao Hong, Yu Jing rang to tell me that Duanmu was dead.

She and I wrote Mrs Duanmu a letter of condolence and sent her a copy of the book. In it was a previously unpublished photograph of Duanmu and Xiao Hong that he had lent me and one of him and me that Yu Jing had taken on our first visit. I thought they, and the physicality of the book, would please her, even if she could not read the text.

Then, yesterday evening, I had a telephone call from Yu Jing who is now studying in Hong Kong. Mrs Duanmu was in town; she wanted to go to St Stephen's to scatter some of Duanmu's ashes over the garden where – somewhere – Xiao Hong's ashes were buried. Yu Jing reported that Xiao Xi, a Hong Kong writer who had written about Xiao Hong and interviewed Duanmu some time before I did, hoped to organise the visit to St Stephen's through the Federation of Hong Kong Writers – which has always maintained a keen interest in its most famous 'Hong Kong' writer. Mrs Duanmu invited me to be present.

At 7.30 this morning, Yu Jing rang to tell me that it had not proved possible to confirm those arrangements but we were all meeting outside the school gates at 10am. Could I do something to make sure the visit could go ahead successfully? Yu Jing herself could not be there.

I have been writing about St Stephen's (starting with *The Private Life of Old Hong Kong*) for even longer than about Xiao Hong. I know the retired headmistress, who now lives in England, through that work. And I know one of the history teachers, Jora Ma, a little better. Courtesy had dictated that I ring Jora after Yu Jing's first call – now I rang her again. Her mother answered the telephone; she spoke only Cantonese; I spoke only English.

When I tracked Jora down at school it was 8.30. 'Ring the headmistress,' she advised. 'And tell her all about the planned visit.' She herself would wait in the staff common room to hear from me. The headmistress was in a meeting with teachers, and unable to talk. Jora rang me at 9. She had, as I had hoped, acted as intermediary.

I arrived at the school at 9.55. Mrs Duanmu, family, friends and luminaries of the Federation of Writers were waiting outside the wrong gate. Yu Jing was, after all, there too. We were at the right gate at 10. Xiao Xi, who lives nearby, arrived bearing one carnation and an air of suppressed emotion a moment later, followed, from within the school, by Jora.

Jora had arranged for the party to be taken to a conference room attached to an embryo school museum and given tea. Another history teacher told us, in Mandarin, a few details of wartime St Stephen's; photographs were taken and a recently-published history of the school by the former headmistress – with a line in it about Xiao Hong – was presented to Mrs Duanmu. Then she was taken on a tour of the old part of the school – in any one of the rooms of which Xiao Hong may have spent her last hours.

The deputy principal arrived and took us towards the garden. By this time it was getting very hot. I could sense Mrs Duanmu flagging – the pink moistness of age and emotion was gathering under her eyes. In the garden, the headmistress joined us. She was responsive on a womanly and historical level but she had not previously understood that Mrs Duanmu had ashes with her. She now assumed that she was being asked permission for a ceremony to take place, and she was not sure that she could allow it like this, without notice and consideration of the implications.

Then there was the question of where Xiao Hong's ashes had been buried 45 years ago. Duanmu, even when I sent him a 1930s map of the grounds, had been completely unsure. Everyone had their own idea of where it might have been.

Mrs Duanmu took all this in. The history teacher said a big tree had recently fallen on one of the slopes. I was talking to the headmistress near the concrete plinth where I felt the burial place had been.* Quickly, Mrs Duanmu made her way through long grass

---

* When I sent this piece to Kay Barker, the former headmistress, in 2006, she wrote in an exchange of emails: 'It is, of course, just possible that Xiao Hung's ashes were buried in the little park just next to the school garden, rather than the garden itself. The wall was moved at one point during my time when Government wanted a bigger area for the public part. So, who knows whether that included the burial plot.' And she added in a later

towards the pile of cut logs. She laid the flower down, and paused a few seconds. Some were quick enough to catch her movements on film. When she came down the slope, her eyes were brimming with tears; there was a trace of ash on her black suit. She had done what she came to do.

Now Mrs Duanmu is finishing the book her husband started not long before he died – telling his version of his love for Xiao Hong. That book will be referred to by future scholars.[†] But it is Mrs Duanmu's gesture this morning that ranks among the most moving in the history of Chinese literature.

AMONG MY SOUVENIRS   *June 1997*

At first, my interest in Wun Yiu pottery was, what part did women play? Now, I seem to be hooked and the women aspect almost doesn't matter. At all events, I am not much further forward to an answer but I have a lovely little collection of folk, or ordinary people's, china.

It all started with a visit to Patrick's house in the New Territories. 'And this,' he proclaimed proudly at the top of the last flight of stairs, 'is my study.' But what immediately caught my eye was the collection of dull blue green grey china of all shapes and sizes displayed on both sides of the doorway. 'What's that?' I asked.

'Part of my Wun Yiu collection,' he replied and I said 'ooooh', and pressed closer. A look crossed his face. 'Here,' he said, 'have this.' He placed a plate in my hands. And I haven't looked back.

When you come to Hong Kong and travel to China, there are endless areas of art, artefacts and furniture to be explored. You have to keep a firm grip on yourself and take some deep breaths before you dive in. Don't start buying reproduction rosewood furniture the moment you arrive, is the advice given to newcomers. And

reply: 'The garden was and still is, I believe, only rented from the Urban Council, so perhaps there is a record of how much we had when we had it. Ellen Li believed that SSGC garden was smaller before the war and that our boundary was extended up the hill during wartime. Was this before or after Xiao Hung died? That seems to me to be rather important. Then later we lost part of it again, as I mentioned. The only thing that is certain is that the boundary was not fixed over the years.' I now pass the parcel, though I shall go on a recce on my next visit.

†   Unfortunately, I don't know if this book was finished or published; I would be glad to know.

we've been *quite* restrained over ten years – my only real obsession being women tomb figures from the various dynasties, and that is a quite recent failure to resist buying.

But what you notice early on is that everything comes from China itself. There are no antique artefacts, except perhaps silk embroidered clothes, that have been made over the centuries in Hong Kong. Now, suddenly, Patrick was explaining that Wun Yiu was a village just south of Tai Po in the New Territories. And there some centuries ago (probably mid-Ming), kilns started to be built (new ones in each generation) and pottery to be produced.

What is more, this pottery epitomises the distinction between imperial porcelain – china produced by the state under the auspices of the emperor – and folk pottery or china produced in private kilns in the countryside in many parts of China for the use of ordinary people.

The folk art started by mimicking the famous imperial blue and white ware which is a conscious development over time towards purity of colour and fineness of glaze. But the private kiln ware did not follow that path towards perfection; the colours are less precise – the white more duck egg blue, the blue more greeny. The materials used are cruder, the design and decoration are less prescribed. Collectors collect imperial ware and pay vast prices; no one, until recently, took any notice of the folk ware.

In Malaysia now they call it 'kitchen Ching' and hold exhibitions, for it turns out that Wun Yiu pottery was exported in specially designed rice bowl boats all over South East Asia, and shards and thousands of whole bowls have been excavated there.

We had, some years ago, been taken by the Royal Asiatic Society to Wun Yiu to see the remains of the kilns, but it didn't mean much to us then and only a residue of memory remained. Now, with Patrick's instructions clasped in our hands, we took the MTR to Tai Po. From there, we walked through a housing estate and across a river towards the village. Up the hill on which Wun Yiu is built we went, round the old and deserted school and into the courtyard of the 1790 temple. Here, there are still offerings laid to Fan Sing the god of potters, though the kilns have not functioned since about 1917. By now we were gripped by excitement, the excitement of the chase. We wanted to find again the kilns – appreciate their significance – and perhaps even find a shard or two. Up through the village, much of it newly built villas, we climbed and along an overgrown path. Now we could see the valley at the head of which used to be the china clay deposits used for the pots.

Along the path, we looked for kilns and shards, without success. We doubled back and took another path, but the remnants of the last kilns are now fenced in to preserve them, and the woods surrounding them were too thick for us to discern them. We did, however, come across pieces of discarded bowls and brought home these mud and insect encrusted shards. Much scrubbed, they form the nucleus of our collection.

As we keep saying, six months later as we leave Hong Kong for good, thank goodness we didn't know about all this earlier! For since then, wherever we have travelled, we have looked for folk pottery, all of it similar in shape, colour, use and design – though Patrick can tell if something comes from Wun Yiu itself.

We started looking first in Hong Kong, of course, but it seems that the Museum of History has bought up most of the available examples of this traditional local artefact. You may find some 'blue and white' folk pottery in the antique shops, but most of it is not from Wun Yiu. Macau is a better bet, and that is where we bought our first whole piece – an oil jar with a slightly Islamic decoration, not from Wun Yiu – and our last – a large plate with wonky colouring – which may be.

But, in between, we have bought a rice bowl from a market in Shanghai, and a large jar said to be Ming. And from Beijing several bowls, one of them squashed in the making. The stallholder who sold us that one said it was from the Sung dynasty. But even I was not born yesterday as she gave it to me for 50 yuan instead of 120 and her neighbour, a bit of an expert from whom Derek was meanwhile negotiating a saucer, declared it Ching.

Now, just before we leave Hong Kong, comes our visit to an exhibition at Tai Po (see the next piece). Here, we see the whole range of wares that were made in Ming and Ching times at Wun Yiu. Fired with renewed passion, we take Young Derek and Vivienne to the village. But it has been raining heavily and the mud and mosquitoes are a deterrent even to these hunters. Nevertheless, we come home with one prize the significance of which, as a result of the exhibition, we now appreciate. A pile of painted bowls was put in the kiln in their saggar – protective earthen overcoat; but the process went wrong in there: the bowls collapsed and melted into each other. They remain fused together, bits of their saggar still stuck to them – an object now of the greatest fascination to us.

And the stripy design on those bowls is magical for it is the final degradation of the original lotus design. One of our shards shows the lotus in its earlier glory – perhaps from Ming times. Each generation simplified the design, or painted it more freely, until it becomes in the early twentieth century little more than a stripe.

The question remains – what part did women play? No one can tell me; it has not seemed important to those retrieving this aspect of China's arts and crafts. The imperial porcelain is known to have been often decorated by named and important male scholar artists. Precise seals are on the bottom of each piece. And paintings show that men worked in the 'factories' that produced the vessels themselves. But those were state-run, public enterprises. What happened within the confines of a village like Wun Yiu? Did the women sit by as men produced from start to finish bowls and other objects for them to prepare the family's food in?

We know that in different parts of China, and at different levels of society, women at home were responsible for hat and mat weaving, spinning and weaving of cotton and silk, and embroidery in silk. Given that Wun Yiu produced enough bowls to export in large numbers, that it was the people's bread and butter, it is unlikely that women were excused labour from all of the several processes. Which part might women, traditionally skilled handworkers, be most suitable for or adept in?

On the island of Peng Chao some years ago (see February 1989) we watched young women handpainting modern bowls that had been manufactured elsewhere. For the historical possibilities, I need my books which have all been sent off to England. However, in a large illustrated book on folk painting on porcelain that I bought in Beijing a couple of weeks ago, I read an account that leaps from the page.

The author describes how, on one of his recent trips to track down the wares, he was taken to a replica kiln, and then, 'In one of the workshops I was perplexed by two younger women sitting by a workbench … the inflexions of the brush lines clearly showed they were no ordinary painters, but had inherited the traditional art from earlier generations.' With this ambiguous reference I have to be content, for the moment.

Postscript

Back in England with my books again I find confirmation that, in exploring the work and crafts of women, most studies concentrate on spinning and weaving. Frustrated, I turn to J. Dyer Ball's *Things Chinese* (1925). In a 24-page historical review of porcelain production, he quotes from the turn-of-the-[twentieth]century account of W.J. Clennel, British consul at Kiukiang. Clennel is writing about Ching-te Chen – today known as Zhingdezhen and traditionally the porcelain capital of China. There, government kilns turned out porcelain for the emperor but there were private kilns as well and, in writing about their production of blue and white porcelain, Clennel notes, 'simple patterns are painted in the moulding shed, but much, and apparently all, the more delicate work is done in shops along the street, much of it done by women'. It is still fairly recent evidence but, finally, I seem to be on to something.

Postpostscript

I sent the above to Patrick who elaborated for me the process from clay to market in which different groups of people would be independently responsible for each part. Some dug the clay, others transported it to the village where it was passed on to the clay-workers. These then crushed it and puddled it to remove every grain of grit, and sold the worked clay to the potters who made it into pots; others again decorated them. Then there were the kiln workers who fired the kilns, and the porters who carried the bowls to the market-towns for sale to the country people. And last, but not least, there were clerks and store-keepers at the kiln offices.

He added very firmly, and in great scholarly detail, concerning my speculation about women's participation:

> I'm not sure you aren't barking up the wrong tree here. In the NT [New Territories], traditionally, if there was wage-labour available, the men took it. The women didn't, though, just sit at home: in such circumstances, they invariably farmed the family land. Normally, wage-labour in the NT closed down at the three harvest periods, so that the wage-labourers could help out with the harvest, but it was usually the women who did the bulk of the farming work. Farming an average sized NT farm needed 4–6 man-hours a day, outside the peak periods, so there was

time for a woman to cope unaided, and look after the children and the house. If both man and wife were wage-labourers they would have to hire a labourer to look after their fields, which would cost as much, probably, as the wife would get in wages. Many of the male wage-labourers at Wun Yiu, especially the less-skilled, were not living with their families. They came from distant villages, and there their wives stayed, to care for the land. In some villages, where most of the men were wage-labourers, it was noted from the earliest days of the British that all the farm work was done by women.

As for decorating the pottery, women were used elsewhere where the decoration was fine: the Wun Yiu decoration is so crude it was probably done by men (we have no hint of women working as decorators there). But women were the normal coolies in the area: carriage of clay from the clay-pits down to the village, of wood to the kilns, and of bowls from the kilns to the market-towns, was probably to a large extent handled by women. (Women could do coolie work after they finished working on the farm.) The wives of the kiln-owners very probably worked in the kiln stores and offices – this, also was not uncommon, as the wife could keep an eye on employees, and stop thievery, etc. (and the kiln-owner was likely to be wealthy enough that he could afford to rent his fields out). But decorating pots might just – although I think it unlikely – have been done by women at Wun Yiu.

So I add, whatever part women played, it appears that they were involved in the process of making the pots from Wun Yiu; I was right to be interested.

THE HANGOVER   *July 1997*

I couldn't get away from it, even if I wanted to. Monday 30 June was a historic day. Hong Kong was returning to Chinese sovereignty after 156 years as a British colony. It was Handover day, as most people call it in English, or Hangover as it's easier to say. Surprisingly, this weak joke does not appear to wear thin. Do I have to be serious about it, or was the Handover to be an occasion for a bumper five day holiday? A bit of both, I suppose.

It's a problem being British and a historian. Whether you like it or not, are sensitive or not, you're part of the colonial past. Everywhere you go you are aware that some people are wholeheartedly in favour of returning to the motherland after suffering under your colonial yoke. Then there are some who 'love China' (that's the expression) but don't want to sweat now under a 'Communist' yoke.

Very few cling to love for Britain but many do feel that British rule may have been fairer than their picture of what 'Communist' rule will be. I put that word in inverted commas as someone who goes regularly to China and knows that even 'Socialism with Chinese characteristics' is somewhat of a misnomer for the current gallop towards Capitalism.

Then there are those who are comfortable with their Chineseness, are able to make use of the good aspects of British colonial rule and put the bad behind them, but feel that Hong Kong people really should be determining the future of their distinctive place. They are struggling to retain a vestige of legislative democracy, together with freedom of speech and assembly which are most obviously under threat.

A hundred polls and surveys have been done, of course. The one that most sticks in my mind is that showing aging businessmen at one end of a continuum and 100 per cent in favour of the return to China. The collaboration between the business elite here and the burgeoning business-political-military elite in China is most marked.

At the other end of this continuum are women students. They feel they have the most to lose. So, men in general gather at one end, women in general at the other. And this is borne out by the Classmates' opinions and that of other women that I talk to. But nothing can compare with the remark of a young girl broadcast among a daily diet of interesting things that children have been saying about the Handover. 'I'm against it because we will lose the freedom to riot.'

As a colonial burdened with a fair amount of 'guilt'; as a women's activist concerned about attempts to reverse some of the advances we have made over the past few years; and as a historian who knows a bit about what exactly happened 156 years ago, I have to absorb and rationalise all these impressions. And, because I am writing about this grand moment of history for these stories, and because I have a family responsibility of trying to keep four of us amused over five days, I kept an eye out for possibilities, and did some judicious organising.

There is the added factor that Derek and I leave for good only ten days into the new order. We leave as Britain leaves – a neat irony. The need to cater to our imminent departure came to the fore as the first day of the Hangover holiday dawned – Saturday 28 June.

On Friday evening, we had been at a farewell dinner for us on Kowloon side (British since 1860), so that night we stayed with Young Derek and Vivienne in Shatin, New Territories (British since 1898). On Saturday, we drove to Tsuen Wan to the Sam Tung Uk Museum which was an old Hakka walled village founded in the eighteenth century. It's always healthy for us colonials to be faced with the fact that Hong Kong did not begin in 1841. Not having a car, we have not explored the New Territories nearly as well as we should have liked – now time has run out.

But at the museum, we saw a stunning exhibition of 'kitchen' pottery made since Ming times in the nearby village of Wun Yiu. We were shown how it was made, exported, used and rediscovered – all of which I am writing about elsewhere, trying to discover what part women played (see my previous piece). The exhibits spoke for themselves but we couldn't help noticing that the fine catalogue was in Chinese alone. The experience was a salutory as well as a most enjoyable beginning to this Handover period.

Continuing the motif of the day, we had lunch at the Yucca de Lac restaurant overlooking the Shatin valley which only 20 years ago was a timeless panorama of agriculture but which is now a concrete new town with a population greater than Birmingham. Not many Westerners come to this place so one didn't feel like an expatriate, let alone a tourist, and the meal was excellent, the sun was warm, but not too hot, and shared family enjoyment added zest to yet another farewell.

After lunch, we took Young Derek and Vivienne to Wun Yiu village where the remnants of the kilns that made the pottery we had seen in the morning are preserved on a wild wooded hillside flanking the village still with its old temple dedicated to the god of potters.

We had not taken into account the recent heavy rain and, as we clambered up the muddy slope, we were attacked by swarms of crazed mosquitoes which forced us to cut short the adventure.

And so home to Hong Kong island, to our place, for the rest of the Handover.

Sunday was still warm and pleasant, not too humid. We had arranged another farewell lunch – the four of us plus two of our dearest historian friends with whom, happily, Young Derek and Vivienne will continue our friendship when we've gone. But before we could leave home, we had a later-than-arranged visit from Pet and her family which now includes not only Peter and the twins but also Helen's firefighter boyfriend Tony.

I was not quite sure of the purpose of this visit but it seemed to be to take photographs in as many group permutations as possible. It was an unsurprisingly awkward yet heartwarming gathering in our funny empty flat; and it was hard to disembarrass ourselves in time for our lunch, so that we had to race to the panoramic restaurant looking back over the harbour to the island.

After fine wine and European food eaten bathed in the reflection of water and sky, we walked for the last time along the quay. We took photographs not just against that unbeatable skyline but also the funnel of the royal yacht *Britannia* which was lying over the other side of the water, almost unobtrusively, ready to carry away the mortal symbols of colonial rule early on Tuesday morning. We topped off Sunday with a visit to the Museum of Art – coveting from afar the Chinese imperial porcelain which is rather different from the pottery of the people that had so fascinated us the day before.

Monday dawned – wet. How were we to know that it would never again stop raining! The rain was to colour everything that happened from then on because there are things you can't or don't want to do in the rain; indeed, many of the hundreds of events had to be cancelled.

I've always thought it was crazy to hold the Handover at the end of June, a time prone to typhoons and inevitably hot, wet and humid. Only once have I heard a reason for the date which everyone poohpoohs when I explain it – the anniversary of the birth of the Chinese Communist Party.

Mid-morning, the two older members of the family took a taxi down to Causeway Bay. Outside the Japanese department store Sogo, the newly-formed Citizens Party had set up camp. Their main spokesperson, Christine Loh, still a member of Legco for another twelve hours, had decided that the Party should do something constructive to mark the Handover – something more than demonstrating against the threat to democracy that others in the pro-democracy camp had planned.

So, banners were strung up in the rain on which passers-by were invited to write their messages to Tung Chee-hwa who would become Chief Executive at midnight. As supporters of Christine personally, and her Party, we braved the elements – rain and vast shopping and milling crowds – to swell the group round this exhibition and add our messages – on women's and more general human rights.

The Great and the Good had, in recent days, received a string of invitations for the public events to mark the Handover. The British event at HMS *Tamar* – metal stands raised round an open air parade ground – at 6.15; a reception and dinner at the brand new Convention Centre jutting out into the harbour at 9pm; the lowering of the flag at midnight there, and the swearing in of the Chief Executive, Provisional Legislative Council, judges etc., thereafter.

As non-persons, we were invited to nothing, so we had planned our own programme. Our friend Neil was a great and good but his companion Paula was excluded. So we invited her to join our family party of four for dinner. To help us avoid the inevitable closed roads, traffic jams and lack of taxis, Neil arranged for his driver to pick us up and drive us to his flat to join Paula to watch the HMS *Tamar* affair on television. We would then walk down on the mid-levels escalator to the Arbitration Centre with its grandstand view of the harbour to watch the fireworks. We could easily then walk up to the restaurant we had chosen and from there walk through events (demonstrations) outside Legco to the FCC (Foreign Correspondents' Club) to watch the Handover on television there.

Television, it seemed, was the only way that 'ordinary people' had access to the official or Territory-wide parts of the Handover. As a bit of a lark, I had even put our identity numbers – unsuccessfully – into the ballot for a few 'ordinary people' places at HMS *Tamar*. Indeed, if we wanted to know what was going on in Hong Kong or Beijing, the best way, as televisionless people, was to ring Mummy in Spain where, day after day, hour after hour, she was dabbing her moist eyes in front of her set.

We got to Paula through the pouring rain and watched as on television, for all the world to see, the Governor and Prince Charles, members of the British armed forces, performers and thousands of guests drowned in an increasingly spirited downpour. We were able, more than ever, to rejoice in being non-persons.

We watched as first the Governor's suit grew darker round the shoulders and his hair clung closer to his head and then as the rain ran like a small waterfall off the peak of the Prince's Royal Navy hat – with his impervious face beneath.

We are told that most spectators, even though they were under umbrellas, found that their gladrags were irredeemably ruined. There was no point in us walking down to the fireworks, though we might have swum. We did find a taxi, however, and got almost to the door of our restaurant.

All the posh restaurants had been promoting their grand dinners for weeks at $1,997 dollars (£170) per couple. Trying to avoid being exploited, we had chosen an Italian restaurant – La Trattoria – well-reviewed and well-placed for our evening programme. But we didn't beat the system. The bill came to $5,000 (£450) for the five of us, the food was execrable, the place was almost empty, the atmosphere non-existent, in spite of hats and balloons. And the service was so slow that we left there too late to see what was going on around Legco. I missed everything I wanted to see, including an alternative women's event.

We just made it to the FCC by 11.30. We had feared it would be so full that we couldn't get in through the front door. At least we got to the crush round the bar television screen, and the heaving and irreverent crowd added an element to the occasion.

We had promised to escort Paula to the Hong Kong Club to meet Neil there at 1.30am. Outside Legco the excitement was very much on the wane. An hour earlier, Martin Lee and other democrats had made their way onto the balcony to address the crowd below and protest at Legco's dissolution at midnight. But by 1.30 only the television cameras being packed away and stragglers and other detritus of a happening remained.

Then we tried to get a taxi home, wearing our fluorescent 1997 glasses, any merriness and bolshiness overlaid by a sense of anti-climax. A choice was soon apparent: since there were no unoccupied Island taxis, should we catch one of the more prevalent Kowloon ones and trail all the way to Shatin. If we did that, we could get up at 6am and watch the 'dreaded' PLA (People's Liberation Army) as they came over the border and along the road that runs below Young Derek and Vivienne's flat. That too would be a historic moment.

We got an Island taxi in the end, so watching the PLA became academic. In the event, the downpour at 6am was so heavy that no mere spectator saw anything of the troops standing bare-headed in the back of open trucks, nor heard the rumble of the armoured cars.

We had planned to go to a Hangover event on one of the small islands on the first morning of Chinese rule, but the rain continued to sheet down, so we stayed tucked up. And I had booked for the six of us to go to a grand 'Dynasty' (Chinese dress) ball at the Cricket Club that evening. At 11am, someone rang to say that during the night, the swimming pool had flooded the marquee – the ball for a thousand was cancelled.

In our flat, where everything but bare essentials and a couple of sticks of furniture had left for England two weeks earlier, we now planned a dinner party for six. Neil and Paula came bearing treats in their own serving dishes. We still had candles and champagne but the large room once so full of books, pictures, rugs and lamps that the sound was muffled, echoed with unaccustomed noises made by shadowy figures.

The rain eased off a little for an even grander firework display than the previous evening but it rained all night and all day next day, and the day after. We make crude jokes about the uncontrollable rain and the ineffectiveness of Chinese rule. Proponents of the Return to the Motherland explain that the rain is washing away all the horrors of British colonial rule. Christine Loh tells me that in Chinese cosmology rain is yin – woman – gentle, healing, conciliatory. She will sit this hangover out and look to the future. We British have occupied a mere speck of time, and we are now the past.

THE LAST GOODBYE   *8 July 1997*

It's my last day on Hong Kong Island. Tomorrow we move into Young Derek and Vivienne's flat in Shatin. The following evening we fly to England. I walk towards the bank to pay in a cheque. It is 5.10 and they are closed – the iron grille pulled down. A sense of desolation – clammy rather than cold but no less mournful for that – is enveloping me. After ten years I am disengaging from Hong Kong.

I walk down the escalator into Episode. How often have I secretly rejoiced as I neared the elegant basement or similar at sale time knowing that I would secure some cunning silk number at 40 per cent off – high fashion clothes made in Hong Kong for the European market and picked up here for a fraction of the price. Today there is no one else there, and I can feel no enthusiasm. I don't even take anything from the rack.

The day started more lively. Just before 10 o'clock, Derek and I arrived at the Foreign Correspondents' Club. There I was giving a farewell lunch for 36 or so Classmates, together with Kavita who is taking over my teaching at the Women's Centre and Rosann who is assuming responsibility for *Stories for Eva*. She hopes to continue its development, to use it, for example, to train volunteer teachers of English to women. All being well, my baby will flourish.

All the Classmates turned up, past and present. More than all, actually. Simon, who has looked after us for nine years at the FCC, tactfully supplied more places and meals. He was touchingly long-suffering as the noise level on the verandah rose. There was no alcohol served but the Classmates are easily able to generate their own excitement without it.

They gave me a beautiful embroidery of peonies and lovebirds – Derek and me they gleefully told us – mounted on silk. At least it isn't framed but somehow in its long card roll it has to be accommodated in our excessive luggage, together with the cricket bat from Derek's team.

At least the AWARE sisters spotted the problem. At our farewell dinner on Friday they gave me a small but impeccable gold dragon to wear on a chain – 24 carat no doubt, the way the Chinese prefer gold. This dragon symbolises many things: Hong Kong, AWARE as an entity, each of us determined and individual women who have striven together for six years and, I suppose, me – a dragon: a deliberate insult and an intentional compliment.

AWARE may or may not continue. I don't flatter myself (as one of the founders) that my departure will hasten its demise but the Handover will change many lives and many organisations. We had a long and heartfelt discussion about the group's future and that of the women's movement under Chinese sovereignty.

I said goodbye to my AWARE sisters, and today to the Classmates, also very much my sisters. But they all have our telephone number in Oxford and many of them will call on us. If any of us really comes into the money they will all come together on a trip for a month. And don't believe it couldn't happen!

We took the last group photographs – Simon pressing the button – or a dozen buttons – somewhat banjaxed; he had not known about this side of my life. Then lots of kisses – the Chinese don't kiss, of course. I had hoped the Classmates would leave first so that I could settle the bill, but no chance. Derek and I had to leave, as if going on honeymoon, then double back. I settled up and paid for a life membership at the same time, so Derek can still rejoice in being a spouse member addressed as Mr Hoe, whatever it says on his card.

Then to my publishers to settle up with them (hence the cheque to be banked) and on to Tosh where I tried once again to have my hair cut for the last time in her inimitable way – scissors held in the air as she tells me the latest of her life, or long ago memories of when her family left China and arrived in Hong Kong.

Unbelievably, I have been unable to ring her to make an appointment. My cardbox was inadvertently packed during the three days of removal in the middle of June. I had dropped by Tosh's place the day before the Handover but the grille was down. This was the second time I had called round today; the grille was still down. I could see straight into her room. It started my desolation. I could not say goodbye to her except by leaving a note and hoping she will write to me.

I worry about why she is not there. Is her mother suddenly too ill to be left alone? Has her new business failed so soon? Six weeks ago, when I last had my hair cut, she was so full of life. She had taken the plunge and set up on her own. She had rented one room and decorated it with unimpeachable taste and practicality – grey and blue, everything just so, as a one-woman hairdressers should be, as she must have dreamed of it for all those years of semi-servitude. She was now answerable to no one but herself, no boss, no partner. But the grille was down, and on a Tuesday afternoon.

It was not only Tosh's card that went with the box in the freight; it was Theresa's too. All I had for her anyway was a pager number and, while Tosh's fortunes seemed to have risen recently, Theresa's had not. Finally, some weeks ago she returned one of my calls. She was working in an office; where? she would tell me when we could talk. Doing what? she would tell me but she couldn't talk now. Was she happy? No. She promised she would ring and explain.

After 25 years of selling flowers, she could no longer continue. She had been forced to move from her position outside the supermarket at the bottom of our road. The supermarket wanted to sell its own Christmas trees and cumquat trees for Chinese New Year. She begged me to find her a job. She would do anything, even be an *amah* – as Pet would put it, clean other people's lavatories.

For a few weeks, Theresa struggled from a corner by the filling station. But it was too off the beaten track for a flower stall and the rain kept falling too. Once I passed when she wasn't there and foraged in the back of her lorry under a dripping red white and blue plastic tarpaulin to find a dozen cream rose buds. I haven't paid her for them yet. And, worse, I haven't had a chance to say goodbye. I feel I have betrayed her.

No wonder, as I walk up Wyndham Street, once called Flower Street because it was lined with flower stalls, I feel this increasing sense of loss. Up Wyndham Street, up the steep heart-pounding flight of steps to Icehouse Street, past the FCC that used to be the ice house, to the good place to catch a taxi.

For the last time I hail a red and cream car – one of the ugliest taxis in the world. I don't jiggle my hand up and down in the peremptory manner of the Chinese, the sight of which has raised my hackles for ten years, but in the languid but firm arm straight out of the Englishwomen. For the last time I do that journey from the FCC home to Jardine's Lookout. Tomorrow is another day, another home, another country, another flag. Goodbye, Hong Kong.

EPILOGUE

'*Jardin San, mgoi,*' I said to the taxi driver. I noticed as we got in how much more attractive the taxis are – silver-roofed instead of a deadening oatmeal above the red. We had been in our hotel only 15 minutes, but I wanted to get to Jardine's Lookout before the light failed; it was my last shot at trying to find Theresa who for ten years sold us flowers from her stall outside the supermarket at the bottom of our road. I knew it was a vain attempt. It was nine years since I had last seen her, four since we had been back to Hong Kong.

After July 1997 we returned several times for Derek's work, giving me the chance to catch up with old friends – with Pet who cleaned for us, Tosh who cut my hair, those left of the AWARE sisters and other activists and scholars, women politicians such as Christine Loh, and with the Classmates. Indeed, the Classmates and I had lunched several times, each occasion as lively and loving as our farewell lunch in 1997. Tosh had cut my hair, and Pet and I had gossiped in hotel lobbies, but Theresa had eluded me, and she did so again.

I debriefed the security guard at the supermarket complex: neither he nor his colleagues had been there longer than two years. I should have done all this on our first return visit. Perhaps I did, it is hard now to remember what is not written down. We wandered almost disconsolately up to Cavendish Heights. It was cold and we didn't hang around; after all, we couldn't see the flat that had been our home for ten years. We went into the residents' club, deserted as always except the gym, and looked through a window down at the swimming pool which had been such a joy – it was winter-empty. We didn't feel up to doing a dog walk, but we passed the cobbler's shack locked for the night. From that glance at our old world, little seemed changed, except the size of the trees planted when Cavendish Heights and we were new. Can the same be said of the whole of Hong Kong?

The structure of this epilogue has taxed me more than I expected. I realise that to try and write about all that has happened in the nine years since we left would require another book, and no doubt others will try their hand at that. Even a series of new sketches such as fill most of this book would not be practical. As the purpose of our visit to Hong Kong in January 2006 was so that I could write this epilogue, so that I could catch up with the women among whom I moved when we lived there and make sure that they are happy with what I have written about them and plan to publish, my best route is, I think, to elaborate in diary form on the notes I made of our meetings. I have also drawn on subsequent emails, telephone conversations, meetings in England and the internet, so that the process has taken several months. As I explain in the Author's Note, to allow time for the publication process, I have stopped writing in July 2006. If anything earth-shattering happens before final proofs, I shall add a postscript to this epilogue. Any further update will be on <www.holobooks.co.uk>.

When I had finished the first draft of the epilogue, I sent it to those mentioned. I have incorporated the responses I received (not all politicians chose to clarify what I had deduced), so that the final process has become organic. Catherine Ng much encouraged me by remarking, 'It's so important for someone to archive Hong Kong women's history. We are making history but sometimes forget to reflect it, to document it.'

SUNDAY

I had written weeks in advance to those I hoped to see; juggling everyone into barely three working days was not going to be easy. The day after our arrival, Sunday, we were determined to return to nearby Macau, a haunt across the wide mouth of the Pearl River that had always meant escape from frenetic Hong Kong and about which I had written historically and once or twice on contemporary issues. What is more, we were to lunch with our dear friend Carl, doyen of Hong Kong's historians and known on women's peace demonstrations as Carla, who is spending his retirement there, looked after by tireless Dolly – she who started Hong Kong life as a Philippine *amah* but graduated seamlessly into Carl's research assistant as well as his eyes, and now his legs.

I didn't want to discuss Philippine domestic helpers over lunch: Dolly is so much more than that, treated rather differently from most of her sisters and, in any case, we were lunching with her as a friend. But I have since rung her to discuss the current position, and there is plenty about it on the internet.

When I wrote the piece in October 1990, there were 60,000 Philippine domestic helpers, mostly women, in Hong Kong. Now there are approximately 240,000 foreign domestic helpers, of which 150,000 or so are from the Philippines (others are from Indonesia, Thailand, Nepal and Sri Lanka). The two week rule still applies and any government-determined increase in wages still only applies to new contracts. But changes in 2003 have made the thought of increase laughable and the position of helpers is even less enviable than before.

In April 2003, the Government slashed wages by $400 a month (11 per cent from $3,670); in October they brought in a levy on employers signing new two-year contracts, or renewing old, for the same amount – thus ensuring that, in fact, the foreign domestic helpers shouldered the levy. The irony is that the amount raised is intended to train local domestic helpers (the legislation is called Employees Retraining Ordinance), thus doing the foreigners out of their traditional jobs, essential both to Hong Kong's economy and to that of the countries to which the foreigners remit funds to support poor families, and struggling economies. Not only can they send less home, but there is less to spend in Hong Kong where the cost of living has continued to rise (wages in December 2004 were the same as they were in 1992).

There was a concerted campaign to prevent the wage cut and levy. The Asia Migrants Co-ordinating Body staged a 12,000 strong protest in February 2003, with such slogans as 'No to Wage Cuts, No to Levy' and 'Blood Money from the Poor', and the President of the Philippines, Gloria Macapagal-Arroyo, barred her compatriots from leaving to work in Hong Kong. This was not a protest that could be sustained for some of them had already paid out money to secure their jobs, and, as was pointed out, their place could well be taken, not so much by local women but by mainlanders from Guangdong Province. In my past experience, local women were not that keen on paid domestic work, though I believe that has changed in view of the economic downturn of 1997 which will come up from time to time as I write. There is, for example, training in professional domestic work at the Women's Centre, suggesting that there is another aspect to this issue. But, as so often, governments are so crass in the way they handle it. An application by five domestic helpers for judicial review of the administrative action of the Chief Executive was unsuccessful (2005).

Although it was splendid to lunch with Dolly and Carl at our favourite restaurant, Macau has changed out of all recognition, and not for the better. It was not human fault that it was cold and miserable that day but, since its return to China from Portugal in 1999, entrepreneurs have turned the once sleepy hollow into a casino and theme-park nightmare, filled with exhaust-emitting coachloads of mainland Chinese and its antique shops without their past allure. Perhaps the rationale – to boost Macau's economy – was well-intentioned but the result is wretched for old timers and aesthetes. That may be our last visit.

MONDAY

Lunch was with the Classmates. Eva had, through the years, remained my contact. After 1997 it was Virginia who organised the venue, at one of her clubs; this time it was Shuk Yin at hers. Nine of the Classmates turned up and four years fell away as I walked towards the round table and the mischievous smiles. The last time we gathered was at the Jockey Club in Shatin where we emptied the dining room as the Classmates rubbished my attempts at Tai Chi and taught me their own versions amid extravagant gestures, pathetic Anglo-Saxon unsuppleness and aging inability to learn, and giggles. The Tai Chi was because I had been unwell and two of them had brought me little statues of a lounging Buddha – one in jade, the other in white porcelain – as traditional get well presents. Now they really did know that they must regularly examine their breasts for lumps, as one of the *Stories for Eva* had dictated.

Only two pieces of news marred the next two hours: Virginia died of lung cancer last year (she was not a smoker); and Linda L, the senior Classmate, died earlier of a stroke. What I always remember about Linda is her beautiful Japanese doll that had to be sacrificed when the Japanese invaded Manchuria in 1937, and how the hurt still showed 60 years later.

I had photocopied all the pieces I had written about the Classmates and started to go through each one with them. But they weren't having it. 'Whatever you've written about us, we're really pleased,' they chorused.

'But some of it's rather personal,' I protested. 'You probably don't remember all you told me.'

'*M'ganyu*' they sang back. This was my catch phrase – 'doesn't matter – don't worry – who cares'. They remembered all our catch phrases from those years – even the special useless words I'd taught them. Now they were ready to add information to what they had told me in the past.

I've already told you how Eva's education was truncated, unlike her brothers'; now it emerged that the same applied to nearly all of them. Few had finished primary school; the schooling of some had been intermittent simply because there wasn't the money that day, week, month. Connie had attended evening classes. At 13, while briefly at primary school during the day, Theresa, who would have liked to be an actress, started work on a treadle sewing machine in a factory. She still does similar work part time. She has changed little since I first knew her years ago, as outrageous, warm, generous as ever with presents: today a warm shawl for Hong Kong's unexpectedly cold snap. She was wearing the same herself. Bonnie and Grace had come – cardigans over their white uniforms – hotfoot from the ear, nose and throat clinic where they work as receptionists. They, like several of the Classmates, had wanted to improve their English for the sake of their work. They brought me a palate of Estee Lauder lipsticks in neat travelling form. Is that a hint that I should wear lipstick?

During one of our early post-1997 gatherings, there were one or two intimations of husbands having lost jobs. There was a sharp economic downturn throughout Asia in the autumn of 1997, particularly affecting Hong Kong which for many years had prospered; the stock market, in which even poorer housewives had invested, and the property market, which underpinned the financial well-being of many, plummeted and much else was affected. That was followed by the SARS epidemic. More recently, to help the economy, the Beijing government has relaxed tourist visas for mainlanders into Hong Kong where they are flocking and spending money. It does not seem so obvious here as it did in Macau, but then the spending area is more diversified in this Special Administrative Region (SAR).

I gather, however, not from the Classmates, that although the economy has been picking up in the past few months, it is benefiting the rich and professionals for whom there are jobs, not the poor and unskilled (women?) for whom there aren't jobs. Is this the economic plan that Margaret Thatcher (and Ronald Reagan) called the trickle-down effect?

Whatever the reason, the Classmates' lives seem much as I knew them before, except that their children are older; many of them wanted better English to help their children. Shuk Yin, our host, asked about her current greatest achievement, said it was to be grandmother of five. It is because of them that her club, where we were lunching, is at BP (Baden Powell) International House; they are attached to the scout movement and use the facilities there.

On one side of me sat Ngan Ieng, who said very little; but then she was always taciturn. I had to wring out of her that she is a happy full time housewife. Cynthia, next to her, always one of the most alert of the Classmates, and still as perky as she was ten years ago when she was the baby of the class, remembered that she is not so much a housewife as a 'domestic manager'. While Connie, who tried to get away with always being 39, remembered Eva's sobriquet and said that she is her husband's 'dogsbody'. 'But that's a joke,' she explained hurriedly. Amy now manages a beauty salon. Both she and Theresa had taken time off to join us that day. Teresina had not been able to.

Eva was sitting the other side of me. She arrived in a flurry and has always declared herself too, too busy in emails. So busy has she been that Theresa is fed up that she never has time to lunch. But she has recently, after three years of study, gained a certificate as a martial arts (*wushi*) coach in seven different forms of the art. Once she dreamed of somehow going to university. With this qualification she has, by more Chinese means, fulfilled the dream. 'I have found my identity,' she told me forcefully, more than once. 'I am finally my own person.' And her beautiful daughter Carmen is at university.

In many ways, the most important results of my seven years of teaching English at the Women's Centre are ones with fancy terminology: raising self-esteem, self-awareness, and consciousness as women; but another, more timeless: warm and lasting relations within a group of women across age, class, education and culture.

I thought I'd lost Tosh again. After July 1997, when I was not able to say goodbye or have a last haircut, we did catch up the following year. But I wrote a letter to the salon well in advance of this visit telling Tosh where we would be staying and heard nothing back. Then, the first evening, on our return to the hotel from dinner, there was a message from her on our voicemail.

Monday is her day off and, as she lives in Kowloon, and as I thought she probably had neither the time nor the money to travel at my convenience, and I wanted to treat her for times past, I suggested tea at the Peninsula Hotel – the poshest place in town for such indulgences. She arrived looking as she often did – not orange hair *en brosse*, but baseball cap, long shorts and trainers. As for my best-laid plans, while I was looking for something in my bag, she grabbed the bill and, in spite of a tussle and my pleading, insisted on paying. 'I've never been to the Peninsula before,' she said serenely, 'and I always thought how nice it would be. It's my pleasure. And, anyway, money is nothing in life – health and happiness are what matters.'

Her mother has had lung cancer since we last talked; she is now in remission but is well into her eighties and more dependent on Tosh than ever. Tosh's life is more circumscribed by her mother than by her salon; indeed, the salon suffers as she continues wholeheartedly to undertake her filial obligations.

When I asked Tosh what she dreams of, it is of a tropical island, set about with flowers and trees – she once had a holiday in the Maldives. Her dream is so reminiscent of that of our flower seller Theresa, and our first domestic helper, the inimitable hard-shelled Danny, that I begin to see a pattern that demands an investigation into the secret dreams of unfulfilled Hong Kong women. For the Classmates, though, it was predominantly education for which they yearned. (Interesting that Theresa, Danny and Tosh all speak English; indeed, Tosh is bi-lingual, having spent several years in North America.)

Monday evening was a slight diversion. The historian of Shanghai, Betty Wei, wrote the first story to arrive for *Stories for Eva* and it was, therefore, the first we discussed in class – showing that the project was likely to be successful. But it was another project, not just friendship, that led us to dinner with her and her family. All being well, Betty will write on Hawaii for the series I have devised, 'Of Islands and Women'. But mostly we reminisced about the trip we once all did, Betty as organiser of a large group, down the Yangtse. It was difficult for me to leave out of this book my pieces on China; but somehow when I tried to fit them in they seemed an intrusion. Hong Kong may be part of China again now, but it wasn't then: it was neat, discrete, unique.

Betty travels at will, is involved in women's issues, and writes scholarly tomes; why didn't I ask her about her dreams? Perhaps writing is dream fulfilment enough; it is for me. Which brings me to Pet on Tuesday morning.

TUESDAY

I lost Pet temporarily too. Having seen her at least once since we left in 1997 and communicated with her by email through her brother, I recently found an email to him returned undelivered, rummaged in past letters that came with photographs and found an email address for her daughter Helen; but that, too, was returned undelivered. So I wrote a note to Pet's last known address and Helen answered by email.

Derek and I went down early to meet Pet because there is an up and a down lobby to our hotel and I thought she would be nonplussed. Not Pet! She was already comfortably installed where she should have been. She did not look the same as ever: I worried that she appeared to have lost a lot of weight which, somehow, didn't suit her. But I said nothing. She gave me a fan that doubles as a hat and two books of Chinese philosophy in Chinese and English. I gave her a box of Harrods chocolates and a *lai see* cheque from an account we keep in Hong Kong for just such a purpose.

Pet explained that she now cleans at the bus terminal between 2 and 10pm each day and when I suggested that sounded like a job such as I hoped she wouldn't have to do any more, she demurred:

'It gives me plenty of time.'

'For what?'

'To write.'

'To write what?' I replied trying to keep astonishment out of my voice.

It is quite clear that Pet gave me the books not just as any old present: she is writing a book on Taoist philosophy – how to live life. She is most anxious that somehow there is an English translation, so that I can read it. Sitting beside me, she marked some relevant passages in the books she was giving me. I hadn't the heart to remind her of my lack of spirituality.

I diverted her into going through every story I'd written about her, explaining carefully how much I had revealed of her life. She listened intently and expressed herself happy about publication, while we reminisced about each incident. But she kept coming back to her own book – the one she is writing – with which she is obviously totally absorbed.

Have I any nurturing responsibility here? I wouldn't presume to claim it. But I always knew there was more to Pet than cleaning our lavatories (and often told her so). Having responsibility for her siblings, and working in a factory from 13, failed to quell or stifle something inside. Another Hong Kong woman's dream, perhaps the most ambitious of them all – and, like the one Eva has realised, totally Chinese. What I hope I may have fostered in both is intrinsic determination and self-belief.

When I wrote to the AWARE sisters and various other scholar friends of the Women's Movement about getting together for lunch, Staci replied by return offering to take the burden of host off my shoulders, as she did four years ago when we had to cancel because Derek and I had to turn back to Europe where my mother was unexpectedly dying.

Staci arrived in Hong Kong later than us but, as a lecturer at Hong Kong University, immediately saw the need for women's history to be taught. Over the years she has been teaching a United States history and American studies programme into which she has woven comparative history, gender at work and other gender related courses, as well as being involved in the work of the Women's Studies Research Centre based at the University. Early on in her endeavours she invited me to lecture to her class – a bit of flattery and fun I never forgot. And when she started her doctorate on American women in Hong Kong and Macau she made it clear that she found my groundwork in *The Private Life of Old Hong Kong* (1991) useful. Poor freelance writers, or, as Staci prefers me to call myself, 'independent scholars', we get so little feedback from our peers that every little is gratefully imbibed.

Thanks to Staci, therefore, we met at Hong Kong University instead of the Foreign Correspondents' Club. Telling you about that lunch not only allows me to catch up with old friends but old and new women's issues too.

There are only two AWARE members left permanently in Hong Kong – Catherine and Tessa. Maria is now based in Oxford, Barbara in Edinburgh, Julie in Canada, Geeta and Linda in the United States and Cecilia moves between Beijing, Australia and Hong Kong. Going round the table at lunch I start with, on my left, Catherine Ng. She is assistant professor in the department of Management and Marketing at Hong Kong Polytechnic University where she is currently doing research into women and small businesses and their expansion, often prompted by the economic downturn of 1997 onwards and layoffs in more conventional employment. Not unnaturally, many women start out without knowledge or experience of running a business.

In a book chapter Catherine wrote with a scholar working in a complementary field, Evelyn Ng – 'Women Micro-entrepreneurs in Hong Kong' – they describe Maureen who set up a garment alteration service. She started work in the garment industry at 12, had a son at 15, divorced after 18 years of marriage and was made redundant by an international sportswear company in her thirties. Maureen explained:

> I thought it might be fun to start my own business. My friends encouraged me and I made the decision in three days ... I had no idea what the economic environment was like. I had no idea if I was in a competitive industry or not. In fact, there were about five to six alteration shops in the mall. I wasn't planning to stay in the business long; in fact I just wasn't planning at all.

Maureen had been running her little business for nine years in 2002 but by then she was at the end of her tether.

Catherine is increasingly interested in the proliferation of women's co-operatives. Of that project, she explained how, since 2005, she has been studying three co-operatives: a domestic household cleaning team, a tuck shop cum student canteen at City University, and a tuck shop plus print shop at Chinese University. She is interested in the women's motivation, their survival tactics, and how they practise workplace democracy. Of course that too is not all sweetness and light but joining a co-operative can be a form of empowerment and the co-op is a support network for its owners.

One of Catherine's other preoccupations has been as founder Chair of HER Fund – part of an international network of women's funds (INWF, 1998) – a women's foundation that aims to fill the funding gap for women's groups and promote philanthropy for women by women. HER (spelling out **H**er **E**mpowering **R**esources) Fund was launched on International Women's Day 2004. When I later told Catherine that I was so impressed by HER Fund and her part in it that I wanted to write about it for this epilogue, she answered, with typical modesty but some firmness, 'I actually came into HER Fund rather late. Please write about the earliest founders *instead of me.*' Those include Linda To Kit-lai, whom I used to know when she ran Harmony House, the first women's refuge, founded under the auspices of the Women's Centre (now the Hong Kong Federation of Women's Centres) about which I often wrote in the past. Linda is now the Chair of HER Fund (and Catherine Vice-Chair). Another founder member, Cecilia Young, the AWARE sister unfortunately absent from our lunch, was Chair of the two-year preparatory committee. Friends of the Fund include Christine Loh, Margaret Ng and Anna Wu.

Whatever Catherine says about her part in the Fund, she has written articles explaining its principles in the *South China Morning Post* which are inspirational. I deliberately leave ambiguous whether or not it is the articles or the principles that are inspirational – because it applies to both! A couple of sentences in an article of 2 October 2004 read 'Feminist philanthropy asks donors to use their money not just for purchasing goods and services. Instead, it is also a tool for social change. Donors' money is an investment in women's wisdom and capability to make decisions for themselves, for their families and the communities they live in.' And another sentiment that strikes a chord: 'In feminist philanthropy, donors and recipients are equal partners.'

HER Fund's importance is made all the clearer when you learn that projects such as Rainlily live from hand to mouth. Rainlily is the 24-hour Rape Crisis Centre of the Association Concerning Violence Against Women. I'm particularly interested in that, not only because of the issue it addresses but because Linda Wong – who used to run the Women's Centre, and who was such a pillar of strength when I taught English there, not just to me but to the Classmates and to Pet – now works there. Since I left, she has also done a Master's degree in England. Women's organisations are as strong as ever they were, and perhaps even more focussed, but increasingly funding is a problem. Any reader who would like to help might like to note these two websites: <www.herfund.org> and <www.rapecrisiscentre.org.hk>.

As Catherine pointed out in an article, 'Don't Abandon Women in Need' (3 December 2005), overseas donors are now less willing to fund local groups because they perceive Hong Kong as a developed city. Of course, in many ways it is but, like many large and apparently prosperous cities, there is a less obvious stratum of poverty, stress and violence. This is not helped when that city has been through a difficult economic period and where there is a cultural timelag concerning marginalised members of society. In Hong Kong's case the marginalised are in many ways women and none more so, I now learn, than certain women from the mainland.

The subject of domestic violence leads me next to Tessa Stewart who was sitting beside Catherine. Tessa teaches general education courses in interpersonal skills at Chinese University, and spouse abuse has been one of her main concerns as long as I have known her (in the Hong Kong Council of Women and then AWARE). A defining incident in Tin Shui Wai came to very public notice, as Tessa has drawn to my attention, in April 2004; she was involved in the consequent submission to Legco of the Hong Kong Federation of Women's Centres, one of several made by women's and other agencies.

Kam Shuk-ying, from mainland Sichuan Province, married Li Pak-sum, a Hong Kong man, in 1991 – what is known as a cross-border marriage. The daughters – twins – who were then born were allowed to settle in Hong Kong with their father, then dependent on welfare, but not Kam Shuk-ying – a policy which has long been blamed for aggravating social problems.

When eventually Kam Shuk-ying was allowed to enter Hong Kong, in January 2004, she was jobless but could not claim benefit because, while such claimants had previously been eligible after 12 months of residence, now it was seven years.

Because of the influx of mainlanders (the term used is 'new arrivals'), often family reunions, following 1997, Tin Shui Wai in the New Territories has become one of the most rapidly developing towns; by 2004, it had a population of 270,000, mostly new arrivals, and lacked much infrastructure and many social services. It was notorious for having the largest number of family abuse cases per head of population, was hardest hit by unemployment, and had the largest number of low-income families. In 2004, there were 3,371 cases of spouse abuse reported, and of the 622 reported cases of child abuse throughout Hong Kong, 93 were from Tin Shui Wai.

Kam Shuk-ying became one of those suffering abuse. On three occasions between her arrival in January and April she spent a few days at a Social Welfare Department Centre, but then returned home. She also sought help from the police and from the Child Protection Services. Li Pak-lam threatened his family to his neighbours. Then, on 12 April, he took an axe and hacked his wife and six-year-old daughters to death.

The case, and the social conditions behind it, created such an uproar that changes are, very slowly, being made. But among the support centres facing closure are those helping new migrants and single-parent families. And the more general background is not promising. Rose Wu, whom I knew as a women's Christian activist, but who has become increasingly mainstream political, tackled the issues in a speech. She highlighted research which shows that only 25–38 per cent of doctors, lawyers and social workers questioned in a poll believe that spouse abuse has a serious impact on society. What is more, 30 per cent of the police questioned in another survey said that husbands were entitled to hit their wives if necessary. And 25.4 per cent of them agreed that husbands should be allowed to have sex with their wives whenever they wanted. The Civil Human Rights Front (founded 13 September 2002), for which umbrella organisation Rose speaks, includes marginalised groups such as sex workers, immigrants, the elderly and the disabled.

That raises another problem facing women coming from the mainland. The Centre of Asian Studies at Hong Kong University, of which I am still an honorary research fellow, and the Women's Studies Research Centre, in which many of the old suspects at the University are still involved, is holding a seminar a week after I am writing this, one of whose papers is entitled 'Bureaucratic Justice: The Incarceration of Mainland Chinese Women Working in Hong Kong's Sex Industry'. One of the authors is law lecturer Carole Petersen who used to work with Derek and was another stalwart of the Women's Movement.

The 2000s have seen a dramatic increase in the number of women sex-workers from the mainland. They cannot get a work visa because these are not issued for sex work, so they are being arrested, prosecuted and sentenced and the women's prison population has leapt. Of course, on a brief visit, however well you knew Hong

Kong, none of this is apparent; but my sisters continue hard at work trying to improve the lot of women of all kinds.

The Civil Human Rights Front includes at least 40 non-governmental organisations one of which, the Association for the Advancement of Feminism (AAF), was much involved in the Women's Movement in my day. I caught up with it by contacting Cheung Choi Wan, author of 'The Right to Talk' (in *Stories for Eva*) about her sexual orientation – a story which so opened the Classmates' minds and enlivened their discussion. Choi Wan now works full time for AAF because she wants to spend her life 'doing something which I think is meaningful'.

Choi Wan's email to me was pessimistic, and she does not mind me quoting from it:

> Young people do not devote themselves as much to feminist causes and other justice issues today. I think we (I mean my generation of Hong Kong people) have ourselves to blame. We know too well that we have taken advantage of the economic expansion since the 70s and have become a new middle class. In order to maintain the advantages gained, we have spent the last 20 years reinforcing the position of the new middle class in the process of which we have sacrificed our time and our lives. We have also helped in nurturing a younger generation of Hong Kong people (especially among the educated) who put self-preservation above taking risks for the benefit of others.

As far as sexual orientation is concerned, Choi Wan suggests that gay people are more visible in Hong Kong, though they are far from gaining equality with heterosexuals. In 2005 Christian fundamentalist groups launched a public campaign against the proposal to outlaw discrimination based on sexual orientation, in the process smearing gay people and reinforcing conservative ideas about sexuality and family. Within families themselves, a gay partner is still unlikely to be invited to their gatherings.

Sitting next to Tessa was Irene Tong, who so endeared herself to me and, indeed, the Classmates, with the story of her lost bear Tung Tung. Irene teaches in the Politics Department at Hong Kong University and, since 1997, has been involved in a number of new courses jointly developed by lecturers in different departments. For solo courses in her own department, she developed a new course called Women and Politics. Meanwhile, Women in the Third World was renamed Gender and Development and that is sometimes cross-listed as Gender and the Global Economy. As one of the sisters pointed out, women's courses are not well-supported; unless that is a course is named Fashion, Women and Health. Gender courses are much better received.

Politics in Hong Kong has moved on in some ways since we were there, and in some ways not. That is to say, there is still not universal and equal suffrage. Indeed, a large demonstration (between 63,000 and 250,000 depending on your point of view) on 4 December 2005, the most recent as I write, was still demanding the right to directly elect the Chief Executive and all seats in the Legislative Council (Legco). A poll published in November suggested that 70 per cent of Hong Kong people want full democracy by 2012.

Among the marchers was Anson Chan, about whose popularity when she was the top civil servant (Chief Secretary) and potential Chief Executive I have written before. She is reported to have said, 'There's a need to fight for democracy. There are moments when you should stand up to be counted.'

Anson Chan resigned as Chief Secretary in January 2001, saying she was leaving for personal reasons, that she wanted to spend more time with her grandchildren. Most believed that she could no longer get on with the Chief Executive since 1997, Tung Chee-hwa. Perhaps it had something to do with the civil service reforms he was trying to push through. As one article put it, following civil service protest rallies, Anson Chan was 'given a humiliating rebuke in Beijing and told to ensure that she and the civil servants gave better support to their master'.

Tung became increasingly unpopular until his resignation ostensibly on health grounds in March 2005. On 1 July 2003, the anniversary of the Handover, 500,000 marched against his proposed legislation on national security. Perhaps as a result, who knows, the votes in Legco no longer stacked up and Tung withdrew the legislation. On 1 July 2004, this time in intense heat and humidity and many sporting 'Power to the People' fans, at least 500,000 again marched against the Chief Executive and the lack of democratic progress. A month earlier, on the fifteenth anniversary of Tiananmen Square, 80,000 or so marched carrying black banners and a coffin, calling upon Beijing 'to vindicate' the memory of the students who died.

Upon Tung's resignation in 2005, his place was taken by Anson Chan's public service successor, Donald Tsang who, in December 2005, went to Beijing ostensibly to try and obtain democratic progress: at least to have the Chief Executive elected by universal suffrage in 2012. One of the purposes of the demonstration on the 4th was to speed him on his way.

One of the outcomes of his trip was a boost to the economy – the relaxation of tourist visas for mainlanders who would flock to Hong Kong and spend money. Tsang came back with ten more proposed functional constituencies (to be elected by special interest groups). As one informant (not one of the sisters) put it, Legco voted on it and told him to stick it; it was perhaps a question of eat your spinach and you might get your ice cream.

But where does Anson Chan fit into all this? I only go by gossip and what I read on the internet. Is she positioning herself to stand as Chief Executive in 2007? Some accuse her of not supporting democratic reform when she had the chance in office. Some have it that she has fallen out with Donald Tsang over his too slow progress towards democracy. In June this year, asked if she would stand for election next year as Chief Executive, she apparently replied 'watch this space.' Unfortunately, both the publication of this book, and the anniversary of the handover, precede that election.

There have been non-democratic Legco elections in 1998, 2000, and 2004. The next are in 2008. Not much has changed so far as women are concerned either, though the number elected has risen slightly; and one or two names have changed. In 1995, the last elections before we left, there were seven women (out of 60); in 1998, ten; in 2000, eleven; and in 2004, ten. In all three terms, Rita Fan has been President of the Council. Miriam Lau and Selina Chow continue to represent business interest functional constituencies. Chan Yuen-han, the (pro-Beijing) Democratic Alliance for the Betterment of Hong Kong (DAB) member for the trade union functional constituency, now takes an independent stand on some issues. She is Chair of the Legco sub-committee on the Tin Shui Wai domestic murder and its social ramifications (Strategy and Measures to Tackle Family Violence).

Emily Lau stood each time as Convenor of the Frontier Party (which she founded in 1996), and won. In an article by her I read while we were in Hong Kong in January she was still railing against the Beijing Government, still calling for freedom of speech, of the press. I asked at lunch how she is now on women's issues – in the past we could call on her; it was she who, in 1992, introduced a Legco Motion calling for the extension of CEDAW to Hong Kong. I gather she represents her constituents' views, so that if a woman issue arises, and it is not of interest to them, or they are against it, she will not support it. I note, though, that she is among the names of Women's Centre supporters.

If Emily's continuing fight for press freedom seems like a hobby horse and her voice sometimes a bit strident, that judgement lacks appreciation of the situation. She spotted well before 1997 that the news media were drawing in their horns, and the dangerous implications. While I did not talk to Emily on this trip, not wanting to disturb a busy Legco member, I have since talked to a journalist – Sharon Cheung – on a Reuters scholarship here in Oxford.

Over the past few years, Sharon's brief has been reporting on politics in China and Taiwan, travelling round with the political leaders; but she is well-versed on Hong Kong where, following a three-year stint on the *South China Morning Post*, she worked, until this research break, for a 24-hour Cantonese television channel.

She has made a study of newspaper coverage going back some years. The news media in Hong Kong tends, as elsewhere, to be part of a business empire. The bigshots who own these conglomerates do big business in China, and are thus dependent on the goodwill of the Beijing authorities for their wider financial endeavours; and, well before 1997, China began to woo them. What is more, there is no legislation to protect journalists, and the Hong Kong Association is weak. The status of journalists is much lower, and the job less well-paid, than previously; increasingly the profession is regarded as part of the entertainment industry; paparazzi proliferate. Beijing wants a harmonious and peaceful society, one in which there is no disturbing criticism or even meaningful debate. When Sharon travelled with the Chinese leadership they refused to answer any questions.

Emily has recently complained that she rarely gets interviewed by the Chinese press, just the English language press. This is a common kind of self-censorship engaged in by the local media. Hong Kong needs Emily more than ever; and she certainly pays for her obduracy: her office has been attacked, I read, and 'Chinese traitors must die' scrawled on the wall outside. I still very much admire her as a doughty and hardworking fighter. If women's issues aren't at the top of her agenda, she has worked out what should be, together with her expertise and her capacity.

Christine Loh's career has been more varied since 1997. She stood and won in 1998 for the Citizens Party which she had founded just before we left. But in 2000 she decided to try pushing for social change from another vantage point. She tells me the party had problems getting members to stand for election and thus would not make much progress. So, that September, she set up Civic Exchange, an independent, non-profit public policy think tank. It advocates cooperative social enterprises for Hong Kong. In a traditional enterprise, the motive is financial return. Civic Exchange argues that the motivation should instead be to meet social needs, and hopes to add intellectual capital to such a venture.

There were articles about the environment by Christine in the *South China Morning Post* while we were there in January. That has always been of great concern to her. In February I read in the *Guardian* how two people were critically ill after running in the Hong Kong marathon, and another 20 taken to hospital, because of the levels of pollution. Christine, I learned from the sisters, is increasingly highly regarded and, as always, open to supporting women's issues. She responded to our campaign for a Women's Commission and was in the forefront of that for inheritance rights for New Territories women. I wonder, upon reflection, if her strong stand then did not mark her out to her political disadvantage in a patriarchal society. Perhaps Emily was always more alert to this danger.

I have a lot of time, personally as well politically, for Christine: she not only wrote for *Stories for Eva* but, as I fondly recall, attended the lunch I gave for the Classmates at Cavendish Heights, giving them untold pleasure. As I write, she is finishing the manuscript of a book about herself and the influences upon her – her first non-policy writing – which I am much looking forward to reading. It is to be called *Being Here: Shaping a Preferred Future* (South China Morning Post, 2006).

A different literary path has been followed by Libby Wong, former Secretary for Health and Welfare who retired early from the public service to become a Legco member in 1995. She left politics in 1997 to write and, at the Hong Kong Literary Festival of 2006, launched her debut novel *Rainbow City* – described as 'A thrilling love story set in Hong Kong as the Chinese take over control from the British.' I'm still trying to get hold of a copy.

Since our visit in January, things have progressed on the political front. One of the rising stars is Audrey Eu SC (Senior Counsel, formerly QC), a former Chair of the Bar Association with whom Derek worked on a sub-committee of the Law Reform Commission. Audrey entered Legco in a by-election in 2000 and was soon making her mark. For a while I'm told, though not by her, she struggled. Appearing as a barrister before a judge, being in control of one's brief, is not quite the same as having to cope with sometimes low level debate that goes nowhere and endless politicking.

In 2002, when the Government intended to introduce Article 23 legislation regarding state secrets and sedition (so-called national security), Audrey, with other members of the Bar such as Margaret Ng (Legco member for the legal functional constituency) set up the Article 23 Concern Group. After those demonstrations of 1 July 2003 which contributed to the withdrawal of that proposal, her popularity increased; she was seen as clean, professional, knowledgeable.

Then concern grew that Articles 45 and 68 of the Basic Law (which came in on 1 July 1997 and under which Hong Kong is governed) were not being acted upon. The ultimate aim of universal suffrage for the Chief Executive and Legco is stipulated under those articles. In order to push for the elections of 2007 (for the Chief Executive) and 2008 (for Legco) to be fully democratic, the same team set up the Article 45 Concern Group. Audrey Eu apparently began to be seen by the pro-Beijing media as an 'Evil Woman'.

The next development came on 19 March 2006: with Audrey Eu as Leader in Legco, a new political party – the Civic Party – was set up. Its Chinese name is short for 'Justice and Democracy'. It has six Legco members and three District Councillors. Among the Legco members are Margaret Ng and Mandy Tam (formerly an independent), and among its supporters is Gladys Li SC (another contributor to *Stories for Eva*). The Civic Party, some say, is likely to replace the Democratic Party – riven as it is by in-fighting and scandal – as the leading advocate of democracy; indeed, many have already switched from one party to the other.

One of the ironies of the electoral system is that in 2004 the second woman member of Emily Lau's Frontier Party – Cyd Ho – lost her seat as a result of tactics which were meant to help a senior and well-regarded member of the Democratic Party – Martin Lee – to retain his. Cyd Ho had been elected in 1998 and retained her seat in 2000. Legco could ill afford to lose a good woman. The Democratic Party, though in the past admirable in many ways, has never been good on women, never had a woman Legco member or, indeed, one in a position of authority within the Party.

Another irony is that Regina Ip, Secretary for Security at the time of the controversial failed security legislation, is now prominent as a television political talk show host whose first interviewee was Audrey Eu; Anson Chan found an excuse to decline her invitation. What is more, not only is Regina being touted as a possible candidate for either the next Chief Executive or as a Legco member, but her recently completed and published Masters thesis has, apparently, captured the political imagination. In it she highlighted the previously rejected idea of a bicameral legislature which could accommodate the functional constituencies and thus, by degrees, lead towards universal suffrage.

Women are still not numerically well-represented in Legco but they seem to be increasingly so as far as quality is concerned. As for role models, it seems that those in Legco and others working in the wider political field might ensure future progress in women voting, and women standing for election – one of the issues that most engaged me during our time in Hong Kong.

There were theoretically two empty chairs at the lunch table which allow me to talk about women's education. One absentee was Kavita who took over my English class at the Women's Centre; she was then teaching at Hong Kong University. Her life changed within the year and she moved on. She now teaches elsewhere, and her class that day prevented her from joining us. But English teaching has continued at the Women's Centre and for some years Elsie Mak has been bravely holding the fort.

Elsie used to be a member of AWARE's sibling AWAKE (Alerting Women About Key Experiences), a group of Chinese middle-class women firmly attached to the Women's Centre in its working class social housing estate as executive committee members, volunteers of the Hotline service or Friends. (I tend to refer to the Women's Centre because there was only one for most of my day; but there are now two centres and the organisation is formally the Federation of Women's Centres; and AWAKE, like AWARE has had its day).

There are also new volunteer teachers who organise elementary English and Cantonese courses for Thai and Indonesian women of Chinese descent. Quite naturally, they devise their own material rather than using *Stories for Eva* which was very much of its time and protagonists. I suspect that 'my' book gathers dust in various cupboards, though Clara Law in charge at the Women's Centre kindly tells me that 'It is a book that helps us and our members reflect'. If that is so, I am happy.

Rosann Kao was supposed to occupy the second empty chair at our lunch table but her mother had just died and she was laid low; I have since talked to her on the telephone. Rosann, not long before we left in 1997, had set up a women's education project as part of Chinese University's Continuing Education Programme. It was at one of Rosann's gatherings for the project that *Stories for Eva* was launched. But with the economic downturn of late 1997, funding became difficult and it was withheld from the women's project.

Like so many tertiary establishments throughout the developed world, making money has taken over from social function and the Chinese University of Hong Kong is no exception. Rosann now works for Hong Kong International School as a family life counsellor, teaching about relations between women and men, including sex education.

So, where do women who missed out on school education now turn? This question allows me to introduce another important development since 1997: on 15 January 2001 a Women's Commission was set up – success after many years of campaigning.

When you have fought long and hard, you are inevitably disappointed if what you are given is not exactly what you asked for. What we always insisted on, and it also applied to the Equal Opportunities Commission which came into being in 1996, was a body with teeth, with power within the government and the will to be radical. But governments rarely work like that; agitation disturbs the status quo and the Women's Commission was set up by the Chief Executive, Tung Chee-hwa, who definitely (from Derek's and my personal experience) prefers harmony.

How the Women's Commission came about I have not really unravelled; you would have thought we would be more likely to succeed pre-1997. One story has it that Anson Chan was behind it; but two other women must have played a major role. Fanny Cheung, first Chair of the Equal Opportunities Commission (EOC), was always a leader in pushing for a Women's Commission. The EOC, with its brief, could not do for women what was expected of it by women. Following her term as Chair of the EOC, and then the setting up of the Women's Commission, Fanny became a member of the latter, but has now returned full time to Chinese University as Professor of Psychology. She has written about both experiences – a chapter in a forthcoming book – which all concerned should look forward to eagerly.

In March 1999, as Fanny's term as Chair of the EOC was ending, Anson Chan approached Anna Wu to succeed her. Anna had been an appointed Legco member between 1992 and the elections of 1995, the year she attempted to introduce full-blooded equal opportunities legislation as a Private Members Bill, after years of intensive work with a team of advisers. It was the first time a legislator had attempted such a policy change and it created a precedent, a legislative option impossible post-1997.

Anna then made a deal with the government that for every portion of her Bill it was willing to take over, she would drop her parallel portion. This is how we came to have the Sex Discrimination Ordinance which set up the EOC, together with other anti-discrimination legislation.

Anna didn't stand for election to Legco in September 1995 because, as a lawyer, having had a chance to look behind legislation and understand better how government worked, she felt she had done her duty by conventional politics. She returned to legal practice and was appointed Chair of a number of major advisory bodies.

The EOC, to which Tung Chee-hwa appointed Anna Chair in August 1999, was an independent statutory body. Although her three-year contract was extended in 2002, something then went wrong: she stood up to the Government, taking the Education Department to court over a policy, extending back over 20 years, of systematic discrimination against girls in high school admissions. From one moment to another, it seemed, Anna was out, a new Chair, a former judge, was in and, almost as quickly, the EOC had lost much of its credibility.

Anna is now Director of the Cheung Kong Centre for Negotiating Skills and Dispute Resolution in the Law School of Shantou University (an institution set up in China by a Hong Kong philanthropist) as well as responsible for the School's strategic development and expansion. She has recently been appointed a member of the Hong Kong Law Reform Commission.

The Women's Commission is differently constituted from the EOC, being an advisory body under the Health and Welfare Department. Anna's official response at the time was that the woman issue was not a welfare issue; it was a matter of rights and there should be a wide representation including, specifically, members from the grass roots. The Commission should have authority and the capacity to transcend government departments (bureaus).

The first Chair of the Women's Commission (2001–06) was Sophie Leung, the Liberal (business) Legco member for the Textile and Garment Functional Constituency who, although she was a founding member of the Beijing-approved Hong Kong Federation of Women (1993), was not involved in campaigning for a Women's Commission (that I know of). AWARE sister Cecilia Young was also a member during the Commission's first term, but the fact that she was seen as a 'useful link' to the progressive women's groups speaks volumes. When asked to serve a second term, it was not mainly Cecilia's increasing absence from Hong Kong that caused her to decline. To be a token representative was alien to someone who had campaigned so long and hard for the women's cause, and who was so conversant with the issues.

The list of new 2006 members contains no names, that I can detect, from the Women's Coalition days, though I note that of the Director of the Hong Kong Federation of Women's Centres, Fong Man-ying. I don't know her but I hear good reports. From 1986, she worked as researcher and assistant to a Legco member in the Hong Kong Federation of Trade Unions (HKFTU), and she organised the 1991 election campaign of Chan Yuen Han (the woman who became the trade union Legco member in 1995). Thereafter, until 1992, she became executive secretary of the HKFTU. Working with Oxfam alerted her to how much poverty affects women and the need for social protection. She is doing a doctorate in social work, has experience as a carer and is interested in women's oral history. Whatever the virtues of the one Commission member I have found out about, members are not only government-appointed but the government decides what the Commission should work on.

One would, of course, like to think that the setting up of the Women's Commission is a step forward. There is some training on gender recognition in the Public Service, and what is termed 'gender mainstreaming' in government departments, whereby the formulation of policies takes into account the perspective of both sexes. I gather, though, there is not the gender auditing that they have, for example, in the Philippines. When a five-day week and flexitime are discussed, it is for the sake of family and social harmony, rather than a firm women's issue. But then that is more likely to be generally acceptable. The Commission recognises the major issue of poverty (particularly among women, particularly among those who missed out on formal education, and of immigrants), but from a middle class perspective, rather than that of the grass roots. I am going by the judgement of others who try to be supportive and get involved where they can.

My own very limited experience is positive. I have introduced the Women's Commission here because the handsome website tells me about something called the 'Capacity Building Mileage Programme' (CBMP). Perhaps it sounds better in Cantonese. As it says, 'An essential aspect of capacity building among women is the provision of adequate education and training programmes'. To this end, the Women's Commission has entered into partnership with the Open University of Hong Kong for a programme, many courses of which are broadcast on the radio. It was launched on 8 March 2004 and its courses include managing health, personal finance, human relationship and communication skills and practical issues in daily lives.

There is something infinitely touching about the script for the television advertisement for the CBMP that came up when I put the name into Google:

Ms Wong: Mr Chan, looking after the stall on your own? Where's your wife?
Mr Chan: She's gone to a self-learning programme seminar.
Ms Wong: You're such a good husband.
Mr Chan: We're a team and working partners. When she has a chance to learn more I should support her.
DJ: Welcome to 'a university a person programme'.
Voice-over: Now there are many women like Mrs Chan who have joined a self-learning programme organised by the Women's Commission to improve their lives.
Ms Wong: What a happy couple you are!

Mrs Chan: To live is to learn!
Voice-over: Capacity Building Mileage Programme.
[And there follow contact details.]

I note the website says that the 'cost would be affordable'. In the past, when I discussed mainstream Open University courses with the Classmates, cost was as much a factor as the academic hurdles to be jumped to get in. Although some of them would have been interested in such courses as are on offer in the CBMP, others had more ambitious intellectual aspirations. Eva tells me that she has not listened to the radio programmes and, knowing how busy she has been with her martial arts training, I'm not surprised. Nor does she think any of the Classmates have.

Failing to get a purchase on the CBMP – though I do know that the Women's Centre helped with putting together material for the courses – I wrote to the new Chair of the Women's Commission – Sophia Kao (whom I don't know). She has been on the Commission since 2001 and convenor of the steering committee on the CBMP. She passed my email to Annie Kong and I must say that I was impressed by the careful and detailed reply; public relations it may be, but well done, and I don't suppose they are overstaffed.

If the Classmates are not engaged, 9,500 women (and men) have registered which, as Annie Kong points out, does not include those who listen without registration. Of course, it is easy for a bureaucrat to reply, 'Student feedback indicates that they have significantly benefited from the course in terms of increased interest in the learning, and enhanced confidence and knowledge in solving daily difficulties.' But, having taught the Classmates, knowing how much women have missed out on education, and the confidence that comes with it, I'm prepared to respond positively to such figures, though I notice that only 127 took part in the first graduation ceremony a year later.

Under another heading, *Adult Education for Women in Hong Kong*, Annie Kong writes,

For adult women who wish to pursue formal education there are many different avenues for them, including evening schools for adults and formal diploma or degree courses offered by local tertiary institutions such as the Open University of Hong Kong. The Government has also set up a number of assistance or funding programmes to encourage adults to pursue continuing education.

For instance, adult women can get financial assistance from the Workplace English Campaign (funded by the Language Fund) if they wish to improve their English language. Under the Adult Education Subvention Scheme, subvention is provided for non-government organisations to run basic adult education programmes within a prescribed purview of the Scheme, such as general education courses and basic literacy in Chinese. The Financial Assistance Scheme for Designated Evening Adult Education Courses provides financial assistance to adult learners attending evening senior secondary courses. In addition, the Continuing Education Fund subsidizes adults with learning aspirations to pursue continuing education and training courses.

I've included that in full, including the rather bureaucratic language, in case what is on offer is not generally known about. Who knows what it all means in practice? I should be glad to hear from anyone who has worked their way through the system.

The Women's Centre or, rather, the Federation of Women Centres, continues to develop many of its education and empowerment programmes, way beyond English language teaching. IT training has gathered momentum. The Centre is involved in helping women, increasingly jobless over the years because of the economic situation and age discrimination, not only to set up co-operatives which allow them to have some control over their lives, but also in sorting out major issues that affect such enterprises – such as insurance, and the fact that co-ops tend not to re-invest, thus inhibiting growth. Poverty among immigrant women is another major concern, as is pressing for social security for homemakers (who used to be called housewives). I'm not so sure about this term 'homemakers'. I have a soft spot for the 'domestic manager' used in 1993 in her Story for Eva by the athlete Wynnie Wing-yee Cosgrove; it so appealed to the Classmates. Making a home is only one aspect of the unpaid work that women do for their families and in running a household – an issue which Cecilia tried to get on the Women's Commission agenda.

The Women's Centre very recently (yesterday as I write) held a seminar on domestic violence – looking at whether or not it should be criminalised, as in China and Taiwan, and making sure that its members understand what the law is. The Free Legal Advice Centre which AWARE sister Julie Macfarlane set up in 1992 is going stronger than ever. And Cecilia and Tessa are still involved with the Women's Centre. AWARE's link with it and even my part in it, was not a wasted effort. Fanny Cheung endeared herself to me for all time when she emailed: 'I still cite your English classes at the Women's Centre as ways how we can build in feminist ideology in everyday life activities, since local women often shy away from the feminist label initially.' And in a later email, '[Your] classes were particularly meaningful to me because they were the embodiment of some of the philosophy and strategies for the Women's Centre when we set it up in the early 1980s. You have made it happen.' How much I gained from my Hong Kong experience, and particularly my work at the Women's Centre, I hope this book makes clear.

And so we came to the end of a re-energising lunch. On my return to Oxford, I wrote to Staci asking her to keep me up to date and give me a few words on her hopes up to July 2007. She delayed replying, hoping to be 'profound' and then wrote, 'Actually, most days my hopes are that my sons turn into men who are not afraid to link their lives with strong-willed women, that I have meaningful work, and can work to make a bit of a difference to the world. But that just sounded so trite.' I'm not sure that I agree, Staci!

From the Elliot (dining) room I slipped through to the Senior Common Room to meet historian Elizabeth Sinn for a glass of hot lemon and honey, and to go over what I had written about her all those years ago. I always remember with affection how kind and helpful she was to the complete stranger with no Hong Kong academic affiliation muscling in on the history of Hong Kong. Elizabeth is now semi-retired from the University and its Centre of Asian Studies, but still involved and writing.

Meanwhile, Derek had been having lunch with Sheree and Dhirendra – his team at City University. Sheree's response to what I wrote about her and her mates in 1993 is all that I could hope for from this book. And she explained why she left as Derek's secretary as she did: the completion of that length of service enabled her to buy a flat. 'That's why I left with thousands of unwillingness. Until I learnt that Derek wanted me back, I jumped up immediately and completed the necessary procedures in order to return "Home"'. Now, in April 2006, Sheree has finally left the Law School, after twenty or so years and transferred to the School of Creative Media at City University.

That evening, Derek and I had dinner with Chris Munn, an English Hong Kong historian and public servant and May Holdsworth, Chris's fellow editor of the *Dictionary of Hong Kong Biography* in preparation. (Elizabeth Sinn is the editor-in-chief, and Christine Loh and Carl Smith are among those on the editorial board.) I have written several entries for them and was informally commissioned to write some more – women about whom I have written before in *The Private Life of Old Hong Kong* and *Chinese Footprints*. Good still to be regarded as part of Hong Kong's scholarly scene. Chris's Thai domestic helper, SunTaree, is another of those leading a happy and secure life in Hong Kong. She has looked after Chris for some years and knows what we like to eat – green papaya salad!

WEDNESDAY

I spent the first part of our last morning in Hong Kong on the telephone. I had left it rather late to ring Far East Media who already distribute two of my books in Hong Kong and that of a friend who had given me a mission with them. My contact was away I learned, and was just about to hang up in despair when I was put through to Shonee Mirchandani. Rather abruptly I asked her who she was, and thus I came to learn of another women's enterprise.

I knew the name Mirchandani because my original dealings some years ago were by email, with a man of that name. What I did not know was that he died in 2003. Nor did I know that his wife, Nisha Mohan Mirchandani, had started the first Bookazine shop in Hong Kong 20 years ago, and continues to run the chain that she has built up, as well as the distribution company, now that her husband is dead. There are two daughters; one is Shonee, who, with her legal and banking background in Boston, is involved in the day to day management of the business and assists in the strategic decisions of the bookshops. She joined the family firm in 2002. Then there is Arti who, with her arts degree from Australia, looks after the retail side. Dealing with the book-trade in Hong Kong is a far cry from teaching arts and crafts to young children and providing special needs teaching assistance, as Arti used to. I am much warmed and encouraged by knowing that these women will look after the distribution and sales of this book.

I was determined also to do some shopping before we left. I had IOU's from Derek left over from Christmas for Hong Kong sale time shopping, preferably at Shanghai Tang where, in the past, I have been delightfully lucky. But it was a fearful disappointment: nothing I liked at a price I wanted to afford, and why were the colours so crude this year?

At Safari, the factory outlet in Pedder Building where I have always shopped, I bought a lovely padded silk jacket in spring colours for my step-daughter Lucy (and now much regret not having bought for myself too). I then pottered around Central and found that there was, since my time, a Harvey Nichols on several floors. I was determined to find something in the sale, but didn't – hardly, at those prices. On all those floors I was pretty well the only shopper. Derek found the same in the posh (expensive) Chinese Arts and Crafts near our hotel where he foolishly thought he could replace the padded silk waistcoat that is his winter-working staple. It was full of assistants, surprisingly polite, but empty of shoppers, explaining the politeness. So where do all the rich mainland tourist/ shoppers go?

An informant tells me that there are three kinds of mainland shopper-tourist. One kind shops in the Landmark and Pacific Place (designer labels or, as one calls them in Hong Kong, famous names). She recalls watching a mainland man in Burberrys buying boxer shorts at $200 a go – one in each colour. Then there are those who have $5 million or more to spend on a house or flat – they are allowed to buy, and that can lead to permanent residence. The third kind are more downmarket – more like those we saw in coachloads in Macau. They come on week-long shopping sprees and are to be found stocking up on electronic goods in Mong Kok and Causeway Bay.

The retailers, not surprisingly, welcome the money. Post-1997 things got really sticky; indeed, the huge demonstration on 1 July 2003, ostensibly against the proposed national security legislation (Article 23), was also against the way Tung Chee-hwa was running the economy. Before 1997, prosperous Hong Kong people tended to look down on mainlanders, because they had less money. Hong Kong is an almost amusingly money-conscious society. People gained their identity and status through their spending power; and it was common currency that China counted on Hong Kong's prosperity post-1997. When it suffered an economic reverse, its people suffered psychologically. Now attitudes are more balanced. That must surely be healthy.

Derek was with me by now and we made our way to Episode in a repeat of my last morning on Hong Kong Island in 1997. Down the escalators, all was just the same: rails of delicate sale goods tastefully colour-coordinated in little nooks. I have trouble these days finding winter trousers in England. Here I found just what I wanted – 50 per cent discount off one pair; 60 per cent off two; 70 per cent off three pairs. Derek insisted I buy them in camel and grey flannel. I felt wicked but marvellous.

And so up Wyndham Street, up the steep steps to the Foreign Correspondents' Club. Immediately we were welcomed back to our family home of nine years ago, even though we had not been there for four. Upstairs we had lunch with Anthony Lawrence, formerly the BBC's Far East Correspondent – a distinctive voice and humanity familiar from many years back, long before I came to Hong Kong. We had a good lunch and a good gossip and then raced to our hotel to pick up our luggage and flee to the airport.

Anthony has since read to Clare Hollingworth what I wrote about her in 1988. We have all aged a bit since then; Clare and Anthony are well into their nineties now. Clare, who doesn't see or hear too well, liked the fact that I had called her a grande dame of British journalism, Anthony tells me; and he is certainly as grand a Correspondent whose Far East diaries should be published. Clare is, not surprisingly, patron of Women in Publishing (WIPS) still, I'm glad to see, going strong.

When I first started writing this epilogue, I planned to be symmetrical, to end as I left Episode and walked up Wyndham Street, as I did in July 1997, though this time feeling less low, for my Hong Kong life is the past and, all being well, we will be back to visit. But I realise that this epilogue and, indeed, the whole book, has had a tendency to be oppositional: agitating in one direction against the Hong Kong Government (and even the Governor, Chris Patten), agitating in favour of women's rights and full democracy. Lavender Patten, on reading the manuscript, chided me in an email ' .. though I was disappointed that you thought so little of Chris's efforts towards democracy or in other areas.' It says much for her generosity that she was still prepared to write kindly about it. And in the other direction I have perhaps been a bit ready to leave out of the picture those who, before 1997, one labelled 'pro-Beijing', and that was in spite of the really happy and fascinating visits we paid to China over the years.

An encounter in Cambridge last week allows me to end on a more positive note. This year is the 100th anniversary of St Stephen's Girls' College which features in the 1997 piece about the writer Xiao Hong. But years earlier, when I was researching *The Private Life of Old Hong Kong*, I was much helped by the headmistress of St Stephen's, Kay Barker.

Kay arrived to teach in Hong Kong in 1958. After two years at St Paul's she moved to St Stephen's and eventually became headmistress, until she retired, much loved, in 1991. Not surprisingly, her former pupils and the school have kept in touch with her ever since and this year she is involved in the anniversary celebrations. She has just returned from one of two lots of celebrations and I wanted her opinion on Hong Kong today.

Because of the status of the school, her former pupils tend to have become rather distinguished. Perhaps the best known in Hong Kong, historically, is Ellen Li, the first woman member of Legco (1966), who died last year aged 97, after a lifetime of public service, including committed campaigning on women's issues. I interviewed Ellen for *The Private Life of Old Hong Kong* for she could not only tell me about the early days of St Stephen's but she had been in Hong Kong for part of the Second World War. As a result of getting to know her then, she wrote a piece for *Stories for Eva* about learning English which became the first in the book. Another grande dame.

Kay tells me that many of her former pupils and friends are working for and in China, in a way that is making a real difference, both to China and to relations between the two places. One has set up a scheme for training social workers in 15 Chinese universities. A former teacher of the deaf is training teachers in China. Another friend, who has a relative in Harbin, is raising funds to build an arts complex and theatre for students from ten new universities there.

When Kay arrived at St Stephen's, the only musical instrument there was a piano. She started an orchestra which this month was distinguished enough to play at the Grand Theatre of the Cultural Centre in Hong Kong, as part of the celebrations, for a production of *My Fair Lady*. But the key scene was not set at Ascot. A member of staff has transposed it to Happy Valley Racecourse, which is very much a centre of Hong Kong life.

Happy Valley was the first place, historically (and the only place for a long time), where the Chinese and the colonial British met as equals. So what one wishes for Hong Kong, on the tenth anniversary of the Handover, is that it can draw on the best of its British colonial heritage, and the best of its Chinese present and future, and be healthy and happy – democratic and prosperous.

Oxford, July 2006

INDEX

*Many women (and a few men) are to be found under their first name,
often with their family name in brackets.*